The Special Education Yellow Pages

Roger Pierangelo, Ph.D.
Rochelle Crane, CSW

The Special Education Yellow Pages is a complete guide for finding sources dealing with specific disabilities, web sites, professional organizations, books, materials, laws, federal agencies, university libraries, medical information, legal issues, transportation issues, adaptive technology, computer resources, assistive technology resources, catalogs, free materials, advocates, employment issues, and more.

Merrill
an imprint of Prentice Hall
Upper Saddle River, New Jersey   Columbus, Ohio

Library of Congress Cataloging-in-Publication Data

Pierangelo, Roger.
    The special education yellow pages / Roger Pierangelo, Rochelle Crane.
       p.   cm.
    Includes index.
    ISBN 0-13-020309-2 (pbk.)
    1. Special education—United States—Directories. 2. Handicapped children—Services for—United States—Directories.
I. Crane, Rochelle. II. Title.
  LC4031.P488   2000
  371.9'025'73—dc21

99-18774
CIP

Editor: Ann Castel Davis
Production Editor: Sheryl Glicker Langner
Editorial Assistant: Pat Grogg
Design Coordinator: Diane C. Lorenzo
Text Designer: Ed Horcharik/Pagination
Cover Designer: Mark Shumaker
Production Manager: Laura Messerly
Electronic Text Management: Marilyn Wilson Phelps, Karen L. Bretz, Melanie King
Director of Marketing: Kevin Flanagan
Marketing Manager: Meghan Shepherd
Marketing Coordinator: Krista Groshong

This book was set in Novarese by Prentice Hall and was printed and bound by Victor Graphics. The cover was printed by Phoenix Color Corp.

ISBN: 0-13-020309-2

Prentice-Hall International (UK) Limited, London
Prentice-Hall of Australia Pty. Limited, Sydney
Prentice-Hall of Canada, Inc., Toronto
Prentice-Hall Hispanoamericana, S. A., Mexico
Prentice-Hall of India Private Limited, New Delhi
Prentice-Hall of Japan, Inc., Tokyo
Prentice-Hall (Singapore) Pte. Ltd., Singapore
Editora Prentice-Hall do Brasil, Ltda., Rio de Janeiro

Dedication

To my loving wife Jackie, and my two beautiful children, Jacqueline and Scott, my parents who got so much pleasure from being parents, my sister Carol who would make any brother proud, and my brother-in-law Dr. George Giuliani, who throughout our relationship has always been there unconditionally.

This book is also dedicated to the memory of Rochelle Crane who always symbolized the word *courageous*. A truly special friend for 25 years, Rochelle's greatness lives on in the hearts of all those who knew her. Her intelligence, wit, perseverence, warmth, and genuine love for people have always been, and will always be, an inspiration for me.

Dr. Roger Pierangelo

This book is dedicated to my parents, the late Harry Drath, my mother Rae Draft, my brother Larry, my children Valerie and Alex whose support and encouragement have been the foundation of my accomplishments, and to my co-author and best friend Roger, who has shown me that what was impossible is possible.

Rochelle Crame

About the Authors

Dr. Roger Pierangelo has more than 25 years of experience as a regular classroom teacher, school psychologist in the Herricks Public School system in New Hyde Park, New York, administrator of special education programs, full professor in the graduate special education department at Long Island University, private practitioner in psychology, member of committees on special education, evaluator for the New York State Education Department, director of a private clinic, and consultant to numerous private and public schools, PTA, and SEPTA groups.

Dr. Pierangelo earned his BS from St. John's University, MS from Queens College, Professional Diploma from Queens College, and Ph.D. from Yeshiva University. Currently he is working as a psychologist both in the schools and in private practice, teaching at the college and working as a director of a private clinic.

He is a member of the American Psychological Association, New York State Psychological Association, Nassau County Psychological Association, New York State Union of Teachers, and Phi Delta Kappa.

Dr. Pierangelo is the author of the *Survival Kit for the Special Education Teacher* and *The Special Education Teacher's Book of Lists*. He co-authored *The Parents' Special Education Survival Kit*, *The Complete Transition Guide for Special Students*, *The Special Educator's Guide to 109 Diagnostic Tests* published by Simon and Schuster, *The Special Educator's Guide to Classroom Management Techniques*, *Basic Classroom Psychology for Elementary School Teachers*, and *Basic Classroom Psychology for Secondary School Teachers*, both to be published by Research Press in 1999. He is also the author of *301 Ways to Be a Loving Parent* published by Shapolsky Publishers of New York.

Rochelle Crane, C. S. W., was a psychiatric social worker for 15 years on the staff of the North Shore Child and Family Guidance Center, a mental health agency on the North Shore of Long Island. From 1985 to 1990, Ms. Crane was the coordinator of its learning disability team before turning to private practice, treating adolescents and adults. In her capacity as a consultant to Boards of Cooperative Educational Services, she led workshops for parents of children with special needs. Ms. Crane also taught in-service courses for teachers and is the co-author of *The Complete Guide to Transition Services* published by Simon and Schuster.

Ms. Crane earned her Masters in Social Work from Adelphi University. She has held memberships in the National Association of Social Workers and the OrthoPsychiatric Association.

About the Special Education Yellow Pages

Purpose of the Guide

With the inclusion of children with disabilities into the mainstream school population, special educators, regular classroom teachers, parents, and students themselves require a vast amount of knowledge. Federal and state laws are continually changing, requiring almost daily monitoring of pertinent issues. The education, health, welfare, and safety of children with disabilities is of paramount importance. Unfortunately, it is impossible for any special educator to keep up with, let alone know where to find, the vast amount of resources available for this population.

Special educators, regular classroom teachers, parents, and students with disabilities are constantly faced with the need to know more about their situation. The more they know, the better chance they will have adapting to the outside world. Many special educators, regular classroom teachers, parents, and students with disabilities find out too late about the tremendous opportunities or resources that exist in today's society for children and adults with disabilities.

In the process of compiling this book, we were amazed by the plethora of data, much of which is lost in the "ocean" we call the Internet. We are not suggesting that the list presented in this book is complete; we decided to select the most relevant resources that are available on a nationwide basis. Bringing them together in an easy-to-read format was our goal.

The *Special Education Yellow Pages* has been developed to help special educators, regular classroom teachers, parents, and students with disabilities through the very difficult and confusing process that a child with a disability faces in their development from birth to adulthood.

Having this guide will be like having an expert in your midst. It will allow special educators, regular classroom teachers, parents, and students with disabilities to be better advocates and reduce their feelings of helplessness which so many times accompany this process.

Many of the places we cite cover several areas. Therefore, we have listed the complete information in the most relevant section, and cross-referenced it to another area. Specific disabilities are listed alphabetically, and agencies that cover a wide range of disabilities have been listed under **Organizations-General**. An alphabetical Index is provided at the back of the book for your convenience.

Helpful and Unique Features

The *Special Education Yellow Pages* contains up-to-date information and the following features:

- An easy-to-follow table of contents and index for quick accessibility
- Explanations of organizations dealing with all facets of disabilities
- Sources dealing with educational issues that affect a disabled child's future
- A complete listing of state and government agencies that offer support and guidance
- Names and addresses of legal agencies and sources that can assist parents
- Medical sources and agencies that can assist parents if they have any questions in this area

- Sources for materials, books, films, and pamphlets dealing with all aspects of a child's disability
- Internet and Web site listings that can be easily accessed on a home computer
- Occupational information that can facilitate the school-to-adult life transition

How to Use This Guide

Parents, children and adults with disabilities, teachers of special education, regular classroom teach and others will find this guide invaluable. Knowing that there are so many resources for children wit abilities and their families will offer a feeling of reassurance and security. Never again will parents, te ers, administrators of special education, or others have to worry about who to ask for information. guide provides them with a resource library to assist them in making the most appropriate decision involving the transition of children from birth to adulthood.

Disclaimer

The information contained in this book is provided for informational purposes only. There is no imp endorsement by the authors. The authors do not promote or endorse participation in any specific nization, agency, or publication. Every effort was made to present the most accurate and up-to-dat information; however, keep in mind that changes in data occur regularly.

We did our best to guarantee that our information is correct. This information does not substitute fc professional advice and counsel of your physician, health care provider, or educator. We assume no liabi any misuse of information in this book, or any information that proves to be incorrect or misleading for reason. The original providers of the content assume full liability for the correctness of their content. Th ters "NA" refer to either non-applicable or inability to secure the information at the time of publication.

Please note that some listed organizations are "member organizations," which means that to re their information and publications one must be a member and pay a fee. You should inquire about requirement when reaching the specific organization.

Acknowledgments

- To all the students, parents, and teachers of the Herricks Public School District, New Hyde Park, York, whom I have had the pleasure of meeting, knowing, and helping in my 23 years in the distri
- Again to Ollie Simmons, an extraordinary individual and personal friend, who always helps me st the day with a smile.
- Helen Firestone, one of the most instrumental individuals in my career, who always believed in r
- In memory of Bill Smyth, a truly "extraordinary ordinary" man and one of the best guidance cour selors and individuals I have ever known.

Roger Pierangelo Ph.D.

- To Dr. David Helfat, who gave me the courage and ability to walk again.
- To Dr. Philip Wilson, who, together with his father, has been my orthopedic support throughout n

Rochelle Crane

Contents

- National Clearinghouse on Family Support and Children's Mental Health
- National Clearinghouse on Women and Girls with Disabilities, c/o Educational Equity Concepts Inc.
- National Diabetes Information Clearinghouse (NDIC)
- National Health Information Center
- National Information Center for Children and Youth with Handicaps (NICHCY)
- National Information Center on Deafness (NICD)
- National Information Clearinghouse on Children Who Are Deaf-Blind (DB-Link)
- National Institute on Deafness and Other Communication Disorders Information Clearinghouse
- National Institute on Disability and Rehabilitative Research (NIDRR)
- National Library Service for the Blind and Physically Handicapped, Library of Congress
- National Maternal and Child Health Clearinghouse
- National Mental Health Consumer Self-Help Clearinghouse
- National Mental Health Services Knowledge Exchange Network (KEN)
- National Organization for Rare Disorders (NORD)
- National Rehabilitation Information Center (NARIC)
- NIH/National Institute of Neurological Disorders and Stroke

College Guides for the Disabled 41

- College Guide for Students with Learning Disabilities
- Help Yourself: Handbook for College-Bound Students with Learning Disabilities
- K&W Guide to Colleges for the Learning Disabled
- Lovejoy's College Guide for the Learning Disabled
- Peterson's Colleges with Programs for Students with Learning Disabilities or Attention Deficit Disor
- Succeeding in College with Attention Deficit Disorders

Colitis and Crohn's Disease 42

- Crohn's and Colitis Foundation of America

Communication Disorders 43

- American Hyperlexia Association
- Cleft Palate Foundation
- Division for Children with Communication Disorders

Communication Disorders: Professional Organizations 44

- American Cleft Palate-Craniofacial Association
- American Speech-Language Association (ASHA)

Communication Disorders Websites 44

- Net Connections for Communication Disorders and Sciences (An Internet Guide by Judith Maginnis Ku

Comprehensive Achievement Assessment Measures 45

- Brigance Diagnostic Inventory of Basic Skills
- Kaufman Tests of Educational Achievement (KTEA)
- Norris Educational Achievement Test (NEAT)

- Government Printing Office (GPO)
- Library of Congress National Library Service for the Blind and Physically Handicapped
- National Cancer Institute (NCI)
- National Center for Education in Maternal and Child Health (NCEMCH)
- National Center for Educational Statistics (NCES)
- National Eye Institute (NEI)
- National Heart, Lung, and Blood Institute (NHLBI)
- National Institute on Alcohol Abuse and Alcoholism (NIAAA)
- National Institute on Allergy and Infectious Diseases (NIAID)
- National Institute of Arthritis and Musculoskeletal and Skin Diseases (NIAMS)
- National Institute of Child Health and Human Development (NICHD)
- National Institute on Deafness and Other Communication Disorders (NIDCD)
- National Institute of Diabetes and Digestive and Kidney Diseases (NIDDK)
- National Institute on Disability and Rehabilitative Research (NIDRR)
- National Institute on Drug Abuse (NIDA)
- National Institute on Early Childhood Development and Education (ECI)
- National Institute on the Education of At-Risk Students (OERI-At Risk)
- National Institute of Environmental Health Sciences (NIEHS)
- National Institute of Health
- National Institute of Mental Health (NIMH)
- National Institute of Neurological Disorders and Stroke (NINDS)
- National Institute on Post Secondary Education, Libraries, and Lifelong Learning (PLLI)
- National Institute on Student Achievement, Curriculum, and Assessment (SAI)
- National Library of Medicine (NLM)
- Office on the Americans with Disabilities Act
- Office of Civil Rights (OCR)
- Office on Disability and Health
- Office of Educational Research and Improvement (OERI)
- Office of Elementary and Secondary Education (OESE)
- Office of Post Secondary Education (OPE)
- Office of Special Education and Rehabilitative Services (OSERS)
- Office of Special Education Programs (OSEP)
- Office of Vocational and Adult Education (OVAE)
- President's Committee on Employment of People with Disabilities
- Rehabilitation Services Administration (RSA)
- Small Business Administration (SBA)
- Social Security Administration (SSA)
- Substance Abuse and Mental Health (SAMHA)

Hearing Impaired   81
- Alexander Graham Bell Association for the Deaf, Inc.
- American Society for Deaf Children
- Better Hearing Institute
- Captioned Films/Videos National Association of the Deaf
- Deafness Research Foundation
- The Ear Foundation

- National Education Association

Publishers and Distributors of Special Education Curriculum Materials Professional Books, and Media Materials   141

- Ablenet, Inc.
- Academic Communication Associates
- Academic Press
- Academic Therapy Publications
- Accelerated Development/A Division of Taylor & Francis Group
- Aquarius Health Care Videos
- A.D.D. WareHouse
- Addison Wesley Longman Publishing Co.
- Allyn & Bacon
- American Guidance Service
- Aspen Publishers Inc.
- Attainment Company
- Boulden Publishing
- Brookline Books
- Brookes Publishing Company
- Brooks/Cole Publishing Co.
- Brunner/Mazel
- Bureau for At-Risk Youth
- C.H. Stoelting Co.
- Cambridge Development Laboratory
- Charles C Thomas
- Child Development Media
- Child's Work Child's Play
- Cognitive Therapeutics
- CompCare Publishers
- Council For Exceptional Children
- Crestwood Catalog Company
- CTB/McGraw-Hill
- Curriculum Associates, Inc.
- Don Johnston Inc.
- EBSCO Curriculum Materials
- Educators Publishing Service, Inc.
- Films for the Humanities and Sciences
- Free Spirit Publishing Inc.
- Funtastic Therapy
- Gallaudet University Press
- Glencoe/McGraw-Hill
- Globe-Fearon Educational Publishers
- Greenwood Publishing Group
- Grey House Publishing
- Guilford Publishing Co.
- Haworth Press

- Hawthorne Educational Services
- Health Source Bookstore
- HRM Video
- Insight Media
- James Stanfield Publishing Co.
- J.E. Stewart Teaching Tools
- Jossey-Bass Inc., Publishers
- J. Weston Walch Publishers
- Kapable Kids
- Kaplan Concepts for Exceptional Children
- Lakeshore Learning Materials
- Love Publishing Co.
- Merrill Publishing Co.
- Multi-Health Systems
- National Professional Resources
- National School Products
- Oryx Press
- PCI Educational Publishing
- Plenum Publishing
- Porter Sargent Publishers
- Prentice Hall
- Prentice Hall/Center for Applied Research in Education/Parker Publishing
- Princeton Review
- Pro-Ed
- Professional Books
- Prufrock Press
- Psychological Assessment Resources
- Psychological Corporation
- Psychological and Educational Publications
- Recorded Books
- Remedia Publications
- Research Press
- Resources for Educators/Prentice Hall
- Riverside Publishing
- Saddleback Education, Inc.
- Scantron Quality Computers
- Scholastic, Inc.
- Scott-Foresman/Addison Wesley
- Self-Esteem Store
- Singular Publishing Group Inc.
- Slosson Educational Publications
- Spring Books
- Springer Publishing Co.
- SRA McGraw-Hill
- Sunburst Communications
- Teachers College Press
- Teacher Ideas Press

A

Acquired Immune Deficiency Syndrome–AIDS

AIDS is an infectious disorder that suppresses the normal function of the immune system. It is caused by the human immunodeficiency virus (HIV), which destroys the body's ability to fight infections. Specific cells of the immune system that are responsible for the proper response to infections (T cells) are destroyed by this virus. Characteristically a person infected with HIV initially experiences no symptoms for a long period of time. This may be followed by the development of persistent generalized swelling of the lymph nodes (AIDS-related lymphadenopathy). Eventually most patients infected with HIV experience a syndrome of symptoms that includes excessive fatigue, weight loss, and/or skin rashes. (From National Organization of Rare Disorders—NORD)

Elizabeth Glaser Pediatric AIDS Foundation
2950 31st Street, Suite 125
Santa Monica, CA 90405
Phone: (310) 314-1459
Fax: (310) 314-1469
E-mail: info@pedaids.org
Internet URL: http://www.pedaids.org
Newsletters/Publications: Call for a list of publications.
Description: A national non-profit organization dedicated to identifying, funding, and conducting basic pediatric AIDS research.

Immune Deficiency Foundation
25 West Chesapeake Avenue, Suite 206
Towson, MD 21204
Phone: (800) 296-4433 or (410) 321-6647 in MD
Fax: (410) 321-9165
e-mail: idf@clark.net
Internet URL: http://www.primaryimmune.org
Newsletters/Publications: *Immune Deficiency Foundation Newsletter*, published six times a year.

Description: The Immune Deficiency Foundation is a national voluntary health organization dedicated to supporting research and training, disseminating information, and conducting educational campaigns.

National Aids Clearinghouse
(See Clearinghouses)

National Foundation for Children with AIDS (NFCA)
3505 South Ocean Drive
Hollywood, FL 33019
Phone: (954) 927-0101
Fax: (954) 927-3091
E-mail: info@childrenwithaids
Internet URL: http://www.childrenwithaids.org
Newsletters/Publications: Call for a list of publications.
Description: The National Foundation for Children with AIDS is a national organization dedicated to providing comfort and assistance to children stricken with AIDS. Efforts for the children come by way of doctors, nursing assistance, medications, field trips, entertainment, reading materials, TV, games, and more.

Ryan White Foundation
1717 West 86th Street, Suite 220
Indianapolis, IN 46260
Phone: (800) 444-RYAN
Fax: (317) 876-3300
E-mail: N/A
Newsletters/Publications: *Ryan White Foundation Newsletter*, published quarterly.
Internet URL: http://www.ryanwhite.org
Description: The Ryan White Foundation is a national non-profit organization established to increase awareness of personal, family, and community issues related to Human Immunodeficiency Virus (HIV) and Acquired Immune Deficiency Syndrome (AIDS).

Adaptive Behavior Assessment Measures

Adaptive Behavior is defined as the effectiveness or degree to which individuals meet the standards of personal independence and social responsibility expected for age and cultural groups. Areas evaluated by adaptive behavior scales include communication, self direction, health and safety, self-care home living, social skills, leisure, work, and so on.

AAMR Adaptive Behavior Scale–Residential and Community-2 (ABS-RC-2)
Authors: Kazuo Nihira, Henry Leland, Nadine Lambert
Publisher: PRO-ED, Inc.
8700 Shoal Creek Boulevard
Austin, TX 78758-6897
Number of Publisher: (512) 451-3246 or (800) 897-3202

Fax of Publisher: (800) FXPROED
Type of Test: Norm-referenced
Administration Time: 15–30 minutes
Type of Administration: Individual
Age/Grade Level: Ages 18 to 80

AAMR Adaptive Behavior Scale–School-2 (ABS-S-2)
Authors: Nadine Lambert, Kazuo Nihira, Henry Leland
Publisher: PRO-ED, Inc.
8700 Shoal Creek Boulevard
Austin, TX 78758-6897
Number of Publisher: (512) 451-3246 or (800) 897-3202
Fax of Publisher: (800) FXPROED
Type of Test: Norm-referenced
Type of Administration: Individual
Administration Time: 15–30 minutes
Age/Grade Level: Ages 3 to 18.11

The Adaptive Behavior Evaluation Scale–Revised (ABES-R)
Author: Stephen B. McCarney
Publisher: Hawthorne Educational Services
800 Gray Oak Drive
Columbia, MO 65201
Number of Publisher: (800) 542-1673
Fax of Publisher: (800) 442-9509
Type of Test: Norm-referenced
Administration Time: 20–25 minutes
Type of Administration: Individual
Age/Grade Level: Grades K-12

Advocacy

This section contains representative organizations, associations, networks, and sites that support the rights of children and adults with disabilities.

American Bar Association
750 North Lake Shore Drive
Chicago, IL 60611
Phone: (312) 988-5000
Fax: N/A
E-mail: info@abanet.org
Internet URL: http://www.abanet.org
Newsletters/Publications: Call for a list of publications.

Description: The ABA provides assistance and information on a variety of issues and areas including legal assistance, lawyer referral, volunteer lawyer programs, lawyer disciplinary agencies, publications for the general public, all ABA publications, additional resources, public services, public education, legal services, domestic violence, mental and physical disability law, children and the law, homelessness and poverty, substance abuse, discussion groups, media information, legal service plans, student educational materials about the law, ABA-approved Law Schools, and the ABA Network Lawyer Locator.

Association for the Severely Handicapped (TASH)
29 West Susquehanna Avenue, Suite 210
Baltimore, MD 21204
Phone: (410) 828-8274
Fax: (410) 828-6706
E-mail: info@tash.org
Internet URL: http://www.tash.org
Newsletter/Publications: Call for a list of publications.
Description: TASH is an international advocacy association of people with disabilities, their family members, other advocates, and people who work in the disability field. It has 38 chapters and members from 34 different countries and territories. Since its inception twenty years ago, TASH has gained international acclaim for an uncompromising stand against separatism, stigmatization, abuse, and neglect. It actively promotes the full inclusion and participation of persons with disabilities in all aspects of life. TASH believes that no one with a disability should be forced to live, work, or learn in a segregated setting; and that all individuals deserve the right to direct their own lives. TASH's mission is to eliminate physical and social obstacles that prevent equity, diversity, and quality of life.

Children's Defense Fund
25 E Street NW
Washington, DC 20001
Phone: (202) 628-8787
Fax: N/A
E-mail: cdfinfo@childrensdefense.org
Internet URL: http://www.childrensdefense.org
Newsletters/Publications: Contact organization for a list of publications.
Description: The Children's Defense Fund (CDF) is a non-profit research and advocacy organization that exists to provide a strong and effective voice for children of America who cannot vote, lobby, or speak out for themselves. The Children's Defense Fund pays particular attention to the needs of poor, minority, and disabled children. CDF's goal is to educate the nation about the needs of children and to encourage investment in children before they get sick, drop out of school, suffer damage breakdown, or get into trouble. The organization has regional offices throughout the United States.

Commission on Mental and Physical Disability Law, American Bar Association
740 Fifteenth Street, NW
Washington, DC 20005-1009
Phone: (202) 662-1570
TTY: (202) 662-1012
Fax: (202) 662-1032

E-mail: cmpdl@abanet.org
Internet URL: http://www.abanet.org/disability/home.html
Newsletters/Publications: Besides a wide variety of publications, the Commission has published the *Mental and Physical Disability Law Reporter,* the nation's longest running and most comprehensive source of disability law, for the last 19 years.
Description: The Commission on Mental and Physical Disability Law has been fulfilling the American Bar Association's commitment to justice and the rule of law for persons with mental and physical disabilities. Established in 1973, it has a great deal of background and references for assisting the disability community.

Disability Rights Education and Defense Fund, Inc. (DREDF)
2212 Sixth Street
Berkeley, CA 94710
Phone: (Voice/TDD) (510) 644-2555
Fax: (510) 841-8645
E-mail: dredf@dredf.org
Internet URL: http://www.dredf.org
Newsletters/Publications: Call for a list of publications.
Description: DREDF is a national law and policy center dedicated to protecting and advancing the civil rights of people with disabilities through legislation, litigation, advocacy, technical assistance, and education and training of attorneys, advocates, persons with disabilities, and parents of children with disabilities.

National Association of Protection and Advocacy Systems (NAPAS)
900 Second Street NE, Suite 211
Washington, DC 20002
Phone: (202) 408-9514 or (202) 408-9521 (TDD)
Fax: (202) 408-9520
E-mail: napas@earthlink.net
Internet URL: http://www.protectionandadvocacy.com/napas.htm
Newsletters/Publications: Call for a list of publications.
Description: NAPAS is a national voluntary membership organization for the federally mandated nationwide network of disability rights agencies, protection and advocacy systems (P&As), and client assistance programs (CAPs).

NAPAS was created to facilitate coordination of its members, represent the needs of members to federal agencies and Congress, and provide technical assistance and training to member agencies to enhance their effectiveness at the state and local levels.

NAPAS has daily contact with P&As and CAPs nationally and has provided training and technical assistance to its members since its inception. NAPAS' goals and activities are based on its understanding of the needs and capacities of the P&A/CAP network. This site provides access to state chapters.

National Association for Rights Protection and Advocacy (NARPA)
NARPA Administrator
P.O. Box 16311
Rumford, RI 02916
Phone: (401) 434-2120

Fax: (401) 431-0043
E-mail: jblaaa@aol.com
Internet URL: http://www.connix.com/~narpa
Newsletters/Publications: Members receive *The Rights Tenet*, the newsletter of the National Association for Rights Protection and Advocacy.
Description: NARPA is dedicated to promoting policies and pursuing strategies that represent the preferred options of people who have been labeled mentally disabled. NARPA is committed to advocating the abolishment of forced treatment laws. NARPA believes the recipients of mental health services are capable of and entitled to make their own choices, and that they are, above all, equal citizens under the law. NARPA is committed to promoting rights protection and advocacy that focuses upon both the right to choose and the specific choices of those who request assistance.

National Parent Network on Disabilities (NPND)
1130 17th Street NW, Suite 400
Washington, DC 20036
Phone: (202) 434-8686
Fax: (202) 638-0509
E-mail: npnd@cs.com
Internet URL: http://www.npnd.org
Newsletters/Publications: *The Friday Fax*, published weekly.
Description: NPND is a membership advocacy organization open to all agencies, organizations, parent centers, parent groups, professionals, and individuals concerned with the quality of life for people with disabilities.

Parent Advocacy Coalition for Educational Rights (PACER)
4826 Chicago Avenue,South
Minneapolis, MN 55417-1098
Phone: (612) 827-2966
Fax: (612) 827-3065
E-mail: webster@pacer.org
Internet URL: http://www.pacer.org
Newsletters/Publications: Call for a list of publications.
Description: This parent-to-parent organization has published numerous items of interest to families of children with disabilities. The center offers training programs for parents and youth, technical assistance, and advocacy information and assistance.

Pete and Pam Wright
c/o The Special Ed Advocate
P. O. Box 1008
Deltaville, VA 23043
Phone: (804) 257-0857
E-mail: pwright@wrightslaw.com
Internet URL: http://www.wrightslaw.com
Newsletter/Publications: Contact organization on-line for publications.
Description: The objective of this organization is to provide parents, educators, attorneys, and other helping professionals with the information they need to be effective advocates for special needs children.

Protection and Advocacy, Inc.
Administrative Offices
100 Howe Avenue, Suite 185-N
Sacramento, CA 95825
All Offices Toll Free: (TTY/TDD) (800) 776-5746
Phone: (916) 488-9955
Fax: (916) 488-2635
E-mail: legalmail@pai-ca.org.
Internet URL: http://www.pai-ca.org
Newsletters/Publications: Call for a list of publications.
Description: Protection and Advocacy, Inc. (PAI) is a non-profit agency that provides legal assistance to people with physical, developmental, and psychiatric disabilities. Services available from PAI include information and referral to other sources of assistance, peer and self-advocacy training, representation in administrative and judicial proceedings, investigation of abuse and neglect, and legislative advocacy.

Albinism and Hypopigmentation

The word "albinism" refers to a group of inherited conditions. People with albinism have little or no pigment in their eyes, skin, or hair. They have inherited genes that do not make the usual amounts of a pigment called melanin.

One person in 17,000 has some type of albinism. Albinism affects people from all races. Most children with albinism are born to parents who have the normal hair and eye color for their ethnic backgrounds.

National Organization for Albinism and Hypopigmentation (NOAH)
1530 Locust Street, Suite 29
Philadelphia, PA 19102
Phone: (800) 473-2310 or (215) 545-2322
Fax: N/A
E-mail: webmaster@albinism.org
Internet URL: http://www.albinism.org
Newsletters/Publications: NOAH publishes *NOAH News* twice yearly, as well as information bulletins on particular topics.
Description: NOAH provides information and support regarding albinism and related conditions, promotes public and professional education about these conditions, and encourages research and funding that will lead to improved diagnosis and management of albinism. NOAH provides networking for those with related albinism, such as minority groups.

NOAH has a network of local chapters and contact persons, and offers referrals to state rehabilitation agencies and providers of equipment and materials.

Americans with Disabilities Act (ADA) Resources

The Americans with Disabilities Act (1990), a Federal law, gives civil rights protections to individuals with disabilities similar to those provided to individuals on the basis of race, color, sex, national origin, age, and religion. It guarantees equal opportunity for individuals with disabilities in public accommodations, employment, transportation, state and local government services, and telecommunications.

The Office of Special Education and Rehabilitation Services (OSERS) is the administrative arm of the ADA.

ADA Homepage
US Department of Justice
Internet URL: http://www.usdoj.gov/crt/ada/adahom1.htm
Description: Contains everything you need to know about ADA.

ADA Information Center OnLine
Internet URL: http://www.public.iastate.edu/%7Esbilling/ada.html
Description: Lists an extensive number of sites for Independent Living Centers, ADA resources, and general disability information.

Office of Special Education and Rehabilitation Services (OSERS)
(See Government Agencies–Federal)

Angelman Syndrome

According to Stephen M. Edelson, Ph.D., at the Center for the Study of Autism, Angelman Syndrome is not considered to be a subtype of autism, but individuals suffering from this disorder exhibit many behaviors characteristic of autism and are sometimes given a secondary diagnosis of autism. Similar to autism, individuals with Angelman Syndrome display the following behaviors: hand-flapping, little or no speech, attention deficits, hyperactivity, feeding and sleeping problems, and delays in motor development. These individuals may also engage in biting and hair pulling.

In contrast to autism, people with Angelman Syndrome are often described as very sociable. They are very affectionate and engage in frequent laughing. The majority of these individuals have abnormal EEGs and epilepsy. Many tend to have a stiff-legged gait and jerky body movements. These individuals also have common facial features, such as a wide smiling mouth, a thin upper lip, and deep set eyes. More than half have low levels of pigmentation in their eyes, hair, and skin.

The prevalence rate of Angelman Syndrome is estimated to be 1 in 25,000 individuals, and the majority are described as severely mentally retarded.

Suggested interventions for Angelman Syndrome include behavior modification, speech therapy, and occupational therapy.

Angelman Syndrome Foundation
P.O. Box 12347
Gainesville, FL 32604

Phone: (800) 432-6435 or (904) 332-3303
Fax: (212) 779-7728
E-mail: dharvey@ucsd.edu
Internet URL: http://www.chemfaculty.ucsd.edu/harvey/asfsite/index.html
Newsletters/Publications: Call for a list of publications.
Description: The foundation provides education on diagnosis, treatment and management, and support and advocacy to regional and local areas.

Anorexia Nervosa and Bulimia

Anorexia Nervosa is characterized by a refusal to maintain body weight at or above a minimally normal weight for age and height, intense fear of gaining weight even though underweight, disturbance in the way one's body weight or shape is experienced, and amenorrhea (absence of at least 3 consecutive menstrual cycles).

Bulimia nervosa is characterized by recurrent episodes of binge eating; recurrent inappropriate behavior to prevent weight gain, such as self induced vomiting misuse of laxatives, diuretics, enemas, or other medications; and fasting or excessive exercise.

Anorexia Nervosa and Bulimia Association
767 Bayridge Drive
P.O. Box 20058
Kingston, Ontario, CANADA
K7P 1C0
Phone: (613) 547-3684
Fax: N/A
E-mail: anab@www.ams.queensu.ca
Internet URL: http://www.ams.queensu.ca/anab
Newsletters/Publications: *Reflections*, published quarterly.
Description: ANAB is a registered, non-profit, community-based organization situated in Kingston, Ontario, Canada that has been active since the fall of 1991. It is comprised of concerned health professionals, volunteers, parents, friends, siblings, and recovered (or recovering) individuals who have had or who do have an eating disorder. Its mission is to facilitate, advocate, and coordinate support for any individual directly or indirectly affected by eating disorders, and to raise public awareness through improved communication and education.

Anorexia Nervosa and Related Eating Disorders, Inc. (ANRED)
P.O. Box 5102
Eugene, OR 97405
Phone: (541) 344-1144
Fax: N/A
E-mail: lpchnedo@ionet.net
Internet URL: http://www.anred.com
Newsletters/Publications: Contact the organization for a list of publications.
Description: ANRED is a non-profit organization that maintains a website on eating disorders and provides a good database.

National Eating Disorders Organization (NEDO)
6655 South Yale Avenue
Tulsa, OK 74136
Phone: (918) 481-4044
Fax: (918) 481-4076
E-mail: N/A
Internet URL: http://www.laureate.com
Newsletters/Publications: *Quarterly National Newsletter.* Contact the organization for a list of publications.
Description: NEDO is one of the oldest eating disorder organizations in the United States. Its focus is on education, prevention, and providing treatment resources. NEDO also disseminates information.

Anxiety Disorders

Everyone faces personal anxieties and fears. They are part of everyday life. But for millions of Americans, anxieties and fears are overwhelming and persistent, often drastically interfering with daily life. These people suffer from anxiety disorders, a widespread group of psychiatric disorders that can be terrifying and crippling. The conditions classified as anxiety disorders include panic disorder, phobia, obsessive-compulsive disorder, post-traumatic stress disorder, and generalized anxiety disorder.

Anxiety Disorders Association of America
11900 Park Lawn Drive, Suite 100
Rockville, MD 20852
Phone: (301) 231-9350
Fax: N/A
E-mail: anxdis.@aol.com
Internet URL: http://www.adaa.org
Newsletters/Publications: Call for a list of publications.
Description: This organization provides information, publications, newsletters, audio tapes, professional therapist listings, and website links to related sites.

National Institute of Mental Health (NIMH)
(See Government Agencies–Federal)

Aphasia

Aphasia is a language disorder that results from damage to the portion of the brain that is dominant for language. For most people, this is the left side of the brain. Aphasia usually occurs suddenly, frequently the result of a stroke or head injury, but it may also develop slowly as in the case of a brain tumor. The disorder may involve aspects of language comprehension and/or expression.

National Aphasia Association (NAA)
P.O. Box 1887
Murray Hill Station
New York, NY 10156-0611
Phone: (800) 922-4622
Fax: (212) 263-7929
E-mail: N/A
Internet URL: http://www.aphasia.org
Newsletters/Publications: Call for a list of publications.
Description: NAA is a non-profit organization that promotes public education, research, rehabilitation, and support services.

Apraxia

Apraxia of speech is considered a motor speech disorder. A child with apraxia of speech has difficulty sequencing the motor movements necessary for volitional speech. Apraxia of speech may also be called verbal apraxia, developmental apraxia of speech, and verbal dyspraxia. No matter which term is used, the most important factor is the root word "praxis." Praxis is the ability to execute skilled movement; therefore, children with the diagnosis of apraxia of speech have varying degrees of difficulty in sequencing and executing speech movements. Apraxia of speech is a specific speech disorder.

Apraxia-Kids
Website only
Phone: N/A
Fax: N/A
E-mail: apraxia@avenza.com
Internet URL: http://www.avenza.com/~apraxia/index.html
Newsletters/Publications: N/A
Description: Apraxia-Kids started as a listserv for parents who have children with apraxia of speech. Such a forum list quickly grew to a vital and busy exchange between parents all over the globe, as well as therapists and other professionals. This organization also provides links to other sites dealing with speech and language disorders.

Arthritis

Juvenile rheumatoid arthritis (JRA) is the most prevalent form of arthritis in children. The most common features of JRA include joint inflammation, joint contracture, joint damage, and altered growth.

Arthritis Foundation
1330 West Peachtree Street
Atlanta, GA 30309

Phone: (404) 283-7800 or (404) 872-7100
Fax: (404) 872-0457
E-mail: webmaster@arthritis.org
Internet URL: http://www.arthritis.org
Newsletters/Publications: *Arthritis Today*, published six times a year.
Description: This organization disseminates information, promotes research, and publishes a newsletter to improve the quality of life for people with arthritis.

American Juvenile Arthritis Organization
1314 Spring Street NW
Atlanta, GA 30309
Phone: (404) 872-7100, extension 6271
Fax: (404) 872-0457
E-mail: webmaster@arthritis.com
Internet URL: http://www.arthritis.org
Newsletters/Publications: *Kids Get Arthritis Too*, published six times a year.
Description: The American Juvenile Arthritis Organization is a council of the Arthritis Foundation devoted to serving the special needs of children, teens, and young adults with childhood rheumatic diseases and their families. The American Juvenile Arthritis Organization offers support and information to parents of children with rheumatic diseases through national and local programs that supports the needs of families, health care professionals, and friends, and provides an effective structure for self-help. The foundation provides staff, funds, and materials for organization activities with volunteers who plan and administer them.

Asperger's Disorder

Asperger's Disorder is a milder variant of Autistic Disorder. Both Asperger's Disorder and Autistic Disorder are subgroups of a larger diagnostic category. This larger category is called either Autistic Spectrum Disorder or Pervasive Developmental Disorders.

In Asperger's Disorder, affected individuals are characterized by social isolation and eccentric behavior in childhood. There are impairments in two-sided social interaction and non-verbal communication. Though grammatical, their speech is peculiar due to abnormalities of inflection and a repetitive pattern. Clumsiness is prominent both in their articulation and gross motor behavior. They usually have a circumscribed area of interest which usually leaves no space for more age appropriate, common interests. Some examples are cars, trains, French Literature, door knobs, hinges, cappuccino, meteorology, astronomy, or history.

Asperger's Disorder Home Page
Author: Kahn R. Ozbayrak, M.D.
E-mail: ozbayrak@aspergers.com
Internet URL: http://www.aspergers.com
Description: This site provides a database, a list of US clinicians, a bibliography, and related websites.

Assistive Technology Websites

Assistive Technology Devices are "Any item, piece of equipment, or product system, whether acquired commercially or off the shelf, modified or customized, that increases, maintains, or improves functional capabilities of individuals with disabilities." (Source: Technology-Related Assistance for Individuals With Disabilities Act of 1988 [Public Law 100-407, August 19, 1988].) Assistive Technology devices can be anything from a simple tool with no moving parts (e.g., a toothbrush with a built-up handle) to a sophisticated mechanical/electronic system (e.g., a robotic arm). Simple, mechanical devices are often referred to as low tech devices while computer-driven or complex assistive technology may be called high tech. However, many people in the assistive technology field have argued that this complexity-based classification is not a useful one as there is no clear division between the devices. With the passage of the Rehabilitation Act Amendments of 1992 (PL 102-569), assistive technology devices and assistive technology services are now included as part of rehabilitation technology.

ABLEDATA Website
Part of The National Institute on Disability and Rehabilitation Research
(See Government Agencies–Federal)
8455 Colesville Road, Suite 935
Silver Spring, MD 20918
Phone: (800) 227-0216 or (301) 608-8998
Fax: (301) 608-8958
E-mail: NA
Internet URL: http://www.abledata.com
Newsletters/Publications: Provides fact sheets, consumer guides, bulletins, and other materials. Call for a complete list of publications, or go online.
Description: ABLEDATA is an electronic database of information on assistive technology and rehabilitation equipment available in the United States. It covers more than 23,000 product listings. ABLEDATA also provides information specialists by appointment who can perform a database search.

Access First
Internet URL: http://www.inforamp.net/~access/af1.htm
Description: Access First provides the best in sales, training, and support for the sight-impaired, print-handicapped and learning-disabled community. Its main services are that of consultants, instructors, and software developers. It has more than 40 years of combined experience in the areas of high technology sales and technical support, applications design, community networking, and funding resources. As end users, Access First understands and addresses the special needs of the student and professional in the workplace.

Adaptive Computing Technology Center
Internet URL: http://www.missouri.edu/~ccact
Description: The mission of the Adaptive Computing Technology Center is to create access to technology in a manner that enhances integration. Adaptive technology makes input to the computer and feedback from the computer accessible to persons with disabilities. This can be achieved by combining adaptive devices with standard computer equipment.

Alliance for Technology Access (ATA)
2175 East Francisco Boulevard, Suite L
San Rafael, CA 94901
Phone: (800) 455-7970 or (415) 455-4575 (Voice)
(TTD): (415) 455-0491
Fax: (415) 455-0654
E-mail: atainfo@ataccess.org
Internet URL: http://www.ataccess.org
Newsletters/Publications: *ATACCESS*, a quarterly newsletter.
Description: The Alliance for Technology Access is a network of community-based resource centers dedicated to providing information and support services to children and adults with disabilities, and to increasing their use of standard assistive and information technologies. The centers can be found across the country.

Apple Computer's Worldwide Disability Solutions Group
Internet URL: http://www.apple.com/disability/welcome.html
Description: This online version of the Mac Access Passport is a place to interactively learn about the kinds of products that make it possible for persons with disabilities to use a Macintosh computer. The latest version of its product database can be downloaded, and links to major organizations and manufacturers can be accessed, along with a collection of software programs from Apple.

Archimedes Project
Internet URL: http://kanpai.stanford.edu/arch/arch.html
Description: Project Archimedes seeks to promote equal access to information for individuals with disabilities by influencing the early design stages of tomorrow's computer-based technology.

Assistive Technology Devices on the Internet
Internet URL: http://www.asel.udel.edu/at-online/devices
Description: This site provides a complete A-Z listing of manufacturers and devices under the following categories:
• Adaptive Toys/Games
• Augmentative Communication
• Cognitive Aids
• Computer Access
• Environmental Controls
• Home Modifications
• Learning Technologies
• Mobility
• Positioning and Seating
• Prosthetics/Orthotics
• Recreation/Sports
• Robotics
• Self-Care
• Sensory Aids
• Telecommunication

Association for the Advancement of Rehabilitation Technology (RESNA)
1700 North Moore Street, Suite 1540
Arlington, VA 22209-1903

Phone: (703) 524-6686 (Voice)
TTY: (703) 524-6639
Fax: (703) 524-6630
E-mail: natloffice@resna.org
Internet URL: http://www.resna.org/resna/reshome.htm
Newsletters/Publications: *Journal of Assistive Technology.*
Contact the organization for a brochure.
Description: Among other areas, RESNA is a resource for educators wishing to ensure that the technology they purchase and use is accessible to all students, including students with disabilities.

AZtech, Inc.
Internet URL: http://cosmos.ot.buffalo.edu/aztech.html
Description: AZtech, Inc. is a community-based enterprise, by and for persons with disabilities. The name AZtech, Inc. stands for A to Z assistive TECHnology. AZtech is operated by the Rehabilitation Engineering Research Center on Technology Evaluation and Transfer (RERC-TET). RERC-TET is supported by a grant from the National Institute on Disability and Rehabilitation Research, U.S. Department of Education.

Center for Information Technology Accommodation (CITA)
Internet URL: http://www.gsa.gov:80/coca
Description: CITA is a clearinghouse of information systems available to all users and includes WWW design guidelines. It is part of the General Services Administration of the federal government.
(See Government Agencies–Federal)

DREAMMS for Kids
Internet URL: http://users.aol.com/dreamms/main.html
Description: DREAMMS for Kids, Inc. (Developmental Research for the Effective Advancement of Memory and Motor Skills) is a non-profit parent and professional service agency that specializes in assistive technology related research, development, and information dissemination. Founded in 1988 by the parents of a Down Syndrome child, DREAMMS is committed to facilitating the use of computers, assistive technologies, and quality instructional technologies for students and youth with special needs in schools, homes, and the community. Services include newsletters, individually prepared Tech Paks, and special programs entitled Computers for Kids and Tools for Transition.

DRM Guide To Disability Resources on the Internet
Internet URL: http://www.geocities.com/~drm/AT.html
Description: Millions of people with disabilities use assistive technology devices to help them live, learn, love, work, and play independently. This section of The DRM WebWatcher accesses online information about assistive technology products and services.

EASI: Equal Access to Software and Information
Address: http://www.isc.rit.edu/~easi
Description: EASI is dedicated to collecting and disseminating up-to-date information about how to provide access for persons with disabilities to computing and technology information resources.

EASI's Seminars on Adaptive Computing
Internet URL: gopher://sjuvm.stjohns.edu/11/disabled/easi/easishop
Description: Gopher server: "EASI's Seminars on Adaptive Computing, EASI's Online Workshops on Adaptive Computing, Article About EASI's Online Workshops on Adaptive Computing, Sample Syllabus of EASI's Online Workshops on Adaptive Computing."

Fortec Institute of Electronics
Internet URL: http://sun4.iaee.tuwien.ac.at/e359.3/abtb/abtb.html
Description: This group was established to intensify and consolidate efforts related to research and development of new technical solutions for disabled and elderly persons.

Mac Access Passport Online
Internet URL: http://www.apple.com/disability/Welcome.html
Description: Mac Access Passport helps consumers and professionals discover assistive technology solutions for Macintosh computers that will allow individuals with disabilities to lead more independent lives.

National Center to Improve Practice
Internet URL: http://www.edc.org/FSC/NCIP
Description: The National Center to Improve Practice (NCIP) promotes the effective use of technology to enhance educational outcomes for students with sensory, cognitive, physical, and social/emotional disabilities.

NCSA Accessibility Project
Internet URL: http://bucky.aa.uic.edu
Description: NCSA Mosaic Access Page is a resource for those interested in how people with disabilities can use the internet and the World Wide Web.

Project Pursuit
Internet URL: http://pursuit.rehab.uiuc.edu/pursuit/homepage.html
Description: Here you will find a wealth of resources including disability information; education accommodation resources; lessons on assistive technology and funding available for this technology; descriptions of careers in science, engineering, and mathematics; high school preparations for these careers; access to countless other information servers; and much more.

Rehabilitation Engineering Research Center on Hearing Enhancement and Assistive Devices (RERC)
Lexington Center, Inc.
30th Avenue and 75th Street
Jackson Heights, NY 11370
Phone: (Voice/TTD) (718) 899-8000, extension 212
Fax: (718) 899-3433
E-mail: lexrsch@transit.appliedtheory.com
Internet URL: http://gramercy.ios.com/~reslex
Newsletters/Publications: *LexAccess* (bi-annual newsletter).
Description: RERC promotes and develops technological solutions to problems confronting individuals with hearing loss. Current projects include assistive devices for hearing impaired individuals with low vision, detection of hearing loss in infants using otoacoustic emissions, developing ASCII standards for TTD modems, and evaluating the use of assistive technologies

in the community and workplace. RERC also provides information and referral for consumer questions on assistive technology and research.

Technical Assistance on Training about the Rehabilitation Act (TATRA)
Part of PACER
(See Pacer–Parent Resources)

Telecommunications for the Deaf, Inc.
8630 Fenton Street, Suite 604
Silver Spring, MD 20910-3803
Phone: (301) 589-3786
TTD: (301) 589-3006
Fax: (301) 589-3797
E-mail: tdial@aol.com
Internet URL: http://www.tdi-online
Newsletters/Publications: *GA-SK* (quarterly), *National Directory of TTD Numbers* (annual).
Description: This non-profit consumer advocacy organization promotes full visual and other access to information and telecommunications for people who are deaf, hard of hearing, deaf-blind, and speech impaired. It supports consumer education and involvement, technical assistance and consulting, and the application of existing programs. Some of these programs are emergency 911 services, relay services, TTD usage and emerging technologies, networking and collaborations, uniformity of TTD standards, and national policy development that aids these goals and services.

WebABLE!
Internet URL: http://www.webable.com
Description: WebABLE! is the World Wide Web information repository for people with disabilities, and accessibility solution providers. WebABLE! is dedicated to promoting the interests of adaptive, assistive, and access technology researchers, users, and manufacturers.

Asthma

Asthma is a disease of the respiratory system. The respiratory system consists of nose, mouth, windpipe (also called trachea), lungs, and many air tubes (or airways) that connect the nose and mouth with the lungs (these tubes are called bronchi and bronchioles).

American Academy of Allergy Asthma and Immunology [AAAAI]
611 East Wells Street
Milwaukee, WI 53202
Phone: (800) 822-2762 or (414) 272-6071
Fax: (414) 276-3349
E-mail: N/A
Internet URL: http://www.aaaai.org
Newsletters/Publications: Call for a list of publications.

Description: AAAAI promotes the early detection and treatment of asthma and other allergic disease; supports local societies through education, marketing and networking activities; and provides a patient's guide to problem foods and food additives, diagnosis, treatment, and resources.

The Food Allergy Network (FAN)

10400 Eaton Place, Suite 107
Fairfax, VA 22030
Phone: (800) 929-4040 or (703) 691-3179
Fax: (703) 691-2713
E-mail: annemffan@aol.com
Internet URL: http://www.foodallergy.org
Newsletters/Publications: *Food Allergy News*, published bi-monthly.
Call for a list of publications.
Description: The mission of The Food Allergy Network is to increase public awareness about food allergies and anaphylaxis, a severe life-threatening reaction. It provides education, emotional support, and coping strategies to individuals with food allergies. FAN works with families, doctors, nurses, dietitians, and the food industry, and furnishes assistance to individuals who wish to start a support group in their locality.

Allergy and Asthma Network/Mothers of Asthmatics [AANMA]

3554 Chain Bridge Road, Suite 200
Fairfax, VA 22030
Phone: (800) 878-4403 or (703) 385-4403
Fax: (703) 352-4354
E-mail: aanma@aol.com
Internet URL: http://www.aanma.org
Newsletters/Publications: The *MA Report* monthly newsletter gives members insider information on medical research, new products, practical how-to-tips and helpful hints, updates on legislation, product recalls, and prevention and coping techniques. AANMA offers many books, pamphlets, and videos, including "Wheeze World," a video for children.
Description: AANMA provides patient education, offers discounts, and advocates for people with asthma and allergies.

Ataxia

Friedreich's and Cerebellar Ataxias are crippling diseases of the nervous system. They share many of the same symptoms, unsteadiness and the inability to coordinate movement being primary. Friedreich's Ataxia usually reveals itself in childhood, while Cerebellar Ataxia more often affects adults. Some people have additional symptoms, but all gradually get worse. Almost everyone eventually needs a wheelchair and has difficulties with their speech, although their mental abilities are unaffected. The causes are unknown and so far there is no treatment.

The National Ataxia Foundation
2600 Fernbrook Lane, Suite 119
Minneapolis, MN 55447
Phone: (612) 553-0020
Fax: (612) 553-0167
E-mail: naf@mr.net
Internet URL: http://www.ataxia.org
Newsletter/Publication: *Generations*, published quarterly.
Description: A non-profit organization that encourages and supports research into primary hereditary ataxia, promotes educational programs, and disseminates information. There are 45 affiliated chapters throughout the United States and Canada.

Attention Deficit Disorder

ADD is a neurobiological disability. It is characterized by attention skills that are developmentally inappropriate, impulsivity, and, in some cases, hyperactivity.

Children with ADD comprise approximately 3 to 5 percent of the school age population. Boys significantly outnumber girls, though girls are more likely to be undiagnosed. As many as 50 percent of children with ADD are never diagnosed.

ADD characteristics often arise in early childhood. ADD is marked by behaviors that are chronic, lasting at least six months with onset before age seven. Characteristics of children with ADD can include:
• fidgeting with hands or feet
• difficulty awaiting turns in games
• difficulty following through on instructions
• shifting from one uncompleted task to another
• difficulty playing quietly
• interrupting conversations and intruding into other children's games
• appearing to be not listening to what is being said
• doing things that are dangerous without thinking about the consequences

The Attention Deficit Information Network, Inc. (AD-IN)
475 Hillside Avenue
Needham, MA 02194
Phone: (781) 455-9895
Fax: (781) 444-5466
E-mail: adin@gis.net
Internet URL: http://www.addinfonetwork.com
Newsletters/Publications: Provides audio tapes, video tapes, information booklets, and articles online.
Description: AD-IN is a non-profit volunteer organization that offers support and information to families of children with attention deficit disorder (ADD), adults with ADD, and professionals through an international network of 60 parent and adult chapters. Contact AD-IN for a list of chapters, as well as to receive cost information for information packets specifically designed for adults with ADD, parents, or educators. AD-IN also provides information to those

interested in starting a new local chapter, and serves as a resource for information on training programs and speakers for those who work with individuals with ADD.

Children and Adults with Attention Deficit Disorder (CHADD)

499 Northwest 70th Avenue, Suite 308
Plantation, FL 33317
Phone: (800) 233-4050
Fax: (954) 587-5499
E-mail: national@chadd.org
Internet: http://www.chadd.org
Newsletters/Publications: CHADD also publishes a newsletter, *Chadderbox*, filled with up-to-date information on ADD issues; a quarterly magazine, *Attention;* and an educator's manual on ADD.
Description: CHADD is a non-profit, parent-based organization that disseminates information on ADD/ADHD, and coordinates more than 500 parent support groups across the country. This site also contains extensive practical information for teachers and parents.

National Attention Deficit Disorder Association (NADDA)

9930 Johnnycake Ridge Road, Suite 3E
Mentor, OH 44060
Phone: (800) 487-2282 to request information packet, or (440) 350-9595
Fax: (440) 350-0223
E-mail: NATLADDA@aol.com
Internet URL: http://www.add.org
Newsletters/Publications: *FOCUS*, published quarterly.
Description: ADDA is a national, non-profit organization that focuses on the needs of adults, young adults, and families with Attention Deficit Disorder. ADDA's mission is to help people with ADD live happier, more successful lives by providing information and resources on treatment and research, as well as workplace, relationship, parenting, and post-secondary educational issues.

Attention Deficit Disorder Websites

The ADDed Line
Internet URL: http://www.mindspring.com/~nlf/ADD/ADDed_Line.html
Description: This online newsletter is published by Thom Hartmann, author of "Attention Deficit Disorder: A Different Perception," "Focus Your Energy: Hunting For Success In Business With ADD," and "ADD Success Stories."

ADDed Reality
Internet URL: http://www.addedreality.com.
E-mail: evelyn@addedreality.com
Description: ADDed Reality is an information source for educators, parents, and young people. It is authored by Evelyn Azbell, a parent/teacher resource in northern Wisconsin.

Attention Deficit Disorder
Internet URL: http://www.ADD.IDsite.com
Description: This site is dedicated to all parents and teachers of children suffering from Attention Deficit Disorder and includes information on ADD, ADHD, ODD, and OCD.

Attention Deficit Disorder Web Site
Internet URL: http://www.ns.net/users/Brandi V
Description: This site is dedicated to all parents and teachers of children suffering from Attention Deficit Disorder.

One ADD Place
Internet URL: http://www.greatconnect.com/oneaddplace
Description: A "virtual neighborhood" consolidating in ONE PLACE information on the Internet relating to Attention Deficit Disorder (ADD, ADHD). One ADD Place includes public information provided by CHADD and ADDA; papers and articles by professionals and experts in the field; products and services (e.g., books, audio tapes, videos, seminars, workshops); calendar of events for seminars, workshops, and other programs; and links to other ADD-related web sites.

Autism

Autism is a nonprogressive neurological disorder characterized by language and communication deficits, withdrawal from social contacts, and extreme reactions to changes in the immediate environment.

Autism Network International (ANI)
P.O. Box 448
Syracuse NY 13210-0448
Phone: (315) 476-2462
Fax: (315) 425-1978
E-mail: jisincla@mailbox.syr.edu
Internet URL: N/A
Newsletters/Publications: ANI's educational materials include a regular newsletter entitled *Our Voice*, brochures, and audiovisual aids.
Description: Autism Network International (ANI) is a self-help and advocacy organization dedicated to supporting individuals with autism and helping them to compensate, navigate, and function in the world. The Network provides a forum for people with autism to share information, peer support, and tips for coping and problem solving. In addition to promoting self-advocacy for high-functioning autistic adults, Autism Network International assists people with autism who are unable to participate directly by providing information and referrals to parents and teachers.

Autism Research Institute (ARI)
4182 Adams Avenue
San Diego, CA 92116

Phone: (619) 281-7165
Fax: (619) 563-6840
E-mail: N/A
Internet URL: http://www.autism-society.org/>
Newsletters/Publications: ARI publishes a quarterly newsletter, *Autism Research Review International,* and has a publication list of information packets.
Description: The Autism Research Institute is primarily devoted to conducting research on methods of preventing, diagnosing, and treating autism and other severe behavioral disorders of childhood. It serves as a link between the parents of affected children, who are widely scattered geographically, and researchers throughout the world who are in need of carefully diagnosed samples of children for research purposes. Such referrals are made only with the prior consent of the parents. ARI assists families directly by providing information by mail or phone and has made the education of these children one of its important functions through literature and worldwide web information sites.

Autism Society of America (formerly NSAC)

7910 Woodmont Avenue, Suite 650
Bethesda, MD 20814-3015
Phone: (301) 657-0881 or (800) 328-8476
Fax: (301) 657-0869
E-mail: NA
Internet URL: http://www.autism-society.org
Newsletters/Publications: The American Autism Society publishes a newsletter called *The Advocate*.
Description: The Autism Society of America, a national not-for-profit advocacy organization established in 1965, is dedicated to providing information, assistance, support, and advocacy services to individuals with autism and their families. The Society supports ongoing medical research into the causes, prevention, and treatment of autism; promotes public awareness; and provides information and advocacy services to help affected individuals become fully participating members of their communities. In addition, the Society makes referrals to appropriate sources of support and treatment. The Society's educational materials include newsletters, brochures, and Spanish language materials.

Families for Early Autism Treatment (FEAT)

PO Box 255722
Sacramento, CA 95865-5722
Phone: (916) 843-1536
Fax: N/A
E-mail: feat@feat.org
Internet URL: http://www.feat.org
Newsletters/Publications: *FEAT Newsletter*
Description: FEAT (Families for Early Autism Treatment) is a non-profit organization of parents and professionals committed to helping families with children who have received the diagnosis of Autism or Pervasive Developmental Disorder (PDD NOS). It offers a network of support where families can meet to discuss issues surrounding autism and its treatment options.

MAAP Services, Inc.

PO Box 524
Crown Point, IN 46307

Phone: (219) 662-1311
Fax: (219) 662-0638
E-mail: chart@netnitco.net
Internet URL: http://www.stepstn.com/nord/org
Newsletters/Publications: *The MAAP* is a quarterly newsletter that allows subscribers to exchange information, learn about issues related to autism, and share with others who face similar challenges. MAAP disseminates specific print materials relevant to high-functioning individuals with autism and distributes a pamphlet entitled "MAAP Services, Inc."
Description: MAAP Services, Inc. is a non-profit organization dedicated to assisting family members of more advanced individuals with autism by offering information and advice on the disorder and by providing the opportunity to network with others in similar circumstances. In addition, MAAP Services works to inform professionals and the general public about more advanced individuals with autism and how to meet their needs. The organization conducts conferences, workshops, and meetings of parent groups; supports education; and provides appropriate referrals.

National Alliance for Autism Research (NAAR)

414 Wall Street, Research Park
Princeton, NJ 08540
Phone: 888-777-NAAR or (609) 430-9160
Fax: (609) 430-9163
E-mail: naar@naar.org
Internet URL: http://babydoc.home.pipeline.com/naar/naar.htm
Newsletters/Publications: *The Narrative*, published quarterly.
Description: The National Alliance for Autism Research (NAAR) is a national non-profit, tax-exempt organization dedicated to finding the causes, prevention, effective treatment and, ultimately, cure of the autism spectrum disorders.

Autism Websites

Autism Resources on the Internet
Internet URL: http://web.syr.edu/~jmwobus/autism/#general
Description: This page provides an organized list of resources about Autism that are available on the net, and an index of online information and resources on the developmental disabilities of autism and Asperger's Disorder.

Blakbird Autism Page
Internet URL: http://www.lasercom.net/blakbird/index.htm
Description: This site is maintained by parents of an autistic child and seems comprehensive.

Dave's Autism Information Page
Internet URL: http://www.lancs.ac.uk/people/cpadak/autism/autism.htm
Description: This international site is dedicated to autism resources.

B

Bilingual Tests

ESL Literacy Scale (ESL)
Author: Michael Roddy
Publisher: Academic Therapy Publications
20 Commercial Boulevard
Novato, CA 94949-6191
Phone: (415) 883-3314 or (800) 422-7249
Fax: (415) 883-3720
Type of Test: Informal assessment
Administration Time: 15–20 minutes
Type of Administration: Individual or group
Age/Grade Level: 16–Adult

Language Proficiency Test (LPT)
Authors: Joan Gerard and Gloria Weinstock
Publisher: Academic Therapy Publications
20 Commercial Boulevard
Novato, CA 94949-6191
Phone Number of Publisher: (415) 883-3314 or (800) 422-7249
Fax of Publisher: (415) 883-3720
Type of Test: Criterion-referenced
Administration Time: 90 minutes
Type of Administration: Individual
Age/Grade Level: Grades 9 and higher

Matrix Analogies Test (MAT)
Author: Jack A. Naglieri
Publisher: The Psychological Corporation
555 Academic Court
San Antonio, TX 78204-2498
Phone: (800) 211-8378
Fax: (800) 232-1223
TDD: (800) 723-1318
Type of Test: Norm-referenced
Administration Time: Short form, 25–30 minutes; Expanded form, 48 minutes.

Type of Administration: Individual
Age/Grade Level: Ages 5.0 to 17.11

Screening Test of Spanish Grammar
Author: Allen S. Toronto
Publisher: Northwestern University Press
625 Colfax Street
Evanston, IL 60201
Phone: (847) 491-5313
Fax: (847) 491-8150
Type of Test: Standardized
Administration Time: 15–25 minutes
Type of Administration: Individual
Age/Grade Level: Spanish-speaking children, ages 3–6

System of Multicultural Pluralistic Assessment (SOMPA)
Authors: Jane R. Mercer and June F. Lewis
Publisher: The Psychological Corporation
555 Academic Court
San Antonio, TX 78204-2498
Phone: (800) 211-8378
Fax: (800) 232-1223
TDD: (800) 723-1318
Type of Test: Norm-referenced
Administration Time: Student assessment, 60 minutes; Parent interview, 20 minutes.
Type of Administration: Individual
Age/Grade Level: Ages 5–11

Brain Injury

Though not always visible, and sometimes seemingly minor, brain injury is complex. It can cause physical, cognitive, social, and vocational changes that affect an individual for a short period of time or permanently. Depending on the extent and location of the injury, symptoms caused by a brain injury vary widely. Some common results are seizures, loss of balance or coordination, difficulty with speech, limited concentration, memory loss, and loss of organizational and reasoning skills.

Brain Injury Association, Inc. (BIA)
105 North Alfred Street
Alexandria, VA 22314
Phone: (703) 236-6000
Fax: (703) 236-6001
Family Helpline: (800) 444-6443

E-mail: N/A
Internet URL: http://www.biausa.org
Newsletters/Publications: BIA publishes a quarterly newsletter, *TBI Challenge*, that is free to members. It also provides brochures and information packets to families and persons with brain injuries at no charge through its Family Helpline.
Description: The Brain Injury Association's mission is to promote awareness, understanding, and prevention of brain injury through education, advocacy, and community support services that lead to reduced incidence and improved outcomes of children and adults with brain injuries. The association supports research for better outcomes to people who sustain a brain injury and promotes prevention of brain injury through public awareness, education, and legislation.

The Brian Injury Association has local support groups and chapters. The Family Helpline will provide information and assistance for starting or joining a local group.

Brain Tumor

A tumor is an abnormal growth caused by cells reproducing themselves in an uncontrolled manner. Tumors in parts of the body other than the brain can be benign (meaning harmless) or malignant (meaning cancerous). These meanings change, however, when referring to tumors in the brain. A benign brain tumor consists of benign (harmless) cells and has distinct boundaries which surgery alone may cure. A malignant brain tumor is life-threatening. It may be malignant because it consists of cancer cells, or it may be called malignant because of its location. In other words, a brain tumor composed of benign cells located in a vital area is considered malignant.

Children's Brain Tumor Foundation (CBTF)
274 Madison Avenue, Suite 1301
New York, NY, 10016
Phone: (212) 448-9494
Fax: (212) 448-1022
E-mail: N/A
Internet URL: http://www.childrensneuronet.org
Newsletters/Publications: Children's Brain Tumor Foundation has a yearly newsletter and a resource guide for parents of children with brain or spinal cord tumors. The first copy is free; there is a charge for additional copies.
Description: Children's Brain Tumor Foundation's mission is to improve treatment, quality of life, and the long-term outlook for children with brain and spinal cord tumors by funding basic, clinical, and applied research; state of the art therapies; professional information and education documents, and patient and family support. Call for the location of the nearest chapter.

National Brain Tumor Foundation
785 Market Street,
Suite 1600
San Francisco, CA 94103
Phone: (415) 284-0208 or (800) 934-2873
Fax: (415) 284-0209

E-mail: nbtf@braintumor.org
Internet URL: http://www.braintumor.org
Newsletters/Publications: A comprehensive guide is available for affected individuals and families who want to learn more about brain tumors. National Brain Tumor Foundation also produces a variety of educational materials, including a newsletter titled *Search*.
Description: National Brain Tumor Foundation, established in 1981, is a national not-for-profit voluntary organization that serves as a center for information regarding resources and support services for lives affected by brain tumor disease. It also provides financial support for investigative studies into the causes, prevention, and treatments of brain tumors. To these ends, the foundation has funded basic and applied laboratory research and clinical trials of new treatments at major institutions in the United States, and supported research for quality of life issues that regularly confront people with brain tumors.

Affected individuals and family members may also receive referrals to a network of support groups throughout the United States.

C

Cancer: Children

Childhood cancer occurs in about 1 in 600 children prior to the age of 15 years. This condition can take many forms including leukemia, lymphoma, and tumors of the central nervous system, bones eyes, and various organs.

American Cancer Society
1599 Clifton Road NE
Atlanta, GA 30329
Phone: (800) ACS-2345
Fax: N/A
E-mail: N/A
Internet URL: http://www.cancer.org
Newsletters/Publications: Contact a local chapter for a list of publications.
Description: American Cancer Society is a community-based voluntary health organization dedicated to eliminating cancer through research, education, advocacy, and service. The society has local chapters throughout the nation.

Candlelighters' Childhood Cancer Foundation
7910 Woodmont Avenue, Suite 460
Bethesda, MD 20814

Phone: (800) 366-CCCF or (301) 657-8401
Fax: (301) 718-2686
E-mail: N/A
Internet URL: http://www.candlelighters.org
Newsletters/Publications: *The Candlelighters' Quarterly*
Description: This leading organization in the field of pediatric cancer provides support, advocacy, and information.

National Cancer Institute
(See Government Agencies–Federal)

National Childhood Cancer Foundation
440 East Huntington Drive, Suite 300
P.O. Box 60012
Arcadia, CA 91066-6012
Phone: (800) 458-6223
Fax: (800) 723-2822
E-mail: N/A
Internet URL: http://www.nccf.org
Newsletters/Publications: *Childhood Cancer Line,* published three times a year.
Description: The foundation is a non-profit organization that supports pediatric cancer treatment and research projects at more than 115 pediatric medical institutions in the United States, Canada, and Australia.

Cardiac

American Heart Association, National Center
7272 Grenville Avenue
Dallas, TX 75231
Phone: (800) 666-7220
Fax: (214) 706-2139
E-mail: N/A
Internet URL: http://www.americanheart.org
Newsletters/Publications: Call for a list of publications.
Description: AHA is a not-for-profit voluntary health organization funded by private contributions. Its mission is to reduce disability and death from cardiovascular diseases and stroke. Programs geared specifically to educational institutions may be available from local chapters.

Mended Hearts (Part of American Heart Association)
Phone: (214) 706-1442
Fax: N/A
E-mail: N/A
Internet URL: http://www.mendedhearts.org

Newsletters/Publications: Contact American Heart Association for a list of publications.
Description: Mended Hearts is a support organization composed of heart patients, spouses, health professionals, and other interested persons. Chapters are available in more than 260 cities throughout the United State and Canada.

Central Auditory Processing Disorder

A CAPD is a physical hearing impairment that does not surface on routine screenings or an audiogram. It affects the hearing system beyond the ear, whose job it is to separate a meaningful message from non-essential background sound and deliver that information with good clarity to the intellectual centers of the brain (the central nervous system). Distorted or incomplete auditory messages prohibits links with the world and other people.

Central Auditory Processing Disorders Web Page
Internet URL: http://www.theshop.net/campbell/central.htm
Description: This web site is dedicated to providing professionals with a place to exchange ideas and information on CAPD. The general public also benefits by having access to better information than may be available from popular news publications.

Cerebral Palsy

Cerebral palsy affects the voluntary muscles and often leads to major problems in communication and mobility. It is caused by brain damage. While it is not "curable," it is also not progressive nor communicable.

United Cerebral Palsy Association
1522 K Street NW, Suite 1112
Washington, DC 20005
Phone: (800) 872-5827 or (202) 776-0406
TTY: (202) 973-7197
Fax: (202) 776-0414
E-mail: ucpnatl@ucpa.org
Internet URL: http://www.ucpa.org
Newsletters/Publications: Call for a publications catalog.
Description: UCP and its nationwide network of 153 affiliates work toward the inclusion of persons with disabilities in every facet of society. UCP provides referral services, legislative advocacy, technology initiatives, and research.

Child Abuse Resources

Administration for Children and Families
(See Government Agencies–Federal)

Child Sexual Abuse
Author: Linda Cain
Internet URL: http://www.commnet.edu/QVCTC/student/LindaCain/sex-abuse.html
Description: This site contains a vast amount of information for parents, teachers, and other professionals on all aspects of child abuse and offers:
- Legal Information on Child Sexual Abuse
- Statistics on Child Sexual Abuse
- Films, Videos, and Presentations on Child Sexual Abuse
- Journals, Newsletters, and Publications on Child Sexual Abuse
- Books, Reviews, and Excerpts About Child Sexual Abuse
- Directories Listing Agencies for Services Related to Child Sexual Abuse
- Self-help Groups for Sexual Abuse
- Services, Agencies, and Private Practice
- Art and Child Sexual Abuse

Children's Bureau
(See Government Agencies–Federal)

Department of Health and Human Services
(See Government Agencies–Federal)

FRIENDS Virtual Resource Center
Internet URL: http://www.famres.org/friends/ntap2.htm
Description: Family Resource Information, Education, and Network Development Services, a program of the National Center on Child Abuse and Neglect, offers a range of services designed to assist states, tribal organizations, and local communities in the development of family resource programs and networks throughout the United States. FRIENDS is a collaborative effort between two organizations with many years of experience in delivering training and technical assistance: Chapel Hill Training-Outreach Project, Inc., and Family Resource Coalition.

Missing Children Web Page
Internet URL: http://www.missingkids.org
Description: Search the National Center for Missing and Exploited Children's (NCMEC) database of current missing children cases and view images of missing children. Their Missing Children Forum, another site feature, aids in finding missing and exploited children, supporting families whose children are missing, and offering child safety assistance. Members can speak with each other and with NCMEC representatives about the images in the forum's libraries.

National Clearinghouse on Child Abuse and Neglect Information
(See Clearinghouses)

National Data Archive on Child Abuse and Neglect
Internet URL: http://www.ndacan.cornell.edu
Description: The mission of the National Data Archive on Child Abuse and Neglect is to facilitate the secondary analysis of research data relevant to the study of child abuse and neglect. The organization's primary activity is the acquisition, preservation, and dissemination of high-quality data sets related to the study of child abuse and neglect. Its Web site provides a listing and brief description of all the studies in the archive along with ordering information. Information on publications and upcoming training institutes and workshops is also offered.

National Indian Child Welfare Association
Internet URL: http://www.nicwa.org
Description: The National Indian Child Welfare Association (NICWA) serves American Indian tribes throughout the country by helping to strengthen and enhance their capacity to deliver quality child welfare services. Among the activities in which NICWA engages are community development, public policy development, and information exchange.

PAVNET Online
Internet URL: http://www.pavnet.org
Description: Pavnet Online is an interagency, electronic resource on the Internet created to provide information about effective violence prevention initiatives. This "virtual library" on violence and youth at risk is designed to give states and local communities a single searchable resource for relevant data from seven federal agencies.

Chronic Pain

With chronic pain, pain signals can keep firing in the nervous system for weeks, months, even years. The pain may have been caused by an initial mishap—a sprained back or serious infection—from which the person has long since recovered. There may be an ongoing cause of pain—arthritis, cancer, or ear infection—though chronic pain in the absence of any past injury or evidence of body damage is possible.

Chronic Pain Links
Internet URL: http://www.crl.com/~rbarnes/pain.html
Description: Contains a complete listing of discussion groups, news organizations, fact sheets, and other pain websites.

National Chronic Pain Outreach Association (NCPOA)
7979 Old Georgetown Road, Suite 100
Bethesda, MD 20814
Phone: (301) 652-4948
Fax: (301) 907-0745
E-mail: N/A
Internet URL: http://neurosurgery.mgh.harvard.edu/ncpainoa.htm
Newsletters/Publications: NCPOA publishes the quarterly (more or less) newsletter, *Lifeline*.

Description: NCPOA serves as a clearinghouse of information on chronic pain. It also maintains a list of support groups in many areas, provides reprints of materials on all aspects of chronic pain, and helps in setting up a local support group. NCPOA provides book reviews to keep patients and loved ones informed about the latest publications on chronic pain. NCPOA lobbies the medical community and the government on the issues of chronic pain, and initiates the legislation necessary to support those afflicted.

Classroom Management Websites

Behavior
Internet URL: http://www.cet.fsu.edu/TREE/behavior.html
Description: Articles from Florida State University concerning behavior problems in the classroom and possible remediations for them are available at this site.

Behavior Home Page Handilinks
Internet URL: http://www.handilinks.com
Description: An interesting resource site on classroom behavior management techniques and articles. To get to this site, click on "EDUCATION," then "SPECIAL EDUCATION," then "BEHAVIOR PAGE."

Better Classroom Discipline: 11 Techniques
Internet URL: http://users.aol.com/churchward/hls/techniques.html
Description: Adapted by Budd Churchward from A *Primer on Classroom Discipline: Principles Old and New* by Thomas McDaniel, these techniques can be used to achieve effective group management and control in the classroom.

Fred Jones Positive Classroom Management
Internet URL: http://www.fredjones.com
Description: These books and tapes focus on the nuts and bolts of classroom application management and are illustrated with real life examples.

Managing Disruptive Behavior in Inclusive Classrooms
Internet URL: http://www.cec.sped.org/bk/focus/daniels.htm
Description: The article by Vera I. Daniels goes beyond the standard classroom discipline problems to focus on disruptive behavior of students with disabilities and the special approaches needed to correct it.

Pennsylvania Resource and Information Service for Special Education (PRISE)
Behavior Management Bibliography List
Internet URL: http://eisc-prise.mciu.k12.pa.us/EISC/PRISE/Catalog-categories/behv_mgmt_bibs.html
Description: This site provides a thorough list of articles and sources dealing with behavior management in the classroom.

Positive Classroom Management
Internet URL: http://www.mindspring.com/~digiulio/ClassMgt/home.htm
Description: Practical strategies to help teachers at all levels manage classrooms effectively without resorting to methods that rob students of their dignity. Features a step-by-step guide with checklists.

Preventing Classroom Discipline Problems
Internet URL: http://www.panix.com/~pro-ed
Description: This training video and book by Dr. Howard Seeman for teachers and prospective educators discusses the diagnoses, prevention, and handling of actual classroom disruptive behavior. The video can be ordered online.

Clearinghouses

A clearinghouse can be defined as a national center for the dissemination of information.

ABLEDATA
(See Assistive Technology)

Distance Education Clearinghouse
University of Wisconsin
432 North Lake Street
Madison, WI 53706
Phone: (608) 262-0737
Fax: N/A
E-mail: N/A
Internet URL: http://www.uwex.edu/disted/home.html
Newsletter/Publications: N/A
Description: The Distance Education Clearinghouse allows users easy access to a wide range of information about distance education. This comprehensive and widely recognized website brings together national and international education information and resources from Wisconsin. New information and resources are being added to the Distance Education Clearinghouse on a continuing basis.

ERIC Clearinghouse on Disabilities and Gifted Education Council for Exceptional Children
(See Professional Organizations)
Phone: (800) 328-0272
Fax: N/A
E-mail: N/A
Internet URL: http://www.cec.sped.org/er-menu.htm
Description: ERIC, a national education information network, is part of the National Library of Education, US Department of Education. The goal of ERIC is to identify, select, process, and disseminate information in education. The ERIC system consists of 16 clearinghouses, each serving a specialized field of education; adjunct clearinghouses on specific aspects of education; and support services. ERIC components offer products and services including ERIC Digests, major publications, user products, bibliographies, referrals, and computer searches on disabilities and gifted education.

ERIC Clearinghouses and other components are listed alphabetically and can be accessed through the following **Internet URL:** http://www.aspensys.com/eric/sites/barak.html

- **Adult, Career, and Vocational Education:** Covers all levels and settings of adult and continuing, career, and vocational/technical education.
- **Assessment and Evaluation:** Seeks to provide balanced information concerning educational assessment and resources to encourage responsible test use.
- **Child Care:** Complements, enhances, and promotes childcare linkages and serves as a mechanism for supporting quality, comprehensive services for children and families. It is sponsored by the National Child Care Information Center (NCCIC).
- **Clinical Schools:** Provides information on clinical schools, professional development schools, partner schools, professional practice schools, and similar institutions.
- **Community Colleges:** Covers development, administration, and evaluation of 2-year public and private community and junior colleges, technical institutes, and 2-year branch university campuses.
- **Consumer Education:** Addresses consumer and personal finance education for life-long application.
- **Counseling and Student Services:** Addresses preparation, practice, and supervision of counselors at all educational levels and in all settings, and theoretical development of counseling and student services.
- **Disabilities and Gifted Education:** Covers all aspects of the education and development of the disabled and gifted, including identification, assessment, intervention, and enrichment, both in special settings and within the mainstream.
- **Educational Management:** Covers all aspects of the governance, leadership, administration, and structure of public and private educational organizations at the elementary and secondary levels, including the provision of physical facilities for their operation.
- **Educational Opportunity:** Strives to increase access to high-quality resources for individuals, parents, and organizations interested in ways and means to enable low-income, first generation, and disabled students to attend college.
- **Elementary and Early Childhood Education:** Covers the physical, cognitive, social, educational, and cultural development of children from birth through early adolescence.
- **Entrepreneurship Education:** Collects, indexes, abstracts, and disseminates information about entrepreneurship education and makes those resources available to the education community.
- **ESL Literacy Education:** Addresses all aspects of literacy education for adults and out-of-school youth with limited English proficiency.
- **Higher Education:** Addresses college and university problems, programs, students, curricular and instructional programs, and institutional research.
- **Information and Technology:** Covers educational technology and library and information science at all levels.
- **International Civic Education:** Acquires, reviews, indexes, and abstracts the English-language literature of civic education in countries throughout the world.
- **Languages and Linguistics:** Covers languages and language sciences, including all aspects of second language instruction and learning in all commonly and uncommonly taught languages.
- **Law-Related Education:** Covers all areas of law-related education, including citizenship education, the US Constitution, the law and legal issues, and the Bill of Rights.
- **National Clearinghouse for Educational Facilities:** Acquires, manages, and disseminates information relating to educational facilities, including the design, construction, equipping, furnishing, maintenance, renovation, rehabilitation, mechanical operation, and demolition of elementary and secondary facilities.

- **National Parent Information Network:** Provides information and communications support to parents and parent support organizations.
- **Reading, English, and Communication:** Covers all aspects of reading, English, and communication (verbal and nonverbal), preschool through college.
- **Rural Education and Small Schools:** Covers economic, cultural, and social conditions related to educational programs and practices for rural residents; American Indians/Alaska Natives, Mexican Americans, and migrants; educational practices and programs in all small schools; and outdoor education.
- **Science, Mathematics, and Environmental Education:** Covers all aspects and levels of science, mathematics, and environmental education.
- **Service Learning:** Provides information about service-learning programs, including organizations, people, calendar events, and literature/multimedia materials.
- **Social Studies/Social Science Education:** Monitors issues about the teaching and learning of history, geography, civics, economics, and other subjects in social studies/social sciences.
- **Teaching and Teacher Education:** Covers teacher recruitment, selection, licensing, certification, training, pre-service and inservice preparation, evaluation, retention, and retirement. Also covers all aspects of health, physical education, recreation, and dance.
- **Test Collection:** Prepares descriptions of commercially available and non-commercially available tests, checklists, instruments, questionnaires, and other assessment and evaluation tools.
- **Urban Education:** Covers programs and practices in urban area schools; education of African-American and Hispanic youth; theory and practice of educational equity; and urban and minority experiences, social institutions, and services.
- **US-Japan Studies:** All aspects of teaching and learning about Japanese society and culture.

Federal Resource Center for Special Education
875 Connecticut Avenue NW, Suite 900
Washington, DC 20009
Voice: (202) 884-8215
TDD: (800) 695-0285
Fax: (202) 884-8443
E-mail: frc@aed.org
Internet URL: http://www.dssc.org/frc/index.htm
Newsletters/Publications: The *RFC Links Online Newsletter* reports the activities of the special education technical assistance and dissemination projects funded by the US Department of Education's Office of Special Education and Rehabilitative Services.
Description: The FRC is a special education technical assistance project funded by the US Department of Education's Office of Special Education and Rehabilitative Services, and is part of the Regional Resource and Federal Centers Network.

HEATH Resource Center, The National Clearinghouse on Post-Secondary Education for Individuals with Disabilities
(See Post-Secondary Education Resources)

National AIDS Clearinghouse Center for Disease Control
PO Box 6003
Rockville, MD 20849-6003
Phone: (800) 458-5231

TTD: (800) 243-7012
E-mail: aidsinfo@cdcnac.aspensys.com
Internet URL: http://www.cdcnac.org
Newsletters/Publications: Call for a list of publications.
Description: The National AIDS Clearinghouse provides resources and information regarding AIDS and HIV. The database includes documents specifically designed for people with disabilities. Geared toward professionals, the materials include tapes, video recordings, brochures, pamphlets, posters, and A/V materials.

National Arthritis and Musculoskeletal and Skin Diseases Information Clearinghouse
(See Government Agencies–Federal, under National Institute of Health)

National Center for Research in Vocational Education (NCRVE)
University of California, Berkeley
2030 Addison Street, Suite 500
Berkeley, CA 94720-1674
Phone: (800) 762-4093 or (510) 642-4004
Fax: (510) 642-2124
E-mail: N/A
Internet URL: http://vocserve.berkeley.edu
Newsletters/Publications: Call for a list of publications.
Description: The center provides a wide range of materials for professionals about curriculum development, technical education, career planning, and preparation for employment.

National Clearinghouse for Alcohol and Drug Information (NCADI)
PO Box 2345
Rockville, MD 20847-2345
Phone: (800) 729-6686
Fax: (301) 468-6433
E-mail: N/A
Internet URL: http://www.health.org
Newsletters/Publications: Call for a list of publications.
Description: One of the largest federal clearinghouses and the world's largest resource for information and materials on substance abuse, the National Clearinghouse for Alcohol and Drug Information (NCADI) is the information arm of the Center for Substance Abuse Prevention.

Services offered by NCADI include an information services staff to respond to public inquiries on alcohol, tobacco, and drugs (ATD); distribution of more than 450 free or low-cost materials on ATD, such as fact sheets, posters, monographs, and video tapes; referrals to prevention, intervention, and treatment resources; access to Prevention Materials and Treatment Resources Databases On-line (PREVILINE); and federal grant announcements for ATD-related projects.

National Clearinghouse for Professions in Special Education (NCPSE)
Council for Exceptional Children
1920 Association Drive
Reston, VA 20191-1589
Phone: (800) 641-7824
Voice: (703) 264-9476

TTD: (703) 264-9480
Fax: (703) 264-1637
E-mail: ncpse@cec.sped.org
Internet URL: http://www.cec.sped.org/cl-menu.htm
Newsletters/Publications: Call for a list of publications.
Description: NCPSE provides information on recruitment, retention, and overall supply of professionals in special educational and related professional fields, with a particular focus on individuals with disabilities and those from culturally/linguistically diverse communities. It maintains a listing of programs of study in colleges and universities at both undergraduate and graduate levels and provides resources for financial aid, nontraditional training programs, alternative certification, and job banks as well as providing specific special education career information.

National Clearinghouse on Child Abuse and Neglect Information
PO Box 1182
Washington, DC 20013-1182
Phone: (800) 394-3366 or (703) 385-7565
Fax: (703) 385-3206
E-mail: nccanch@calib.com
Internet URL: http://www.calib.com/nccanch
Newsletters/Publications: Call for a list of publications.
Description: The National Clearinghouse on Child Abuse and Neglect Information, a national resource for professionals seeking information on the prevention, identification, and treatment of child abuse and neglect, and related child welfare issues.

National Clearinghouse on Family Support and Children's Mental Health
Portland State University
PO Box 751
Portland, OR 97207-0751
Phone: (800) 628-1696 or (503) 725-4040
TTD: (503) 725-4165
Fax: (503) 725-4180
Internet URL: http://www.rtc.pdx.edu
Newsletters/Publications: Call for a list of publications.
Description: The center's activities focus on improving services to families whose children have mental, emotional, or behavioral disorders through a set of related research and training programs. Research efforts are clustered around five themes:

- Family Participation in Services
- Family Participation at the Policy Level
- Families and Out-of-Home Care
- Evaluation of Family Organizing Efforts
- Interventions in Professional Education

National Clearinghouse on Women and Girls with Disabilities c/o Educational Equity Concepts Inc.
114 East 32nd Street, Suite 701
New York, NY 10016
Phone: (212) 725-1803
Fax: (212) 725-0947

E-mail: 75507.1306@compuserve
Internet URL: http://www.onisland.com/eec
Newsletters/Publications: Call for a list of publications.
Description: This clearinghouse provides a catalog of manuals, teen supplements, videos, and directories, many of which deal with sexuality issues faced by women and girls with disabilities.

National Diabetes Information Clearinghouse
(See Government Agencies–Federal under National Institute of Diabetes and Digestive and Kidney Diseases)
1 Information Way
Bethesda, MD 20892-3560
Phone: (301) 654-3327
Fax: N/A
E-mail: ndic@info.niddk.nih.gov
Internet URL: http://www.niddk.nih.gov/health/diabetes/ndic.htm
Newsletter/Publications: *Diabetes Dateline*, a quarterly newsletter. Call for other information.
Description: The goal of the clearinghouse is to increase knowledge and understanding about diabetes. NDIC works with the diabetes community to identify and respond to informational needs about diabetes and its management. It also provides an online database.

National Health Information Center
PO Box 1133
Washington, DC 20013-1133
Phone: (800) 336-4797 or (301) 565-4167
Fax: (301) 984-4256
E-mail: nhicinfo@health.org
Internet URL: http://nhic-nt.health.org
Newsletters/Publications: Call for a list of factsheets and publications.
Description: National Health Information Center (NHIC) is a health information referral service. NHIC puts health professionals and consumers who have health questions in touch with organizations that are best able to provide answers. It was established in 1979 by the Office of Disease Prevention and Health Promotion (ODPHP), Office of Public Health and Science, Office of the Secretary, US Department of Health and Human Services.

National Information Center for Children and Youth with Handicaps (NICHCY)
PO Box 1492
Washington, DC 20013-1492
Phone: (800) 695-0285
Voice/TTD: (202) 884-8200
Fax: (202) 884-8441
E-mail: nichcy @aed.org
Internet URL: http://www.aed.org/nichcy
Newsletters/Publications: NICHCY offers publications in all disability areas.
Description: NICHCY is an information clearinghouse that provides information on disabilities and related issues. Children and youth are the special focus. NICHCY has an extensive database on all disabilities and technical assistance to parents and professional groups.

National Information Center on Deafness (NICD)
Gallaudet University
800 Florida Avenue NE
Washington, DC 20002-3695
Voice: (202) 651-5051
TTD: (202) 651-5052
Fax: (202) 651-5054
E-mail: nicd@gallux.gallaudet.edu
Internet URL: http://www.gallaudet.edu/~nicd
Newsletters/Publications: NICD provides a publications catalog.
Description: NICD collects, develops, and shares information on all aspects of hearing loss and deafness, and offers programs and services for people who are deaf and hard of hearing.

National Information Clearinghouse on Children Who Are Deaf-Blind (DB-Link)
Teaching Research
345 North Monmouth Avenue
Monmouth, OR 97361
Voice: (800) 438-9376
TTD: (800) 854-7013
Fax: (503) 838-8150
E-mail: dblink@tr.wosc.osshe.edu
Internet URL: http://www.tr.wosc.osshe.edu/tr/dbp/index.htm
Newsletters/Publications: *Deaf-Blind Perspectives*. Call for a list of other publications.
Description: The organization collects and disseminates information related to children and youth (newborn-21) who are deaf-blind and connects consumers of deaf-blind information to sources of information about deaf blindness, assistive technology, and deaf-blind people. DB-LINK is a collaborative effort involving the Helen Keller National Center, Perkins School for the Blind, and Teaching Research.

National Institute on Deafness and Other Communication Disorders Information Clearinghouse
(See Government Agencies–Federal)

National Institute on Disability and Rehabilitative Research (NIDRR)
(See Government Agencies–Federal)

National Library Service for the Blind and Physically Handicapped, Library of Congress
(See Government Agencies–Federal)

National Maternal and Child Health Clearinghouse
2070 Chain Bridge Road, Suite 450
Vienna, VA 22182-2536
Phone: (703) 356-1964
Fax: (703) 821-2098
E-mail: nmchc@circsol.com

Internet URL: http://www.circsol.com/mch
Newsletters/Publications: Call for a publications catalog.
Description: The National Maternal and Child Health Clearinghouse disseminates information about maternal and child health across the nation. It provides publications, posters, videotapes, and many materials for professional use.

National Mental Health Consumer Self-Help Clearinghouse
1211 Chestnut Street
Philadelphia, PA 19107-4103
Phone: (215) 751-1810 or (800) 553-4539
Fax: (215) 636-6310
E-mail: thekey@delphi.com
Internet URL: http://www.kibertynet.org/~mha/cl_house.html
Newsletters/Publications: *The Key* is a quarterly newsletter.
Description: This clearinghouse handles thousands of inquiries annually from health care consumers, affected individuals, family members, professionals, and others interested in mental health issues. Information and technical assistance for starting or locating local groups is also available, as well as on-site consultations to individuals and groups interested in mental health self-help group development.

National Mental Health Services Knowledge Exchange Network (KEN)
Part of the Center for Mental Health Services (CMHS)
PO Box 42490
Washington, DC 20015
Phone: (800) 789-2647
TDD: (301) 443-9006
Fax: (301) 984-8796
E-mail: ken@mentalhealth.org
Internet URL: http://www.mentalhealth.org/index.htm
Newsletters/Publications: KEN has an online publications list.
Description: This network provides information about mental health via toll-free telephone services, an electronic bulletin board, and publications. The National Center for Mental Health Services developed KEN for users of mental health services and their families, the general public, policy makers, providers, and the media. KEN is a national source of information and resources on prevention, treatment, and rehabilitation services for mental illness.

National Organization for Rare Disorders (NORD)
100 Route 37, PO Box 8923
New Fairfield, CT 06812-8923
Phone: (800) 999-6673
Voice: (203) 746-6518
TTD: (203) 746-6927
Fax: (203) 746-6481
E-mail: orphan@nord-rdb.com
Internet URL: http://www.nord-rdb.com/~orphan
Newsletter/Publications: *Orphan Disease Update*
Description: This is a unique federation of more than 140 not-for-profit voluntary health organizations serving people with rare disorders and disabilities. NORD has databases on specific rare disorders and drugs.

The National Rehabilitation Information Center (NARIC)
8455 Colesville Road, Suite 935
Silver Spring, MD 20910
Phone: (301) 588-9284
Voice: (800) 346-2742
TTD: (301) 495-5626
Fax: (301) 587-1967
E-mail: N/A
Internet URL: http://www.naric.com/naric
Newsletters/Publications: NARIC's information resources include its Directory of National Information Sources on Disabilities, Guide to Disability and Rehabilitation Periodicals, and NIDRR Program Directory and Compendium.
Description: NARIC provides information and referral services on disability and rehabilitation, including quick information and referral; database searches of the bibliographic database, REHABDATA; and document delivery. It also provides the NIDRR Program Directory and the Compendium of Products by NIDRR Grantees and Contractors.

NIH/National Institute of Neurological Disorders and Stroke
(See Government Agencies–Federal)

College Guides for the Disabled

College Guide for Students with Learning Disabilities (12th ed.)
Publisher: Laurel Publishers
Authors: Annette Joy Sclafani and Michael J. Lynch
Format: Paperback
Published: 1996
ISBN: 093324309X

Help Yourself: Handbook for College-Bound Students with Learning Disabilities
Publisher: Princeton Review
Authors: Erica-Lee Lewis and Eric L. Lewis
Format: Paperback
Published: 1996
ISBN: 0679764615

K&W Guide to Colleges for the Learning Disabled 1998 (4th ed.)
Publisher: Princeton Review
Authors: Marybeth Kravets and Imy F. Wax
Format: Paperback
Published: 1997
ISBN: 0375750436

Lovejoy's College Guide for the Learning Disabled
Publisher: Prentice Hall
Author: Charles T. Straughn
Format: Paperback
Published: 1993
ISBN: 0671847716

Peterson's Colleges with Programs for Students with Learning Disabilities or Attention Deficit Disorders (5th ed.)
Publisher: Peterson's Guides
Authors: Charles T. Mangrum and Stephen Strichart
Format: Paperback
Published: 1997
ISBN: 156079853X

Succeeding in College with Attention Deficit Disorders: Issues and Strategies for Students, Counselors and Educators
Publisher: Specialty Press Inc.
Author: Jennifer S. Bramer, Ph.D.
Format: Paperback
Published: 1996
ISBN: 1886941068

Colitis and Crohn's Disease

Colitis is an inflammation of the colon wall and can result in inflammatory bowel disease. Crohn's Disease is characterized by an inflammation of any part of the gastrointestinal tract.

Crohn's and Colitis Foundation of America
386 Park Avenue South, 17th Floor
New York, NY 10016-8804
Phone: (800) 932-2424 or (212) 685-3440
Fax: (212) 779-4098
E-mail: info@ccfa.org
Internet URL: http://www.ccfa.org
Newsletters/Publications: Call for a list of publications.
Description: The purpose of the organization is to support research into the cause and cure of colitis and Crohn's Disease, provide educational programs to families, and furnish an updated medical database.

Communication Disorders

Hyperlexia is a syndrome observed in children who have the following characteristics:

- precocious ability to read words
- intense fascination with numbers or letters
- significant difficulty using verbal or non-verbal language
- difficulty in reciprocal interaction

American Hyperlexia Association

479 Spring Road
Elmhurst, IL 60126
Phone: (630) 415-2212
Fax: (630) 530-5909
E-mail: president@hyperlexia.org
webmaster@hyperlexia.org
Internet URL: www.hyperlexia.org
Newsletters/Publications: Call for a list of publications.
Description: American Hyperlexia Association is dedicated to educating parents and professionals with a common goal of identifying this disorder and facilitating effective teaching techniques both at home and at school.

Cleft Palate Foundation
National Office

1829 East Franklin Street, Suite 1022
Chapel Hill, NC 27514
Phone: (800) 242-5338 or (919) 933-9044
Fax: (919) 933-9604
Internet URL: http://www.cleft.com
Newsletters/Publications: The foundation provides free fact sheets and brochures.
Description: The Cleft Palate Foundation is a non-profit public service affiliate of the American Cleft Palate–Craniofacial Association dedicated to assisting individuals with birth defects of the head and neck, and their families.

Division for Children with Communication Disorders (See Council for Exceptional Children–Organizations)

Communication Disorders: Professional Organizations

American Cleft Palate–Craniofacial Association
National Office
1829 East Franklin Street, Suite 1022
Chapel Hill, NC 27514
Phone: (800) 242-5338 or (919) 933-9044
Fax: (919) 933-9604
E-mail: N/A
Internet URL: http://www.cleft.com/acpa2.htm
Newsletters/Publications: *ACPA/CPF Newsletter*, published quarterly; and a professional journal, *Cleft Palate Craniofacial Journal.*
Description: The Cleft Palate–Craniofacial Association is an international non-profit medical society of health care professionals who treat and research birth defects of the head and face.

American Speech–Language Association (ASHA)
10801 Rockville Pike
Rockville, MD 20852
Phone: (800) 638-8255
Voice/TTD: (301) 897-5700
Fax: (301) 571-0457
E-mail: N/A
Internet URL: http://www.asha.org
Newsletters/Publications: *Journal of Speech-Language-Hearing Research; American Journal of Audiology; American Journal of Speech-Language Pathology; Language Speech and Hearing Services in the Schools; ASHA Magazine; ASHA Leader*
Description: ASHA is a professional credentialing and scientific organization for speech-language pathologists and audiologists concerned with communication disorders. It provides informational materials and a toll-free HELPLINE number for consumers to inquire about speech, language, or hearing problems, and offers referrals to audiologists and speech-language pathologists in the United States.

Communication Disorders Websites

Net Connections for Communication Disorders and Sciences
Author: Judith Maginnis Kuster
Internet URL:
http://www.mankato.msus.edu/dept/comdis/kuster2/welcome
Description: This site provides access to resources for professionals and students in the area of communication disorders, as well as for persons with communication disabilities.

Comprehensive Achievement Assessment Measures

Comprehensive achievement tests cover a variety of academic skills including but not limited to reading, math, spelling, and writing.

Brigance Diagnostic Inventory of Basic Skills
Author: Albert Brigance
Publisher: Curriculum Associates, Inc.
5 Esquire Road, North
Billerica, MA 01862-2589
Phone: (800) 225-0248
Fax: (800) 366-1158
Type of Test: Criterion-referenced
Administration Time: Specific time limits are listed on many tests; others are untimed.
Type of Administration: Individual or group
Administrator: Special education teacher, classroom teacher
Age/Grade Level: Grades K through 6. It is also used for academic assessment of older students functioning below sixth-grade academic levels.

Kaufman Tests of Educational Achievement (KTEA)
Authors: Alan S. Kaufman and Nadren L. Kaufman
Publisher: American Guidance Service
4201 Woodland Road
Circle Pines, MN 55014-1796
Phone: (612) 786-4343 or (800) 328-2560
Fax: (612) 786-9077
Type of Test: Norm-referenced, standardized
Administration Time: 60–75 minutes
Type of Administration: Individual
Administrator: Special education teacher, classroom teacher
Age/Grade Level: Grades 1–12

Norris Educational Achievement Test (NEAT)
Author: Jane Switzer
Publisher: Western Psychological Services
12031 Wilshire Boulevard
Los Angeles, CA 90025
Phone: (310) 478-2061 or (800) 648-8857
Fax: (310) 478-7838
Type of Test: Norm-referenced
Administration Time: 30 minutes
Type of Administration: Individual
Administrator: Special education teacher, classroom teacher

Age/Grade Level: Preschool–12

Peabody Individual Achievement Test—Revised
Author: Frederick C. Markwardt, Jr.
Publisher: American Guidance Service
4201 Woodland Road
Circle Pines, MN 55014-1796
Phone: (612) 786-4343 or (800) 328-2560
Fax: (612) 786-9077
Type of Test: Norm-referenced, standardized
Administration Time: 50–70 minutes
Type of Administration: Individual
Administrator: Special education teacher, classroom teacher
Age/Grade Level: Level 1, Grades K–1; Level 2, Grades 2–12

Test of Academic Achievement Skills–Reading, Arithmetic, Spelling, and Listening Comprehension (TAAS-RASLC)
Author: Morison. F. Gardner, Ed.D.
Publisher: Psychological and Educational Publications
PO Box 520
Hydesville, CA 95547-0520
Phone: (800) 523-5775
Fax: (800) 447-0907
Type of Test: Norm-referenced
Administration Time: 15–25 minutes; scoring time is approximately 15 minutes.
Type of Administration: Individual
Administrator: Special education teacher, classroom teacher
Age/Grade Level: Ages 4.0 to 12.0

Wechsler Individual Achievement Test (WIAT)
Author: The Psychological Corporation
Publisher: The Psychological Corporation
555 Academic Court
San Antonio, TX 78204-2498
Phone: (800) 211-8378
Fax: (800) 232-1223
TDD: (800) 723-1318
Type of Test: Norm-referenced
Administration Time: 30–75 minutes
Type of Administration: Individual
Administrator: Special education teacher, classroom teacher
Age/Grade Level: Ages 5 to 19

Wide Range Achievement Test–3 (WRAT–3)
Author: Gary S. Wilkinson
Publisher: Wide Range Inc.
PO Box 3410
Wilmington, DE 19804-0250

Phone: (800) 221-9728
Fax: (302) 652-1644
Type of Test: Norm-referenced
Administration Time: Each form of the WRAT–3 takes aproximately 15–30 minutes to administer; however, age, ability, and behavioral style of the student will vary the length.
Type of Administration: Primarily individual, although certain portions of the test can be administered to small groups (spelling and math).
Administrator: Special education teacher, classroom teacher
Age/Grade Level: Ages 5 to 75

Comprehensive Perceptual Assessment Measures

Comprehensive perceptual tests measure the various aspects of the learning process including modalities, the channels through which information is received (i.e., visual, auditory); and process areas, the psychological processes that give meaning to received information (i.e., reception, association, memory, expression).

Bruininks-Oseretsky Test of Motor Proficiency
Author: Robert Bruininks
Publisher: American Guidance Service
4201 Woodland Road
Circle Pines, MN 55014-1796
Phone: (612) 786-4343 or (800) 328-2560
Fax: (612) 786-9077
Type of Test: Standardized
Administration Time: Complete battery takes 45–60 minutes; short form, 15–20 minutes.
Type of Administration: Individual
Age/Grade Level: Ages 4.5 to 14.5

Detroit Tests of Learning Aptitudes–Third Edition (DTLA–3)
Author: Donald D. Hammill
Publisher: PRO-ED, Inc.
8700 Shoal Creek Boulevard
Austin, TX 78758-6897
Number of Publisher: (512) 451-3246 or (800) 897-3202
Fax of Publisher: (800) FXPROED
Type of Test: Standardized
Administration Time: 50–120 minutes
Type of Administration: Individual
Age/Grade Level: Ages 6.0 to 17.11

Illinois Test of Psycholinguistic Abilities (ITPA)
Authors: S.A. Kirk, J.J. McCarthy, and W.D. Kirk
Publisher: University of Illinois Press
54 East Gregory Drive
Champaign, IL 61820
Phone: (217) 333-0950
Fax: N/A
Type of Test: Standardized
Administration Time: 60–90 minutes
Type of Administration: Individual
Age/Grade Level: Ages 2 to 10

Slingerland Screening Tests for Identifying Children with Specific Language Disability
Author: Beth H. Slingerland
Publisher: Educators Publishing Service, Inc.
31 Smith Place
Cambridge, MA 02138
Phone: (800) 225-5750
Fax: (617) 547-0412
Type of Test: Informal diagnostic
Administration Time: 60–80 minutes for Forms A, B, and C; 110–130 minutes for Form D.
Type of Administration: Individual or group
Age/Grade Level: Grades 1–6

Test of Gross Motor Development (TGMD)
Author: Dale A. Ulrich
Publisher: PRO-ED, Inc.
8700 Shoal Creek Boulevard
Austin, TX 78758-6897
Phone: (512) 451-3246 or (800) 897-3202
Fax: (800) FXPROED
Type of Test: Standardized
Administration Time: 15 minutes
Type of Administration: Individual
Age/Grade Level: Ages 3 to 10

Woodcock Johnson Psychoeducational Battery–Revised (WJ-R)
Authors: Richard W. Woodcock and Mary Bonner Johnson
Publisher: The Riverside Publishing Company
8420 Bryn Mawr Avenue
Chicago, IL 60631
Phone: (800) 323-9540
Type of Test: Norm-referenced
Administration Time: Part I, 60–90 minutes; Part II, 30–45 minutes; Part III, 15–30 minutes.

Type of Administration: Individual
Age/Grade Level: Ages 3 to 80

Conduct Disorders

Conduct disorders are a complicated group of behavioral and emotional problems in young people. The diagnosis of a conduct disorder usually refers to a child who has great difficulty following rules and behaving in a socially acceptable way. However, it is important to recognize that all young people who misbehave do not have a conduct disorder. The expression of anger for children with this disorder is the outstanding feature. They are often aggressive with others and they may lie, steal, destroy property, and misbehave sexually.

American Academy of Child and Adolescent Psychiatry
(See Professional Organizations)

Internet Mental Health
(See Mental Health Websites)

Curriculum Resource Finders

Eisenhower National Clearinghouse for Science and Math Education (ENC)
Internet URL: http://www.enc.org/enctext.htm
Description: ENC lists areas of educational materials on its site. Continue through the site and log on http://watt.enc.org/mcquery2.html for a selection of materials by grade, or http://wattenc.org/cgibin/tree0.pl?file=&11=159 for integrated/interdisciplinary materials.

Cystic Fibrosis

Cystic fibrosis is an inherited, fatal disease that results in an abnormal amount of mucus throughout the body, most often affecting the lungs and digestive tract.

Boomer Esiason Foundation
One World Trade Center, 101st Floor
New York, NY 10048
Phone: (800) 789-4376 or (212) 938-4376
Fax: (212) 938-7123
E-mail: esiason@eaison.org
Internet URL: http://www.esiason.org

Newsletters/Publications: Call for a list of publications.
Description: An online resource that includes cystic fibrosis. It is a partnership of leaders in the medical and business communities, along with volunteers, to provide financial support for research aimed at finding a cure for cystic fibrosis.

National Cystic Fibrosis Foundation
6931 Arlington Road
Bethesda, MD 20814
Phone: (800) 344-4823 or (301) 951-4422 (Both have Voice/TTD)
Fax: (301) 951-6378
E-mail: info@cff.org
Internet URL: http://www.cff.org
Newsletters/Publications: The foundation provides booklets and videos.
Description: CFF promotes research and education in the area of cystic fibrosis.

D

Deaf–Blind

American Association of the Deaf–Blind
814 Thayer Avenue, Suite 302
Silver Spring, MD 20910
Phone: (800) 735-2258
TTD: (301) 588-6545
Fax: (301) 588-8705
E-mail: N/A
Internet URL: http://www.tr.wosc.osshe.edu/dblink/aadb.htm
Newsletters/Publications: N/A
Description: A national consumer advocacy organization for people with combined hearing and vision impairments. The organization seeks to encourage independent living, for which it provides technical assistance.

Helen Keller National Center for Deaf–Blind Youths and Adults
111 Middle Neck Road
Sands Point, NY 11050
Phone: (516) 944-8900
TTD: (516) 944-8637
Fax: (516) 944-7302

E-mail: abigailp@aol.com
Internet URL: http://www.helenkeller.org
Newsletters/Publications: *The Nat-Cent News, National Family Association for the Deaf–Blind Newsletter*
Description: The national center and its 10 regional offices provide diagnostic evaluations, comprehensive vocational and personal adjustment training, and job preparation and placement for people (from every state and territory) who are deaf-blind. Field services include information and referral, and advocacy and technical assistance to professionals, consumers, and families.

Depression

Depressive and manic depressive illnesses are the two major types of depressive illness also known as affective disorders or mood disorders. Symptoms of depression may include:

- prolonged sadness or unexplained crying spells
- significant changes in appetite and sleep patterns
- irritability, anger, worry, agitation, anxiety
- pessimism, indifference
- loss of energy
- feelings of guilt, worthlessness
- inability to concentrate, indecisiveness
- inability to take pleasure in former interests
- social withdrawal
- unexplained aches and pains
- recurring thoughts of death and suicide

American Academy of Child and Adolescent Psychiatry
(See Mental Health–Professional Organizations)

Internet Mental Health
(See Mental Health-Websites)

National Depressive and Manic-Depressive Association
730 North Franklin Street, Suite 501
Chicago, IL 60610-3526
Phone: (800) 826-3632
Fax: (312) 642-7243
E-mail: myrtis@aol.com
Internet URL: http://wwwndmda.org
Newsletters/Publications: *Outreach*, published quarterly.
Description: The mission of the National Depressive and Manic-Depressive Association is to educate patients, families, professionals, and the public concerning the nature of depressive and manic-depressive illness as treatable medical diseases; to foster self-help for patients and families; to eliminate discrimination and stigma; to improve access to care; and to advocate for research toward the elimination of these illnesses.

National Institute of Mental Health (NIMH)
(See Government Agencies–Federal)

Diabetes

Diabetes is a metabolic disorder in which the pancreas cannot produce sufficient insulin to process food. Children with certain types of diabetes must take daily injections of insulin.

American Diabetes Association (ADA)
Diabetes Information Service Center
1660 Duke Street
Alexandria, VA 22314
Phone: (800) ADA-DISC
Fax: (703) 549-6995
E-mail: N/A
Internet URL: http://www.diabetes.org
Newsletters/Publications: *Diabetes Forcast,* a monthly magazine; and the *Diabetes Advisor,* a bimonthly newsletter.
Description: The ADA is a non-profit health organization providing research, information, and advocacy on diabetes. It has programs in all 50 states.

Juvenile Diabetes Foundation International (JDF)
120 Wall Street
New York, NY 10005-3904
Phone: (212) 785-9500
Voice/TTD: (800) 223-1138
Fax: (212) 785-9595
E-mail: N/A
Internet URL: http://www.jdfcure.org
Newsletters/Publications: *Countdown Magazine,* and *Countdown Magazine for Kids* published quarterly.
Description: JDF is a not-for-profit voluntary health agency with chapters and affiliates throughout the world. Its main objective is to fund research.

Distance Education

Distance Education courses are offered by educational institutions, businesses, or other entities away from the regular campus sites by using computer conferencing, cable TV, telephone conference calling, video cassettes, correspondence courses, or any combination of these.

Distance Education Clearinghouse
(See Clearinghouses)

Heritage on Line
Heritage Institute
2802 East Madison Avenue, Suite 187
Seattle, WA 98112
Phone: (800) 445-1305
Fax: (206) 322-0996
E-mail: mail@hol.edu
Internet URL: http://www.hol.edu
Newsletters/Publications: The Heritage Institute Continuing Education catalog is published three times a year. Contact the organization for a catalog.
Description: Heritage on Line specializes in Internet-assisted distance education for teachers.

United States Distance Learning Association (USDLA)
1240 Central Boulevard, Suite A
Brentwood, CA 94513
Phone: (925) 513-4253
Fax: (925) 513-4255
E-mail: charles@usdla.org
Internet URL: http://www.usdla.org
Newsletters/Publications: *ED, Education at a Distance* magazine and journal is the official publication of the United States Distance Learning Association (USDLA). Published monthly, ED covers the latest devlopments in the field of distance learning with up-to-date and thoughtful articles from top names in the field, and features such as the Teachers Forum. The ED journal is the only academic journal specifically for distance learning.
Description: USDLA is a non-profit association whose purpose is to promote the development of distance learning for application and training for K-12 education, higher education, continuing education, corporate training, and military and government training. It has chapters in all 50 states.

Down Syndrome

(See Mental Retardation)

Drug and Alcohol Abuse and Prevention

Mothers Against Drunk Drivers (MADD)
National Office
511 East John Carpenter Freeway, Suite 700
Irving, Texas 75062
Phone: (214) 744-6233

Fax: N/A
E-mail: info@madd.org
Internet URL: http://www.madd.org
Newsletters/Publications: Contact local chapter for a list of publications. The local chapter can be found through MADD's website.
Description: MADD is a non-profit grass roots organization with 600 chapters nationwide. Its focus is to find solutions to drunk driving and underage drinking problems. MADD provides information and education opportunities, and helps to establish support groups.

National Clearinghouse for Alcohol and Drug Information (NCADI)
(See Clearinghouse)

National Council on Alcoholism and Drug Dependence
12 West 21st Street
New York, NY 10010
Phone: (212) 206-6770
Fax: (212) 645-1690
E-mail: N/A
Hope Line (24-hour): (800) NCA-CALL
Internet URL: http://www.ncadd.org
Newsletters/Publications: *The Alcoholism Report,* a monthly newsletter.
Description: The council is a voluntary health organization with a nationwide network of affiliates. It provides community prevention/intervention/education programs, a resource center for audio visual materials, and advocacy efforts with local and state governments. Representatives of the council will also (make presentations at schools.)

National Institute on Alcohol Abuse and Alcoholism (NIAAA)
(See Government Agencies–Federal)

National Institute on Drug Abuse (NIDA)
(See Government Agencies–Federal)

E

Early Childhood

Center for Disability Studies at the University of Hawaii at Manoa
1110 University Avenue, Suite 302

Honolulu, HI 96822
Phone: (808) 956-6449
Fax: 808-956-4734
E-mail: dotty@hawaii.edu
Internet URL: http://www.hawaii.edu
Newsletters/Publications: Call for a list of publications.
Description: The Center for Disability Studies at the University of Hawaii at Manoa contributes expertise in community-based inclusive services and provides special linkages to NECTAS's diverse clients in the Pacific Basin. It is part of the NECTAS Consortium.

Federation for Children with Special Needs
(See Parenting Resources)

Georgetown University Child Development Center
3307 M Street NW, Suite 401
Washington, DC 20007-3935
Phone: (202) 687-5000
Fax: (202) 687-1954
E-mail: gucdc@gunet.georgetown.edu
Internet URL: http://www.dml.georgetown.edu/depts/pediatrics/gucdc/nectas.html
Newsletters/Publications: Call for a list of publications.
Description: The Georgetown University Child Development Center contributes expertise in interagency coordination, finance, and cultural appropriateness and provides special linkages to the maternal and child health and mental health communities. It is part of the NECTAS Consortium.

National Early Childhood Technical Assistance System (NECTAS) Coordinating Office
500 Nations Bank Plaza
137 East Franklin Street
Chapel Hill, NC 27514
Voice: (919) 962-2001
TTD: (919) 962-8300
Fax: (919) 966-7463
E-mail: nectas@unc.edu
Internet URL: http://www.nectas.unc.edu
Newsletters/Publications: Call for a list of publications.
Description: NECTAS is housed at the Frank Porter Graham Child Development Center (FPG) at the University of North Carolina at Chapel Hill. FPG contributes broad expertise in policy, service planning, and implementation for states and early childhood projects. It has extensive skills in the technical assistance process and expertise in research and development. FPG provides the NECTAS consortium with special linkages to other research, technical assistance, and professional organizations.

ZERO TO THREE: National Center for Infants, Toddlers and Families
734 15th Street NW, Suite 1000
Washington, DC 20005-1013

Phone: (202) 638-1144
Fax: (202) 638-0851
E-mail: 0to3@zerotothree.org
Internet URL: http://www.zerotothree.org
Newsletters/Publications: Call for a list of publications.
Description: As part of the NECTAS consortium, ZERO TO THREE National Center for Infants, Toddlers and Families contributes expertise in policies, programs, and practices, including promoting mental health for infants and toddlers. It provides the consortium with special linkages to the Head Start and child-care communities.

Early Childhood Assessment Measures

Early childhood measures assess the developmental and academic skills of young children, approximately birth to age 8.

Bayley Scales of Infant Development–2nd Edition (BSID-II)
Author: Nancy Bayley
Publisher: The Psychological Corporation
555 Academic Court
San Antonio, TX 78204-2498
Phone: (800) 211-8378
Fax: (800) 232-1223
TDD: (800) 723-1318
Type of Test: Norm-referenced
Administration Time: Under 15 months, 25–30 minutes; over 15 months, up to 60 minutes.
Type of Administration: Individual
Age/Grade Level: Ages 1–42 months

Boehm Test of Basic Concepts–Revised (BTBC-R)
Author: Ann F. Boehm
Publisher: The Psychological Corporation
555 Academic Court
San Antonio, TX 78204-2498
Phone: (800) 211-8378
Fax: (800) 232-1223
TDD: (800) 723-1318
Type of Test: Standardized
Administration Time: 0–40 minutes for form C or D; 15–20 minutes for Applications form.
Type of Administration: Group
Age/Grade Level: Grades K–3

Bracken Basic Concept Scale (BCDP)
Author: Bruce A. Bracken
Publisher: The Psychological Corporation
555 Academic Court
San Antonio, TX 78204-2498
Phone: (800) 211-8378
Fax: (800) 232-1223
TDD: (800) 723-1318
Type of Test: Standardized
Administration Time: 20–40 minutes
Type of Administration: Group
Age/Grade Level: Age 2.6 to 7.11

Child Behavior Checklist (CBCL)
Authors: Thomas H. Achenbach and Craig Edelbrock
Publisher: University Associates in Psychiatry
1 South Prospect Street
Burlington, VT 05401
Phone: (802) 656-4563
Fax of Publisher: (802) 656-8747
Type of Test: Norm-referenced
Administration Time: Varies with age
Type of Administration: Individual
Age/Grade Level: Ages 4 to 18

Degangi-Berk Test of Sensory Integration (TSI)
Authors: Ronald A. Berk and Georgia A. De Gangi
Publisher: Western Psychological Services
12031 Wilshire Boulevard
Los Angeles, CA 90025
Phone: (310) 478-2061 or (800) 648-8857
Fax: (310) 478-7838
Type of Test: Norm-referenced
Administration Time: 30 minutes
Type of Administration: Indivdual
Age/Grade Level: Ages 3 to 5

The Denver Developmental Screening Test–Revised Denver-2
Author: William K. Frankenburg
Publisher: Denver Developmental Materials Inc.
PO Box 6919
Denver, CO 80206-0919
Phone: (303) 355-4729
Fax of Publisher: (303) 355-5622
Type of Test: Standardized
Administration Time: 10–20 minutes
Type of Administration: Individual

Age/Grade Level: Birth to age 6

Kindergarten Readiness Test (KRT)
Authors: Sue L. Larson and Gary Vitali
Publisher: Slosson Educational Publications
PO Box 280
East Aurora, NY 14052-0280
Phone: (888) SLOSSON
Fax: (800) 655-3840
Type of Test: Standardized
Administration Time: 15–20 minutes
Type of Administration: Individual
Age/Grade Level: Ages 4 to 6

Metropolitan Readiness Tests–5th Edition (MRT–5)
Authors: Joanne R. Nurss and Mary E. Mc Gauvran
Publisher: The Psychological Corporation
555 Academic Court
San Antonio, TX 78204-2498
Phone: (800) 211-8378
Fax: (800) 232-1223
TDD: (800) 723-1318
Type of Test: Standardized
Administration Time: Approximately 90 minutes per level; 5 minutes for practice booklet for each level.
Type of Administration: Group administered
Age/Grade Level: Pre-kindergarten through grade 1
a.   Level 1 - Beginning and middle of kindergarten
b.   Level 2 - Middle and end of kindergarten, and beginning of grade 1

The Preschool Evaluation Scales (PES)
Author: Stephen B. McCarney
Publisher: Hawthorne Educational Services
800 Gray Oak Drive
Columbia, MO 65201
Phone: (800) 542-1673
Fax: (800) 442-9509
Type of Test: Norm-referenced
Administration Time: 20–25 minutes
Type of Administration: Individual
Age/Grade Level: Birth to 72 months

Preschool Language Scale 3 (PLS–3)
Authors: Irla Lee Zimmerman, Violette G. Steiner, and Roberta L. Evatt
Publisher: The Psychological Corporation
555 Academic Court
San Antonio, TX 78204-2498

Phone: (800) 211-8378
Fax: (800) 232-1223
TDD: (800) 723-1318
Type of Test: Norm-referenced, criterion
Administration Time: 30 minutes
Type of Administration: Individual
Age/Grade Level: Birth to 6.11

Early Childhood and Elementary Websites

Early Childhood Education On-Line Website
Internet URL: http://www.ume.maine.edu/~cofed/eceol/website.html
Description: This site provides information on developmental guidelines, diversity, observation and assessment, curriculum, issues in early childhood settings, advocacy, professional development, and more.

Early Childhood Educators and Family Web Corner
Internet URL: http://www.nauticom.net/www/cokids/index.html
Description: This site provides a vast database of information for teachers and parents on numerous topics dealing with early childhood.

Educational Resources on the Internet
Internet URL: http://ericeece.org/ed2link.html
Description: This page contains links to Internet sites that have some connection with the development and education of children from birth through adolescence.

Eating Disorders Websites

These sites cover a variety of disorders including anorexia nervosa, bulimia nervosa, binge-eating disorder (compulsive eating), anorexia athletica (compulsive exercising), night-eating syndrome, nocturnal sleep-related eating disorder, gourmand syndrome, and muscle dysmorphia (bigarexia).
(See Anorexia and Bulimia)

Illnesses–Health Care Resources on the Internet
Internet URL: http://www-hsl.mcmaster.ca/tomflem/backup/eatdis.html
Description: A Canadian-based database located at McMaster University Health Sciences Library in Hamilton, Ontario. This site offers a wide range of information on numerous health care issues.

Educational Software Publishers Directory

Educational Software Institute–ESI Online
Internet URL: http://www.edsoft.com
Description: This site is an educational software resource center containing an extensive collection of K-12 educational software for parents, students, and teachers.

PEP Registry of Educational Software Publishers
Phone: (415) 382-1818
Fax: (415) 382-1717
E-mail: N/A
Internet URL: The PEP Website is maintained by Anne Bubnic at www.microweb.com/pepsite/Software/publishers.html
Newsletters/Publications: N/A
Description: PEP is the acronym for the resources available to Parents, Educators & Publishers. The PEP Registry is a comprehensive listing of more than 1000 Educational Software Companies, with direct links to their sites. It does not imply endorsement of a product or company.

Employment Resources for the Disabled

(See Transition Services)

Epilepsy

Epilepsy is a seizure disorder resulting in recurrent seizures. These seizures are attributable to a massive abnormal electrical discharge.

Epilepsy Foundation of America (EFA)
4351 Garden City Drive, 5th Floor
Landover, MD 20785-4941
Phone: (800) 332-1000
TTD: (800) 332-2070
Fax: (301) 577-2684
E-mail: postmaster@efa.org
Internet URL: http://www.efa.org
Newsletters/Publications: Call for a list of publications.
Description: The Epilepsy Foundation of America is a national not-for-profit voluntary organization that works for people affected by seizures through programs of research, education, advocacy, and service. The Foundation seeks to improve quality of life, facilitate access to reliable information, and act as a voice for people affected by seizures. The Foundation supplies

informational materials to the public and to health care professionals. In addition, the National Epilepsy Library and Resource Center provides authoritative information to professionals and the public by means of computer access to major collections of medical information.

Estate Planning for the Disabled

Future Planning Resources from The Arc
Internet URL: http://www.thearc.org/misc/futplan.html
(See The Arc–Mental Retardation/Developmental Disabilities)

Life Services for the Handicapped
Phone: (800) 995-0066 or (212) 532-6740
Fax: (212) 532-6740
E-mail: disabledandalone@juno.com
Internet URL: http://www.hsca.org/disabledandalone.htm
Newsletter/Publications: *Lifelines,* published three times a year or as needed.
Description: This organization helps families to plan the future for a family member with a disability. It will also carry out the plan in the event that the family cannot.

National Institute on Life Planning for Persons with Disabilities
PO Box 5093
Twin Falls, ID 83303-5093
Fax: (208) 735-8562
E-mail: rfee@sonic.net
Internet URL: http://www.sonic.net./nilp
Newsletter/Publications: *Life Planning Newsletter,* published monthly online.
Description: NILP is a national clearinghouse for professional members on all aspects of life planning for the disabled, including guardianship, conservators, special needs trust, and more. It also provides links to other sites on this topic.

F

Fibrodysplasia Ossificans Progressiva

Fibrodysplasia Ossificans Progressiva (FOP) is a very rare inherited connective tissue disorder characterized by the abnormal development of bone in areas of the body where bone is not normally present (heterotopic ossification), such as the ligaments, tendons, and muscles. Major symptoms may include skeletal malformations and/or abnormally short and malformed toes and fingers. The abnormal development of bone may lead to stiffness in affected areas and may also limit movement in affected joints (e.g., knees, wrists, shoulders, spine, and/or neck).

Fibrodysplasia Ossificans Progressive usually begins during early childhood and progresses throughout life. Most cases of FOP occur randomly (sporadic). However, researchers believe that the defective gene(s) responsible for this disorder may be inherited as an autosomal dominant genetic trait.

International Fibrodysplasia Ossificans Progressiva Association
PO Box 3578
Winter Springs, FL 32708
Phone: (407) 365-4194
Fax/Voice: (407) 365-4194
E-mail: ifopa@vol.com
Internet URL: http://www.med.upenn.edu/ortho/fop
Newsletters/Publications: IFOPA recently published two very special books: *What is FOP? A Guidebook for Families* (available in an online version) and *What is FOP? Questions and Answers for the Children*. This is the first comprehensive resource package written specifically for families dealing with FOP.

The IFOPA publishes *The FOP Connection*, a quarterly newsletter for FOP families and other interested individuals.
Description: The International Fibrodysplasia Ossificans Progressiva (FOP) Association is a voluntary not-for-profit organization. The association is dedicated to promoting and funding research on FOP and making medical resources available to affected individuals. The organization assists individuals with FOP in any manner reasonably related to their medical concerns, including making adaptive equipment and transportation available.

Fragile X Syndrome

Fragile X syndrome, also called Martin-Bell syndrome, is a genetic disorder and is the most common form of inherited mental retardation. Approximately 15 percent to 20 percent of those with Fragile X Syndrome exhibit autistic-type behaviors, such as poor eye contact, hand-flapping or odd gesture movements, handbiting, and poor sensory skills. Behavior problems and speech/language delay are common features of Fragile X Syndrome.

People with Fragile X syndrome also have a number of recognizable physical features, including a high arched palate, strabismus (lazy eye), large ears, long face, large testicles in males, poor muscle tone, flat feet, and sometimes mild heart valve abnormalities. Although most individuals with Fragile X syndrome have a characteristic "look" (long face and large ears), there are some who do not have the typical features of the syndrome.

National Fragile X Foundation
1441 York Street, Suite 303
Denver, CO 80206-2127
Phone: (800) 688-8765 or (303) 333-6155
Fax: (303) 333-4369

E-mail: natlfx@sprintmail.com
Internet URL: http://www.nfxf.org
Newsletters/Publications: Call for a list of publications.
Description: The National Fragile X Foundation provides advocacy, consultation, referral, information, research, newsletter and educational resources.
(See also Mental Retardation/Developmental Disorders)

Free Materials for Educators Websites

Free Education on the Internet
Internet URL: http://www.free-ed.net/fr04/fr0403.htm
Description: Free online courses, tutorials, and activities.

National Education Association
(See Professional Organizations)
Internet URL (for free materials): http://www.nea.org/resources/free.html
Description: Numerous free classroom materials for educators.

The Perpetual Preschool
Free Stuff for Teachers on the Internet
Internet URL: http://members.aol.com/aactchrday/free/internet.htm
Description: An excellent link to numerous free material sites.

G

Gifted and Talented

There are many definitions for giftedness. They all have one element in common: A gifted person is someone who shows, or has the potential for showing, an exceptional level of performance in one or more areas of expression. Some of these abilities are very general and can affect a broad spectrum of the person's life, such as leadership skills or the ability to think creatively. Some are very specific talents and are only evident in particular circumstances, such as a special aptitude in mathematics, science, or music. The term giftedness provides a general reference to this spectrum of abilities without being specific or dependent on a single measure or index. It is generally recognized that approximately five percent of the student population, or three million children, in the United States are considered gifted. (Source: National Association for Gifted Children; 1998)

American Association for Gifted Children (AAGC)

1121 West Main Street, (Suite 100)
Durham, NC 27701
Phone: (919) 683-1400
Fax: N/A
E-mail: N/A
Internet URL: http://www.jayi.com/jayi/aagc
Newsletters/Publications: Three newsletters a year.
Description: AAGC is an advocacy organization for gifted children. It publishes materials for the educational research community, health professionals, and for parents and teachers of gifted children.

Council for Exceptional Children

(See professional Organizations—GENERAL)

National Association for Gifted Children (NAGC)

1707 L Street NW, (Suite 550)
Washington, DC 20036
Phone: (202) 785-4268
Fax: (202) 785-4248
E-mail: nagc@nagc.org
Internet URL: http://www.nagc.org
Newsletters/Publications: *Gifted Child Quarterly.* Call the association for a list of other publications.
Description: The NAGC is an organization of parents, educators, other professionals, and community leaders who unite to address the needs of gifted children. It provides publications, materials, and parenting information as well as involvement in public policy and advocacy.

Gifted Websites

Gifted Links
Ohio Association of the Gifted
Internet URL: http://www.oagc.com/links
Description: This site has an extensive link to numerous other gifted sights.

Gifted Resources Home Page
Internet URL: http://www.eskimo.com/~user/kids.html
Description: Contains links to all known online gifted resources, enrichment programs, talent searches, summer programs, mailing lists, and early acceptance programs. It also contains contact information for many local and state gifted programs and associations.

TAG Family Network
Website Only

Phone: N/A
Fax: (503)378-7851 (membership)
E-mail: rkaltwas@teleport.com
Internet URL: http://www.teleport.com/~rkaltwas/tag
Newsletters/Publications: Call for a list of publications.
Description: TAG is a parent organization run by and for parents of gifted children. It disseminates information, supports parents, and monitors and influences legal issues. TAG offers articles and links to other resources on the internet. Membership is free, and contact is by e-mail only.

Yahoo Education K–12: Gifted Youth
Internet URL:
http://www.yahoo.com/education/k_12/gifted_youth
Description: Excellent links to numerous sites dealing with gifted education including university sites, organizations, foundations, and more.

Government Agencies (Federal)

U.S. Federal Government Agencies Directory
Internet URL: http://www.lib.lsu.edu/gov/fedgov.html
Description: This site contains a complete list of all federal agencies, departments, and institutes. It is a comprehensive site and assists in locating appropriate resources.

The federal government is comprised of hundreds of agencies and departments. We have chosen the most relevant departments and their agencies that relate to the needs of special education. The reader should note that these agencies may have state counterparts.

Department of Education (DoE)
400 Maryland Avenue, SW
Washington, DC 20202-0498
Phone: (800) USA-LEARN
Fax: N/A
E-mail: N/A
Internet URL: http://www.ed.gov
Newsletters/Publications: Contact the agency for a catalog.
Description: The department administers over 200 programs that assist state and local education agencies to improve the achievement of elementary and secondary school students.

The following six agencies (and their subagencies) included under the DOE that may be relevant include:

1. **Office of Civil Rights (OCR)**
   US Department of Education, OCR
   330 C Street SW, Suite 5000
   Washington, DC 20202-1100
   Phone: (202) 205-5413
   Fax: (202) 205-9862
   TDD: (202) 205-5166

E-mail: ocr@ed.gov
Internet URL: http://www.ed.gov/offices/OCR
Newsletters/Publications: Contact the agency for a catalog.
Description: This agency ensures equal access to education and promotes educational excellence throughout the country through vigorous enforcement of civil rights. Its primary responsibility is to resolve complaints of discrimination. To file a formal civil rights complaint (i.e. Section 504 complaint), contact this office or the regional office servicing your area.

2. **Office of Special Education and Rehabilitative Services (OSERS)**
    Mary E. Switzer Building
    330 C Street SW, Suite 3006
    Washington, DC 20202
    Phone: (202) 205-5465 (Voice and TDD)
    Fax: (202) 205-9252
    E-mail: N/A
    Internet URL: http://www.ed.gov/offices/**OSERS**
    Newsletters/Publications: Contact the agency for a catalog.
    Description: This office supports programs that assist in educating children with special needs, provides for the rehabilitation of youth and adults with disabilities, and supports research to improve the lives of individuals with disabilities.
    OSERS consists of three program-related components:
    1. Office of Special Education Programs (OSEP) (this section)
    2. Rehabilitation Services Administration (RSA) (this section)
    3. National Institute on Disability and Rehabilitation Research (NIDRR) (this section)

Note: The following 5 agencies are under OSERS.

A. **Office of Special Education Programs (OSEP)**
    Mary E. Switzer Building
    330 C Street SW, Room 3086
    Washington, DC 20202-9754
    Phone: (202) 205-5507
    TDD: (202) 205-9754
    Fax: N/A
    E-mail: N/A
    Internet URL: http://www.ed.gov
    Newsletters/Publications: Contact the agency for a catalog.
    Description: The Office of Special Education Programs (OSEP) has primary responsibility for administering programs and projects relating to the free, appropriate public education of all children, youth, and adults with disabilities from birth through age 22. The bulk of special education funds is administered by OSEP's Division of Assistance to States, which provides grants to states and territories to assist them in providing a free, appropriate public education to all children with disabilities.

B. **Rehabilitation Services Administration (RSA)**
    Mary E. Switzer Building
    330 C Street SW, Room 3026
    Washington, DC 20202

Phone: (202) 205-5482
TDD: (202) 205-8352
Fax: (202) 260-9424
E-mail: N/A
Internet URL: http://www.ed.gov/offices/OSERS/RSA/rsa.html
Newsletters/Publications: Contact the agency for a catalog.
Description: The Rehabilitation Services Administration (RSA) oversees programs that help individuals with physical or mental disabilities to obtain employment through the provision of such supports as counseling, medical and psychological services, job training, and other individualized services. RSA's major formula grant program offers funds to state vocational rehabilitation agencies to provide employment-related services for individuals with disabilities, giving priority to individuals who are severely disabled. It administers the principal federal service programs designed to rehabilitate, employ, and promote the independent living of people with disabilities.

C.   **National Institute on Disability and Rehabilitative Research (NIDRR)**
Mary E. Switzer Building
330 C Street SW, Room 3060 MES
Washington, DC 20202-2572
Phone: (202) 205-8134
Fax: (202) 205-8515
TDD: (202) 205-9136
E-mail: N/A
Internet URL: http://www.ed.gov/offices/OSERS/NIDRR/nidrr.html
Newsletters/Publications: Contact the agency for a catalog.
Description: National Institute on Disability and Rehabilitation Research (NIDRR) administers the principal federal disability research programs, the Technology Related Assistance for Individuals with Disabilities Act, and ADA technical assistance centers.

3.   **Office of Educational Research and Improvement (OERI)**
555 New Jersey Avenue, NW
Washington, DC 20208
Phone: (202) 219-1385
Fax: N/A
E-mail: N/A
Internet URL: http://www.ed.gov/offices/OERI
Newsletters/Publications: Contact the agency for a catalog.
Description: The Office of Educational Research and Improvement provides national leadership for educational research and statistics. It offers a variety of services through its library, institutes, and program-specific services.

Note: The following agencies are under OERI.

A.   **National Center for Educational Statistics (NCES)**
555 New Jersey Avenue, NW
Washington, DC 20208
Phone: (800) 424-1616
Fax: (202) 219-1696

67

E-mail: Library@inet.ed.gov
Internet URL: http://nces.ed.gov
Newsletters/Publications: Contact the agency for a list of publications.
Description: NCES is the primary federal agency for collecting and analyzing data related to education in the US and other nations.

B. **National Institute on Early Childhood Development and Education (ECI)**
    555 New Jersey Avenue, NW
    Washington, DC 20208
    Phone: (202) 219-1935
    Fax: (202) 273-4768
    E-mail: eci@inet.ed.gov
    Internet URL: http://www.ed.gov/offices/OERI/ECI
    Description: ECI sponsors comprehensive and challenging research that investigates the most effective strategies and practices that affect young children and their families.

C. **National Institute on the Education of At-Risk Students**
    OERI At Risk, Room 610
    555 New Jersey Avenue, NW
    Washington, DC 20208
    Phone: (202) 219-2239
    Fax: (202) 219-2030
    E-mail: N/A
    Internet URL: http://www.ed.gov/offices/OERI/At-Risk
    Newsletters/Publications: Contact the agency for a catalog.
    Description: The institute supports a range of research and activities designed to improve the education of students at risk of educational failure.

D. **National Institute on Post Secondary Education, Libraries, and Lifelong Learning (PLLI)**
    555 New Jersey Avenue, NW
    Washington, DC 20208
    Phone: (202) 219-2207
    Fax: (202) 219-3005
    E-mail: N/A
    Internet URL: http://www.ed.gov/offices/OERI/PLLI
    Newsletters/Publications: Contact the agency for a catalog.
    Description: PLLI seeks to expand knowledge about the education and training of adults in a variety of settings including post secondary institutions, community-based education programs, libraries, and the workplace.

E. **National Institute on Student Achievement, Curriculum and Assessment (SAI)**
    OERI/Student Achievement Institute
    555 New Jersey Avenue, NW
    Washington, DC 20208
    Phone: (202) 219-2079

Fax: (202) 219-2135
E-mail: sai@ed.gov
Internet URL: http://www.ed.gov/offices/OERI/SAI
Newsletters/Publications: Contact the agency for a list of publications.
Description: The institute's purpose is to carry out a coordinated and comprehensive program of research and development in core content areas and to integrate these areas to enhance student learning.

4. **Office of Elementary and Secondary Education (OESE)**
   Portals Building
   600 Independence Avenue, SW
   Washington, DC 20202
   Phone: (202) 401-0113
   Fax: (202) 205-0303
   E-mail: oese@ed.gov
   Internet URL: http://www.ed.gov/offices/OESE
   Newsletters/Publications: Contact the agency for a catalog.
   Description: OESE promotes academic excellence and enhances educational opportunities, and seeks to improve the quality of teaching and learning.

5. **Office of Post Secondary Education (OPE)**
   Regional Office Building 3 (ROB-3)
   7th and D Streets, SW
   Washington, DC 20202
   Phone: (202) 708-5547
   Fax: N/A
   E-mail: N/A
   Internet URL: http://www.ed.gov/offices/OPE
   Newsletters/Publications: Contact the agency for a catalog.
   Description: OPE is responsible for formulating policy and directing and coordinating programs for financial assistance to post-secondary educational institutions.

6. **Office of Vocational and Adult Education (OVAE)**
   Mary E. Switzer Building
   330 C Street SW, Room 4090
   Washington, DC 20202
   Phone: (202) 205-5451
   Fax: (202) 205-8973
   E-mail: ovae@net.ed.gov
   Internet URL: http://www.ed.gov/offices/OVAE
   Newsletters/Publications: Contact the agency for a catalog.
   Description: This clearinghouse links the adult education community with existing resources in adult education and provides information that deals with programs funded under the Adult Education Act (P.L. 100-297). The clearinghouse provides a number of free publications, fact sheets, bibliographies, directories, and abstracts available for the adult with special learning needs.

Department of Health and Human Services
200 Independence Avenue, SW
Washington, DC 20201
Phone: (202) 619-0257
Fax: N/A
E-mail: N/A
Internet URL: http://www.os.dhhs.gov
Publications: Contact the agency for specific publications catalogs.
Description: The DHHS is the US government's principal agency for protecting the health of all Americans and providing essential human services. The department includes more than 300 programs and a wide spectrum of activities. The most relevant agencies for special educators are:

1. **Administration for Children and Families**
   370 Promenade
   Washington, DC 20047
   Phone: (202) 401-9215
   Fax: (202) 205-9688
   E-mail: N/A
   Internet URL: http://www.acf.dhhs.gov
   Description: The Administration for Children and Families (ACF) is the agency within the Department of Health and Human Services that brings together the broad range of federal programs and services that address the needs of children and families. Some of the services that are funded include foster care, adoption assistance, independent living, child abuse and neglect programs, child welfare services, Head Start, and developmental disabilities support programs.

   Two of the agencies under the Administration for Children and Families are:

A. **Children's Bureau**
   330 C Street, SW
   Washington, DC 20201
   Phone: (202) 205-8618
   Fax: N/A
   E-mail: gharden@acf.dhhs.gov
   Internet URL: http://www.acf.dhhs.gov/programs/cb
   Newsletters/Publications: Contact the agency for a catalog.
   Description: Children's Bureau is the oldest federal agency specifically charged with the responsibility of looking after the well-being of the nation's children. The bureau helps the states to deliver child welfare services, such as the protection of children and the strengthening of families (child protective services), family preservation and support, foster care, adoption, and independent living.

B. **National Center for Education in Maternal and Child Health**
   2200 15th Street N, Suite 701
   Arlington, VA 22201
   Phone: (703) 524-7802
   Fax: (703) 524-9335
   E-mail: N/A

Internet URL: http://www.ncemch.org
Newsletters/Publications: Call for a publications catalog.
Description: The center provides information publications, program development, and policy analysis and education.

2. **National Institute of Health (NIH)**
Bethesda, Maryland 20892
Phone: (301) 496-4000
Fax: N/A
E-mail: N/A
Internet URL: http//www.nih.gov
Newsletters/Publications: Call for a complete list of publications.
Description: The NIH mission is to uncover new knowledge that will lead to better health for everyone. NIH works toward that mission by conducting research in its own laboratories; supporting the research of non-federal scientists in universities, medical schools, hospitals, and research institutions throughout the country and abroad; helping in the training of research investigators; and fostering communication of biomedical information. It offers a wealth of information on illnesses and disabilities. This information is available for use by both professionals and nonprofessionals.

NIH is comprised of 24 separate Institutes and Centers and is one of 8 health agencies that is part of the US Department of Health and Human Services. The relevant sites for special educators, with their website address, are:

A. **National Cancer Institute (NCI)**
9000 Rockville Pike, Room 10A16
Bethesda, MD 20892
Phone: (301) 496-5583
Fax: N/A
E-mail: N/A
Internet URL: http://www.nci.nih.gov
Newsletters/Publications: Contact the agency for a catalog.
Description: The National Cancer Institute (NCI) coordinates the government's cancer research program. NCI is the largest of the 17 biomedical research institutes and centers at the National Institutes of Health (NIH).

B. **National Eye Institute (NEI)**
9000 Rockville Pike
Building 31, Room 6A06
Bethesda, MD 20892
Phone: (301) 496-4876
Fax: N/A
E-mail: N/A
Internet URL: http://www.nei.nih.gov
Newsletters/Publications: Contact the agency for a catalog.
Description: NEI provides research, educational programs, publications, and conferences to professionals and the public.

C. **National Heart, Lung, and Blood Institute (NHLBI)**
9000 Rockville Pike
Building 31, Room 5A48
Bethesda, MD 20892
Phone: (301) 496-2411
Fax: N/A
E-mail: N/A
Internet URL: http://www.nhlbi.nih.gov/nhlbi/nhlbi.htm
Newsletters/Publications: Contact the agency for a catalog.
Description: The National Heart, Lung, and Blood Institute (NHLBI) provides leadership
for a national education program in diseases of the heart, blood vessels, lungs, and
blood resources; and sleep disorders.
    For health professionals and the public, the NHLBI conducts educational
activities, including development and dissemination of materials in the above areas,
with an emphasis on prevention.

D. **National Institute on Alcohol Abuse and Alcoholism (NIAA)**
(Willco Building)
6000 Executive Boulevard
Bethesda, MD 20892-7003
Phone: (301) 443-3860
Fax: N/A
E-mail: N/A
Internet URL: http://www.niaaa.nih.gov
Newsletters/Publications: Contact the agency for a catalog.
Description: The National Institute on Alcohol Abuse and Alcoholism (NIAAA) supports
and conducts biomedical and behavioral research on the causes, consequences, treatment,
and prevention of alcoholism and alcohol-related problems. NIAAA also provides leadership
in the national effort to reduce the severe and often fatal consequences of these problems.

E. **National Institute of Allergy and Infectious Diseases (NIAID)**
9000 Rockville Pike
Building 31
Bethesda, MD 20892
Phone: (301) 496-5717
Fax: N/A
E-mail: N/A
Internet URL: http://www.niaid.nih.gov
Newsletters/Publications: Contact the agency for a catalog.
Description: NIAID is the leading research and information center on HIV and AIDS. It
also offers information on advisory allergy and infectious diseases as well as research
on minority and women's health.

F. **National Institute of Arthritis and Musculoskeletal and Skin Diseases Information Clearinghouse**
Building 31, Room 4C05
31 Center Drive, MSC 2350
Bethesda, MD 20892-2350

Phone: Voice (301) 495-4484 or (301) 495-4484
TTD: (301) 565-2966
Fax: N/A
Internet URL: http://chid.nih.gov/subfile/contribs/ar.html
Newsletters/Publications: Contact the organization for list of publications.
Description: The National Arthritis and Musculoskeletal and Skin Diseases Information Clearinghouse (NAMSIC) was established in 1978 as the Arthritis Information Clearinghouse; its scope expanded in 1987 to include musculoskeletal (including sports-related injuries) and skin diseases. The purpose of the clearinghouse is to identify, collect, process, and disseminate information about print and audiovisual educational materials concerned with arthritis, musculoskeletal diseases, skin diseases, and sports-related injuries. The clearinghouse serves health professionals, health educators, patients, and the general public. The information in the database includes references to books, journal articles, audiovisuals, directories, bibliographies, manuals, brochures and pamphlets, computer programs, monographs, newsletters, and other educational materials.

G. **National Institute of Child Health and Human Development (NICHD)**
9000 Bockville Pike
Bethesda, MD 20892
Phone: (301) 496-5133
Fax: N/A
E-mail: N/A
Internet URL: http://www.nih.gov/nichd
Newsletters/Publications: Contact the agency for a catalog.
Description: The National Institute of Child Health and Human Development (NICHD) seeks to assure that every individual is born healthy, is born wanted, and has the opportunity to fulfill his or her potential for a healthy and productive life unhampered by disease or disability. In pursuit of this mission, NICHD conducts and supports laboratory, clinical, and epidemiological research on the reproductive, neurobiologic, developmental, and behavioral processes that determine and maintain the health of children, adults, families, and populations.

An overarching responsibility of NICHD is to disseminate information emanating from the institute's research programs to researchers, practitioners, and other health professionals and to the general public.

H. **National Institute on Deafness and Other Communications Disorders (NIDCD)**
Bethesda, MD 9000 Rockville Pike 20892
Phone: (301) 496-7243
Fax: N/A
E-mail: N/A
Internet URL: http://www.nih.gov/nidcd
Newsletters/Publications: Contact the agency for a catalog.
Description: The institute is mandated to conduct and support biomedical and behavioral research and research training in the normal and disordered processes of hearing, balance, smell, taste, voice, speech and language. The institute also conducts and supports research and research training related to disease prevention and health promo-

tion, addresses special biomedical and behavioral problems associated with people who have communication impairments or disorders, and supports efforts to create devices that substitute for lost and impaired sensory and communication function.

I.   **National Institute of Diabetes and Digestive and Kidney Diseases (NIDDK)**
Bethesda, MD 9000 Rockville Pike 20892
Phone: (301) 496-3583
Fax: N/A
E-mail: N/A
Internet URL: http://www.niddk.nih.gov
Newsletters/Publications: Contact the agency for a catalog.
Description: The National Institute of Diabetes and Digestive and Kidney Diseases conducts and supports research on many of the most serious diseases affecting public health. It also supports much of the clinical research on the diseases of internal medicine and related subspecialty fields as well as many basic science disciplines.

The institute's Division of Intramural Research encompasses the broad spectrum of metabolic diseases such as diabetes, inborn errors of metabolism, endocrine disorders, mineral metabolism, digestive diseases, nutrition, urology and renal disease, and hematology. Basic research studies include biochemistry, nutrition, pathology, histochemistry, chemistry, physical, chemical, and molecular biology, pharmacology, and toxicology.

J.   **National Institute on Drug Abuse (NIDA)**
Bethesda, MD 5600 Fischers Lane 20857
Phone: (301) 443-6245
Fax: N/A
E-mail: N/A
Internet URL: http://www.nida.nih.gov
Newsletters/Publications: Contact the agency for a catalog.
Description: NIDA supports more than 85 percent of the world's research on the health aspects of drug abuse and addiction. NIDA-supported science addressing the most fundamental and essential questions about drug abuse, ranging from the molecule to managed NIDA, is not only seizing upon unprecedented opportunities and technologies to further understanding of how drugs of abuse affect the brain and behavior, but also is working to ensure the rapid and effective transfer of scientific data to policy makers, drug abuse practitioners, other health care practitioners, and the general public.

K.   **National Institute of Mental Health (NIMH)**
Bethesda, MD 5600 Fischers Lane 20857
Phone: (301) 443-4513
Fax: N/A
E-mail: N/A
Internet URL: http://www.nimh.nih.gov
Newsletters/Publications: Contact the agency for a catalog.
Description: NIMH is the foremost mental health research organization in the world, with a mission of improving the treatment, diagnosis, and prevention of mental disorders such as schizophrenia and depressive illnesses, and other conditions that affect millions of Americans, including children and adolescents.

L. **National Institute of Neurological Disorders and Stroke (NINDS)**
Bethesda, MD 9000 Rockville Pike 20892
Phone: (301) 496-5751
Fax: N/A
E-mail: N/A
Internet URL: http://www.ninds.nih.gov
Newsletters/Publications: Contact the agency for a catalog.
Description:
- Conducts, fosters, coordinates, and guides research on the causes, prevention, diagnosis, and treatment of neurological disorders and stroke, and supports basic research in related scientific areas.
- Provides grants-in-aid to public and private institutions and individuals in fields related to its areas of interest, including research projects, program projects, and research center grants.
- Operates a program of contracts for the funding of research and research-support efforts in selected areas of institute need.
- Provides individual and institutional fellowships to increase scientific expertise in neurological fields.
- Conducts a diversified program of intramural and collaborative research in its own laboratories, branches, and clinics.
- Collects and disseminates research information related to neurological disorders.

M. **National Library of Medicine (NLM)**
Bethesda, MD 8600 Rockville Pike 20894
Phone: (301) 496-6308
Fax: N/A
E-mail: N/A
Internet URL: http://www.nlm.nih.gov
Newsletters/Publications: Contact the agency for a catalog.
Description: The National Library of Medicine's World Wide Web site includes MEDLINE. Every significant program of the Library is represented, from medical history to biotechnology.

3. **Center For Disease Control and Prevention (CDC)**
1600 Clifton Road, NE
Atlanta, GA 30333
Phone: (404) 639-3311
Fax: N/A
E-mail: N/A
Internet URL: http://www.cdc.gov
Newsletters/Publications: Contact the agency for a list of publications and its catalog.
Description: CDC is the nation's prevention agency for disease. It is part of the Department of Health and Human Services and has 11 centers, institutes, and offices. Some of these follow:

A. **National Institute of Environmental Health Sciences (NIEHS)**
PO Box 12233
Research Triangle Park, NC 27709

Phone: (919) 541-2605
Fax: N/A
E-mail: N/A
Internet URL: http://www.cdc./gov/ncehhome.htm
Newsletters/Publications: Contact the agency for a catalog.
Description: NCEH promotes health and quality of life by preventing and controlling disease, birth defects, disability, and death resulting from interactions between people and their environment.

Note: The following agency is under the NCEH and may provide important information for special education:

B.   **Office on Disability and Health**
4770 Buford Highway (F-29)
Atlanta, GA 30341
Phone: (770) 488-7082
Fax: (770) 488-7075
E-mail: N/A
Internet URL: http://www.cdc.gov/nceh/programs/disabil/overvwt.htm
Newsletters/Publications: Contact the agency for a catalog.
Description: ODH provides public health leadership to promote understanding about disabilities, and coordinates relevant federal disability and health activities.

4.   **Substance Abuse and Mental Health Administration**
5600 Fischers Lane
Rockville, MD 20857
Phone: (301) 443-8956
Fax: (301) 443-9050
E-mail: padams@samhsa.gov
Internet URL: http://www.samhsa.gov
Newsletters/Publications: Call for a list of publications.
Description: SAMHA's mission within the nation's health system is to improve the quality and availability of prevention, treatment, and rehabilitation services order to reduce illness, death, disability, and the cost to society resulting from substance abuse and mental health.

Note: The following three centers are a part of SAMHA.

A.   **Center for Mental Health Services**
5600 Fischers Lane
Rockville, MD 20857
Phone: (301) 443-2792
Fax: (301) 443-5163
E-mail: N/A
Internet URL: http://www.samhsa.gov/cmhs/cmhs.htm

Newsletters/Publications: Contact the agency for its publications list on the National Mental Health Services Knowledge Exchange Network (KEN). (See Mental Health.)

Description: CMHS oversees a variety of service-related programs and conducts several new programs mandated by Congress. The center also funds KEN, a National Mental Health Services Knowledge Exchange Network. (See Clearinghouses.)

B. **Center for Substance Abuse Prevention (CSAP)**
5600 Fischers Lane
Rockville, MD 20857
Phone: (301) 443-0365
Fax: N/A
E-mail: nnadal@samsha.gov
Internet URL: http.www.samsha.gov/csap
Newsletters/Publications: Contact the center for information.
Description: CSAP provides national leadership in the federal effort to prevent alcohol, tobacco, and illicit drug problems. It participates in the development of new information about prevention and disseminates it in a "user friendly" manner to encourage its application in settings applicable to the prevention or reduction of substance abuse.

C. **Center for Substance Abuse Treatment (CSAT)**
5600 Fischers Lane
Rockville, MD 20857
Phone:
Fax:
E-mail: lyoung@samsha.gov
Internet URL: http://www.samsha.gov/csat
Newsletters/Publications: Contact the center for information.
Description: CSAT works to develop and support policies, approaches, and programs that enhance and expand treatment services for individuals who abuse alcohol and other drugs.

> **Note: The following are other agencies of the federal government that may be of service to special educators:**

5. **Census Bureau**
Phone: (301) 457-4100
FAX: (301) 457-4714
TDD: (301) 457-4611
E-mail: N/A
Internet URL: http://www.census.gov
Newsletters/Publications: N/A
Description: The mission of the Census Bureau is to be the preeminent collector and provider of timely, relevant, and quality data about the people and economy of the United States.

6. **Department of Justice**
   Phone: (800) 514-0301
   TTD: (800) 514-0383
   Fax: N/A
   E-mail: N/A
   Internet URL: http://www.usdoj.gov
   Newsletters/Publications: Contact the agency for a list of publications to obtain answers to general and technical questions about the ADA, and to order technical assistance materials.
   Description: The Department enforces ADA requirements in three areas:
   Title I: Employment practices by units of state and local government
   Title II: Programs, services, and activities of state and local government
   Title III: Public accommodations and commercial facilities (private businesses and non-profit service providers)

   Office of the Americans with Disabilities Act
   US Department of Justice
   Civil Rights Division
   PO Box 66118
   Washington, DC 20035-6118
   Phone: (202) 514-0301
   TTD: (202) 514-0383
   Fax: N/A
   E-mail: N/A
   Internet URL: www.doj.gov
   Newsletters/Publications: Call for a list of publications.
   Description: This office is responsible for monitoring actions involving Americans with Disabilities Act.

7. **Equal Employment Opportunity Commission (EEOC)**
   1801 L Street, NW
   Washington, DC 20507
   Phone: (202) 663-4900
   For information and publications:
   Phone: (800) 669-EEOC
   TDD: (800) 800-3302
   Fax: (513) 489-8692
   For local agency referral and addresses:
   Phone: (800) 669-4000
   TTD: (800) 669-6820
   E-mail: N/A
   Internet URL:
   Newsletters/Publications: Call the agency for a list of publications.
   Description: EEOC promotes equal opportunity in employment by enforcing the federal civil rights employment laws.

8. **Federal Communications Commission (FCC)**
   1919 M Street, NW
   Washington, DC 20554

Phone: (202) 418-200
TDD: (202) 632-6999
Fax: N/A
E-mail: N/A
Internet URL: http://www.fcc.gov
Newsletters/Publications: Call the agency for list of its publications.
Description: The FCC develops and implements policy concerning interstate and international communications by radio, television, wire, satellite, and cable.

9. **General Services Administration**
Center for IT Accommodation (CITA)
1800 F Street NW, Room 1234
Washington, DC 20405-0001
Phone: (202) 501-4906
TTD: (202) 501-2010
Fax: (202) 501-6269
E-mail: N/A
Internet URL: http://www.gsa.gov
Newsletters/Publications: Call for a list of publications.
Description: CITA is a clearinghouse of information systems available to all users, including WWW design guidelines. It is part of the General Services Administration of the federal government.

10. **Government Printing Office**
Superintendent of Documents
US Government Printing Office
Washington, DC 20402
Phone: (888) 293-6498 or (202) 512-1530
Fax: (202) 512-1262
E-mail: gpoaccess@gpo.gov
Internet URL: http://www.access.gpo.gov/su_docs
Newsletters/Publications: Call the agency for a list of publications.
Description: This site contains everything that is published by the federal government. Several databases may have to be explored for specific information.

11. **Library of Congress National Library Service for the Blind and Physically Handicapped**
1291 Taylor Street, NW
Washington, DC 20542
Phone: (800) 424-8567
TDD: (202) 707-0744
Fax: (202) 707-0712
E-mail: N/A
Internet URL: http://www.loc.gov/nls
Newsletters/Publications: Call the agency for a list of publications.
Description: This national library service provides Braille and recorded books and magazines on free loan to anyone who cannot read standard print because of visual or physical disabilities. It publishes Talking Books and Reading Disabilities, a fact sheet

that outlines eligibility requirements for persons with learning disabilities interested in borrowing talking books.

12. **President's Committee on Employment of People with Disabilities**
1331 F. Street NW, Third Floor
Washington, DC 20004
Phone: (202) 376-6200
TDD: (202) 376-6219
Fax: N/A
E-mail: N/A
Internet URL: http://janweb.icdi.wvu.edu/english/pcepd.html
Newsletters/Publications: Call the agency for a list of publications.
Description: Technical assistance on employment provisions of ADA is available directly and through the agency's Governors' Committees on Employment of People with Disabilities.

13. **Small Business Administration (SBA)**
Office of Advocacy
Office of Economic Research
409 Third Street SW, Suite 7600
Washington, DC 20416
Phone: (800) 8 ASK-SBA or (202) 376-6200
TDD: (202) 205-7333
Fax: (202) 205-7064
E-mail: N/A
Internet URL: http://www.sbaonline.sba.gov
SBA On-Line (electronic bulletin board): (800) 697-4636 (limited access) or (900) 463-4636 (full access)
Gopher: gopher://gopher.sbaonline.sba.gov
Telnet: telnet://sbaonline.sba.gov
FTP: ftp://ftp.sbaonline.sba.gov
Newsletters/Publications: Call the agency for a list of publications.

14. **Social Security Administration (SSA)**
6401 Security Boulevard
Baltimore, MD 21235
Phone: 800-772-1213
TDD: 800-325-0778
Fax: N/A
E-mail: N/A
Internet URL: http://www.ssa.gov
Description: The mission of this agency is to administer the national Social Security programs as prescribed by legislation. The Social Security programs that were established to protect Americans against the loss of income include retirement, survivor, and disability benefits, as well as health insurance coverage through the Medicare program.

H

Hearing Impaired

Alexander Graham Bell Association for the Deaf, Inc.
3417 Volta Place, NW
Washington, DC 20007
Phone (Voice/TTD): (202) 337-5220
Fax: (202) 337-8314
E-mail: agbell@aol.com
Internet URL: http://www.agbell.org
Newsletters/Publications: *The Volta Review* (journal), *Volta Voices* (magazine).
Description: The association gathers and disseminates information on hearing loss, promotes better public understanding of hearing loss in children and adults, provides scholarships and financial and parent-infant awards, promotes early detection of hearing loss in infants, publishes books on deafness, and advocates for the rights of children and adults who are hard of hearing or deaf.

American Society for Deaf Children
1820 Tribute Road, Suite A
Sacramento, CA 95815
Phone (Voice/TTY): (916) 641-6084
Fax: (916) 641-6085
E-mail: ASDC1@aol.com
Internet URL: http://www.deafchildren.org
Newsletters/Publication: *The Endeavor*
Description: ASDC is a non-profit, parent-helping-parent organization promoting a positive attitude toward signing and deaf culture. It also provides support, encouragement, and current information about deafness to families with deaf and hard of hearing children.

Better Hearing Institute
5021-B Backlick Road
Annandale, VA 22003
Phone (Voice/TTD): (703) 642-0580 or (800) EAR-WELL (Hearing Helpline)
Fax: (703) 750-9302
E-mail: mail@betterhearing.org
Internet URL: http://www.betterhearing.org
Newsletter/Publications: *Better Hearing News*

Description: BHI is a non-profit educational organization that implements national public information programs on hearing loss through television, radio, and print media public service messages. It also provides information about available medical, surgical, hearing aid, and rehabilitation assistance for millions with uncorrected hearing problems. BHI maintains a toll-free "Hearing Helpline" telephone service with information on hearing loss, sources of assistance, lists of local hearing professionals, and other available hearing for callers from anywhere in the United States and Canada.

Captioned Films/Videos
National Association of the Deaf
1447 East Main Street
Spartanburg, SC 29307
Phone (Voice): (800) 237-6213
TTD: (800) 237-6819
Fax: (800) 538-5636
E-mail: info@cfv.org
Internet URL: http://www.nad.org
Newsletters/Publications: Free-Loan Captioned Films/Videos Catalog. Also call for a list of publications.
Description: Free loans of educational and entertainment captioned films and videos for deaf and hard of hearing people.

Deafness Research Foundation
15 West 39th Street
New York, NY 10018
Phone (Voice/TTD): (212) 768-1181 or (800) 535-3323
Fax: (212) 768-1782
E-mail: drf@drf.org
Internet URL: http://www.drf.org
Newsletters/Publications: *The Hearing Advocate*, published twice a year.
Description: The nation's largest voluntary health organization providing grants for fellowships, symposia, and research into causes, treatment, and prevention of all ear disorders. The DRF also provides information and referral services.

The Ear Foundation
1817 Patterson Street
Nashville, TN 37203
Phone (Voice/TTD): (800) 545-HEAR or (615) 329-7809
Fax: (615) 329-7935
E-mail: N/A
Internet URL: http://www.earfound.org
Newsletters/Publications: *Otoscope, Steady*
Description: The foundation is a national, not-for-profit organization committed to integrating the hearing- and balance-impaired person into the mainstream of society through public awareness and medical education. It also administers The Meniere's Network, a national network of patient support groups that provides people with the opportunity to share experiences and coping strategies.

Gallaudet University
(See University-based Sites)

Hear Now
9745 East Hampden Avenue, Suite 300
Denver, CO 80231
Phone Voice/TTD: (800) 648-HEAR or (303) 695-7797
Fax: (303) 695-7789
E-mail: 127737.1272@compuserve.com
Internet URL: http://www.leisurelan.com~hearnow
Newsletters/Publications: *Hear Now*. Also call for a list of publications.
Description: Hear now is committed to making technology accessible to deaf and hard of hearing individuals throughout the United States. It provides hearing aids and cochlea implants for very low income, hard of hearing and deaf individuals.

League for the Hard of Hearing
71 West 23rd Street
New York, NY 10010-4162
Phone (Voice): (212) 741-7650
TTD: (212) 255-1932
Fax: (212) 255-4413
E-mail: postmaster@lhh.org
Internet URL: http://www.lhh.org
Newsletters/Publications: *Hearing Rehabilitation Quarterly (journal), abc Reports* (newsletter).
Description: The mission of the league is to improve the quality of life for people with all degrees of hearing loss. It offers comprehensive hearing rehabilitation and human services programs for infants, children, and adults and their families, regardless of age or mode of communication. The League promotes hearing conservation and provides public education about hearing.

National Association of the Deaf (NAD)
814 Thayer Avenue
Silver Spring, MD 20910-4500
Phone (Voice): (301) 587-1788
TTD: (301) 587-4875
Fax: (301) 587-4873
E-mail: Juniornad@juno.com
Internet URL: http://www.nad.org
Newsletters/Publications: *The NAD Broadcaster*, published 11 times a year.
Description: The association develops and promotes citizenship, scholarship, and leadership skills in deaf and hard of hearing students (grades 7–12) through chapter projects, national conventions, contests, and other activities. NAD also sponsors a month-long Youth Leadership Camp Program each summer in Oregon.

National Technical Institute for the Deaf
(See University-based Sites)

Rehabilitation Engineering Research Center on Hearing Enhancement and Assistive Devices (RERC)
(See Assistive Technology)

Self Help for Hard of Hearing People, Inc.
7910 Woodmont Avenue, Suite 1200
Bethesda, MD 20814
Phone (Voice): (301) 657-2249
TTD: (301) 657-2249
Fax: (301) 913-9413
E-mail: N/A
Internet URL: http://www.shhh.org
Newsletters/Publications: *Hearing Loss: The Journal of Self Help for Hard of Hearing People*
Description: The organization promotes awareness and information about hearing loss, communication, assistive devices, and alternative communication skills through publications, exhibits, and presentations.

Hearing Impaired Assessment Measures

Auditory Perception Test for the Hearing Impaired (APT/HI)
Authors: Susan G. Allen and Thomas S. Serwatka
Publisher: Slosson Educational Publications
PO Box 280
East Aurora, NY 14052-0280
Phone: (888) SLOSSON
Fax: (800) 655-3840
Type of Test: Criterion-referenced
Administration Time: 30 minutes
Type of Administration: Individual
Age/Grade Level: ages 5 and above

Carolina Picture Vocabulary Test For Deaf and Hearing Impaired (CPVD)
Authors: Thomas L. Layton and David W. Holmes
Publisher: PRO-ED, Inc.
8700 Shoal Creek Boulevard
Austin, TX 78758-6897
Phone: (512) 451-3246 or (800) 897-3202
Fax: (800) FXPROED
Type of Test: Norm-referenced
Administration Time: 10–30 minutes
Type of Administration: Individual
Age/Grade Level: Ages 4 to 11.5

Hiskey-Nebraska Test of Learning Aptitude
Author: Marshall S. Hiskey
Publisher: Marshall S. Hiskey
5640 Baldwin
Lincoln, NE 68507
Phone: (402) 466-6145
Fax: N/A
Type of Test: Standardized
Administration Time: Approximately 60 minutes
Type of Administration: Individual
Age/Grade Level: Ages 2 to 18

Leiter-R International Performance Scale
Authors: Russel Graydon Leiter and Grace Arthur
Publisher of Test: C.H. Stoelting Co.
620 Wheat Lane
Wood Dale, IL 60191
Phone: (630) 860-9700
Fax: (630) 860-9775
Type of Test: Standardized
Administration Time: 30–60 minutes
Type of Administration: Individual
Age/Grade Level: Ages 2 to 17

Rhode Island Test of Language Structure (RITLS)
Authors: Elizabeth Engen and Trygg Engen
Publisher: PRO-ED, Inc.
8700 Shoal Creek Boulevard
Austin, TX 78758-6897
Phone: (512) 451-3246 or (800) 897-3202
Fax: (800) FXPROED
Type of Test: Criterion-referenced and norm-referenced
Administration Time: 25–35 minutes.
Type of Administration: Individual
Age/Grade Level: Hearing-impaired children, ages 3 to 20; hearing children, (ages) 3 to 6.

Screening Instrument for Targeting Educational Risk (SIFTER)
Author: Karen Anderson
Publisher: PRO-ED, Inc.
8700 Shoal Creek Boulevard
Austin, TX 78758-6897
Number: (512) 451-3246 or (800) 897-3202
Fax: (800) FXPROED
Type of Test: Rating scale
Administration Time: Untimed
Type of Administration: Individual

Age/Grade Level: Elementary school age.

Test of Early Reading Ability–2, Deaf or Hard of Hearing (TERA-2 D/HH)
Authors: D. Kim Reid, Wayne P. Jiresko, Donald D. Hammill, and Susan Wiltshire
Publisher: PRO-ED, Inc.
8700 Shoal Creek Boulevard
Austin, TX 78758-6897
Phone: 512 451-3246 or (800) 897-3202
Fax: (800) FXPROED
Type of Test: Norm-referenced
Administration Time: 15–30 minutes
Type of Administration: Individual
Age/Grade Level: Deaf and hard of hearing children ages 3.0 to 10.

Hearing Impairments: Professional Organizations

American Academy of Audiology
8201 Greensboro Drive, Suite 300
McLean, VA 22102
Phone (Voice/TTD): (800) 222-2336 or (703) 610-9022
Fax: (703) 610-9005
E-mail: lac@audiology.com
Internet URL: http://www.audiology.org
Newsletters/Publications: *Audiology Today* (magazine), *Journal of AAA* (journal), and *Audiology Express* (newsletter).
Description: The academy is a professional organization of individuals dedicated to providing high quality hearing care to the public. It provides professional development, education, and research and promotes increased public awareness of hearing disorders and audiologic services.

American Deafness and Rehabilitation Association (ADARA)
PO Box 6956
San Mateo, CA 94403
Phone (Voice/TTD): (650)372-0620
Fax: (650)372-0661
E-mail: adaraorgn@aol.com
Internet URL: N/A
Newsletters/Publications: *JADARA*, a journal for professionals, and *ADARA UPDATE* (newsletter).
Description: This organization promotes and participates in quality human services delivery to deaf and hard of hearing people through agencies and individuals. ADARA is a networking partnership of national organizations, local affiliates, professional sectors, and individual members working together to support social services and rehabilitation delivery for deaf and hard of hearing people.

American Sign Language Teacher's Association (ASLTA)
814 Thayer Avenue
Silver Spring, MD 20910-4500
Phone (TTY only): (301) 587-0628
Fax: N/A
E-mail: ASLTA@aol.com
Internet URL: http://www.nad.org/aslta.htm
Newsletters/Publications: Publishes a quarterly newsletter.
Description: This national organization of teachers of American Sign Language (ASL) operates under the auspices of the National Association of the Deaf. ASLTA certifies teachers, recommends teaching programs, provides professional development activities, and seeks to advance the recognition of ASL in the schools.

International Hearing Society
16880 Middlebelt Road, Suite 4
Livonia, MI 48154
Phone: (800) 521-5247 (Helpline) or (734) 522-7200
Fax: (810) 478-4520
E-mail: N/A
Internet URL: http:///www.hearingihs.org
Newsletters/Publications: *Audecibel*
Description: Professional association of specialists who test hearing and select, fit, and dispense hearing instruments. The society conducts programs of competence qualifications, education, and training and promotes specialty-level accreditation. The Hearing Aid Helpline provides consumer information and referral.

Registry of Interpreters of the Deaf, Inc.
8630 Fenton Street, Suite 324
Silver Spring, MD 20910
Phone (Voice/TTD): (301) 608-0050
Fax: (301) 608-0508
E-mail: N/A
Internet URL: http://www.rid.org
Newsletters/Publications: *Views*
Description: This organization certifies interpreters, provides information about interpreting to the general public, publishes a national directory of certified interpreters, and makes referrals to interpreter agencies.

Human Growth

There are many diseases and disorders that can cause short stature and growth failure. A balanced diet with adequate calories and protein is essential for growth. There are a number of intestinal disorders that may lead to poor absorption of food. Failure to absorb nutrients and energy from food then leads to growth failure. Children with these conditions may have complaints that involve the stomach or intestines (bowels) and may have bowel movements that are unusual in pattern, appearance, and odor. Treatment of these conditions often involves a special diet. Normal growth usually resumes after the condition has been treated.

Human Growth Foundation

7777 Leesburg Pike
Falls Church, VA 22043
Phone: (800) 451-6434 or (703) 883-1773
Fax: (703) 883-1776
E-mail: webmaster@genetic.org
Internet URL: genetic.org/hgf
Newsletters/Publications: HGF publishes *Fourth Friday*, a bi-monthly newsletter, and *Outreach for Growth* a semiannual publication.
Description: Human Growth Foundation is a voluntary, non-profit organization dedicated to helping medical science better understand the process of growth. It is composed of concerned parents and friends of children with growth problems and interested health professionals. Its objectives are:
- Support of research
- Family education and service
- Public education
- Support of training for growth specialists
- Education of the medical profession
- Parent-to-parent support/networking programs
  The foundation helps individuals with growth-related disorders, their families, and health care professionals through education, research, and advocacy.

Hydrocephalus

Hydrocephalus is an abnormal accumulation of fluid—cerebrospinal fluid, or CSF—within cavities called ventricles inside the brain. CSF is produced in the ventricles, circulates through the ventricular system, and is absorbed into the bloodstream. CSF is in constant circulation and has many important functions. It surrounds the brain and spinal cord and acts as a protective cushion against injury. CSF contains nutrients and proteins that are needed for the nourishment and normal function of the brain. It also carries waste products away from surrounding tissues. Hydrocephalus occurs when there is an imbalance between the amount of CSF that is produced and the rate at which it is absorbed. As the CSF builds up, it causes the ventricles to enlarge and the pressure inside the head to increase.

Hydrocephalus Association

870 Market Street, Suite 955
San Francisco, CA 94102
Phone: (415) 732-7040
Fax: (415) 732-7044
E-mail: hydroassoc@aol.com
Internet URL: http://neurosurgery.mgh.harvard.edu/ha
Newsletters/Publications: A 12-page newsletter is published quarterly.

Description: The goal of this association is to ensure that families and individuals dealing with the complexities of hydrocephalus receive personal support, comprehensive educational materials, and on-going quality medical care.

Hyperlexia

Hyperlexia is a syndrome observed in children who have the following characteristics:
- precocious ability to read words
- intense fascination with numbers or letters
- significant difficulty using verbal or non-verbal language
- difficulty in reciprocal interaction

American Hyperlexia Association
479 Spring Road
Elmhurst, IL 60126
Phone: (630) 415-2212
Fax: (630) 530-5909
E-mail: president@hyperlexia.org or webmaster@hyperlexia.org
Internet URL: http://www.hyperlexia.org
Newsletters/Publications: Call for a list of publications.
Description: American Hyperlexia Association is dedicated to educating parents and professionals with a common goal of identifying this disorder and facilitating effective teaching techniques both at home and at school.

I

Inclusion Resources

Inclusive education means disabled and non-disabled children and young people learning together in ordinary pre-school provision, schools, colleges, and universities, with appropriate networks of support.

Inclusion means enabling pupils to participate in the life and work of mainstream institutions to the best of their abilities, whatever their needs.

Inclusive Education Web Site/Renaissance Group
College of Education
University of Northern Iowa
Cedar Falls, IA 50614
Phone: (319) 273-2717
Fax: (319) 273-2607
E-mail: N/A
Internet URL: http://www.uni.edu/coe/inclusion
Description: The Renaissance Group is a consortium of universities noted for their teacher education programs. This group has many resources for learning more about inclusive education.

Inclusion Sites on the World Wide Web
Collected by Denise Hunnie
Internet URL: http://www3.mb.sympatico.ca/~dhoney/sites.html
Description: This site contains numerous links to other inclusion sites, along with articles.

Kids Together, Inc.
(See Individuals with Disabilities Education Act [IDEA] Information.)

Resources for the Inclusion of Students with Disabilities into Math and Science Education
Internet URL: http://www.atlanta.arch.gatech.edu/BFE
Description: The principal philosophy of the developers of this site is that the academic community must assume a leadership role in creating accessible environments. Specifically, the text and links at this site are intended to assist teachers, parents, and students to fulfill the promise of universal access to education in middle-school and high-school environments.

Utah's Project for Inclusion: Products and Materials Internet URL:
http://www.usoe.k12.ut.us/sars/inclusion/library/library2.html
Description: This site offers materials, techniques, resources, curriculum, and strategies.

Independent Living Centers

Centers for independent living (CIL) are private, non-profit, consumer-controlled, community-based organizations providing services and advocacy by and for persons with all types of disabilities. Their goal is to create opportunities for independence, and to assist individuals with disabilities to achieve their maximal level of independent functioning within their families and communities.

Centers for Independent Living–Listed By State
From ADA and Disability Info
Internet URL: http://www.public.iastate.edu:80/~sbilling/cil.html
Description: Here is a very thorough listing of centers for independent living in the United States and Canada.

Design Linc–Accessibility and Design Resources
Internet URL: http://www.designlinc.com/designlinc/centers.htm
Description: Design Line an on-line interior design resource and information service, geared to locate products and services geared for individuals with all disabilities. It lists independent living centers by state.

Independent Living Centers on the Internet
Internet URL: http://www.lsi.ukans.edu/rtcil/ilcs.htm
Description: This site sorts independent living centers by state. It also provides listings for independent living organizations and associations.

Independent Living Research Utilization Project
The Institute for Rehabilitation and Research (TIRR)
2323 South Sheppard, Suite 1000
Houston, TX 77019
Phone: (713) 520-0232
TTD: (713) 520-5136
Fax: (713) 520-5785
E-mail: ilru@bcm.tmc.edu
Internet URL: http://www.bcm.tmc.edu/ilru
Newsletters/Publications: *Insights,* published twice a year. Call for a list of publications.
Description: TIRR provides a directory of independent living centers and related organizations nationwide.

Internet Resources for Special Children (IRSC)
Internet URL: http://www.irsc.org/centers.htm
Description: This site sorts independent living centers by state. It also provides listings for Canada and international centers. For the Home Page URL, see Websites–General.

Individuals with Disabilities Education Act (IDEA) Information

Kids Together, Inc.
PO Box 574
Quakertown, PA 18951
Phone: (800) 879-2301
Fax: N/A
E-mail: staff@kidstogether.org
Internet URL: http://www.kidstogether.org/idea.html
Description: Kids Together, Inc. is a non-profit organization co-founded by parents and organized by volunteers. The goals of Kids Together, Inc. include a desire to remove barriers that exclude people with disabilities.

This site provides helpful information and resources to enhance the quality of life for children and adults with disabilities, and communities as a whole.

Office of Special Education Programs
(See Government Agencies—Federal)

Intelligence Tests

The Wechsler Scales of Intelligence
Author: David Wechsler
Publisher: The Psychological Corporation
555 Academic Court
San Antonio, TX 78204-2498
Phone: (800) 211-8378
Fax: (800) 232-1223
Type of Test: Standardized
Administration Time: 60–75 minutes
Type of Administration: Individual
Administrator: Psychologist
Age/Grade Level: The three tests are designed for children and adults, ages 4½ to adult. The age ranges for the three Wechsler tests are:
- Wechsler Preschool and Primary Scale of Intelligence (WPPSI), ages 4½ to 6½
- Wechsler Intelligence Scale for Children–III (WISC–III), ages 6½ to 16½
- Wechsler Adult Intelligence Scale–Revised (WAIS–R), ages 16½ and above

The Stanford-Binet Intelligence Scale (Fourth Edition)
Authors: R.L. Thorndike, E.P. Hagen, and J.M. Sattler
Publisher: The Riverside Publishing Company
8420 Spring Lake Drive
Itasca, Illinois 60143-2079
Phone: (800) 323-9540
Fax: (630) 467-7192
Type of Test: Standardized
Administration Time: 45–90 minutes
Type of Administration: Individual
Administrator: Psychologist
Age/Grade Level: Ages 2 to adult

Kaufman Assessment Battery for Children (K–ABC): Mental Processing Scales
Authors: Alan S. Kaufman and Nadeen L. Kaufman
Publisher: American Guidance Service
Publishers Building
Circle Pines, MN 55014-1796
Phone: (800) 328-2560

Fax: (512) 786-5603
Type of Test: Standardized
Administration Time: 35–85 minutes, depending upon age group
Type of Administration: Individual
Administrator: Psychologist
Age/Grade Level: Ages 2½ to 12½

Kaufman Brief Intelligence Test (KBIT)
Authors: Alan S. Kaufman and Nadeen L. Kaufman
Publisher: American Guidance Service
4201 Woodland Road
PO Box 99
Circle Pines, MN 55041-1796
Phone: (800) 328-2560
Fax: (512) 786-5603
Type of Test: Individual
Administration Time: 15–30 minutes
Type of Administration: Individual
Administrator: Psychologist
Age/Grade Level: Ages 4 to 90

Columbia Mental Maturity Scale (CMMS)
Authors: Bessie B. Burgemeister, Lucille Hollander Blurn, and Irving Lorge
Publisher: The Psychological Corporation
555 Academic Court
San Antonio, TX 78204-2498
Phone: (800) 211-8378
Fax: (800) 232-1223
TDD: (800) 723-1318
Type of Test: Standardized
Administration Time: 15–30 minutes
Type of Administration: Individual
Administrator: Psychologist
Age/Grade Level: Ages 3½ to 10

McCarthy Scales of Children's Abilities
Author: Dorothea McCarthy
Publisher: The Psychological Corporation
555 Academic Court
San Antonio, TX 78204-2498
Phone: (800) 211-8378
Fax: (800) 232-1223
TDD: (800) 723-1318
Administration Time: 45–60 minutes
Type of Administration: Individual
Administrator: Psychologist
Age/Grade Level: Ages 2.4 to 8.7

Slosson Intelligence Test–Revised (SIT–R)
Authors: Richard L. Slosson, revised by Charles L. Nicholson and Terry L. Hibpschman
Publisher: Slosson Educational Publications
PO Box 280
East Aurora, NY 14052-0280
Phone: (888) SLOSSON
Fax: (800) 655 -3840
Type of Test: Norm-referenced
Administration Time: 15–30 minutes
Type of Administration: Individual
Administrator: Psychologist, special education teacher, classroom teacher
Age/Grade Level: Ages 4 to 65

Comprehensive Test of Nonverbal Intelligence (CTONI)
Authors: Donald D. Hammill, Nils A. Pearson, and Lee Wiederholt
Publisher: PRO-ED, Inc.
8700 Shoal Creek Boulevard
Austin, TX 78758-6897
Phone: (512) 451-3246 or (800) 897-3202
Fax: (800) FXPROED
Type of Test: Norm-referenced
Administration Time: 60 minutes
Type of Administration: Individual
Administrator: Psychologist
Age/Grade Level: Ages 6 to 18

Test of Nonverbal Intelligence (TONI-3)
Authors: Linda Brown, Rita J. Sherbenou, and Susan Johnsen
Publisher: PRO-ED, Inc.
8700 Shoal Creek Boulevard
Austin, TX 78758-6897
Phone: (512) 451-3246 or (800) 897-3202
Fax: (800) FXPROED
Type of Test: Norm-referenced
Administration Time: 15–20 minutes
Type of Administration: Individual
Administrator: Psychologist
Age/Grade Level: Ages 5 to 85

Otis-Lennon School Ability Test (OLSAT)
Authors: Arthur S. Owen and Roger T. Lennon
Publisher: The Psychological Corporation
555 Academic Court
San Antonio, TX 78204-2498
Phone: (800) 211-8378
Fax: (800) 232-1223
TDD: (800) 723-1318

Type of Test: Standardized
Administration Time: Levels A–C (grades K–2), 75 minutes over two sessions; Levels D–G (grades 3–12), 60 minutes
Type of Administration: Group
Administrator: Psychologist, special education teacher,classroom teacher
Age/Grade Level: Grades K–12

J

Journals

Following is a list of journals that are not published by specific disability organizations and associations.

disAbility Resources Inc.
Internet URL: http://www.eskimo.com/~jlubin/disabled/newslett.htm
Description: This section of Jim Lubin's disAbility Resources Inc. (see Websites-General) provides extensive information on magazines, journals, and newsletters in the area of disabilities.

Journal of Applied Behavior Analysis
Publisher: The Society for the Experimental Analysis of Behavior, Inc.
Department of Psychology
Indiana University
Bloomington IN 47405-1301
Description: Journal of Applied Behavior Analysis publishes experimental research about applications of the experimental analysis of behavior to problems of social importance. It is published quarterly.

Journal of Educational Psychology
Publisher: American Psychological Association
750 First Street, NE
Washington, DC 20002
Phone: (202) 336-5500
Fax: N/A
E-mail: N/A
Internet URL: http://www.apa.org
Description: This research journal pertains to education at every level, from intervention during early childhood to educational efforts directed to elderly adults. It includes topics such as

research on learning, cognition, motivation, instruction, social issues, individual differences in teachers, and individual differences in learning.

Journal of Educational Research

Publisher: Heldref Publications
1319 18th Street, NW
Washington, DC 20036-1802
Phone: (202) 296-6267
Fax: (202) 296-5149
E-mail: N/A
Description: This bimonthly journal publishes intervention studies in public elementary and secondary schools. Its authors experiment with new procedures, evaluate traditional practices, replicate previous research for validation, and perform work essential to understanding and improving the education of students and teachers.

Pro-Ed (also see section on Publishers)

Internet URL: http://www.proedinc.com/intro.html
Pro-Ed offers a variety of journals including:

• Focus on Autism and Other Developmental Disabilities

Description: Focus on Autism and Other Developmental Disabilities gives practical elements of management, treatment, planning, and education. The articles cover a variety of topics including assessment, vocational training, curricula, educational strategies, treatments, integration methods, and parent/family involvement. It is published quarterly.

• Intervention in School and Clinic

Description: Intervention in School and Clinic is a practitioner-oriented journal designed to provide practical, research-based ideas to those who work with students with learning disabilities and emotional/behavioral problems for whom minor curriculum and environmental modifications are ineffective. The journal is published five times a year.

• Journal of Emotional and Behavioral Disorders

Description: The international, multi-disciplinary Journal of Emotional and Behavioral Disorders (JEBD) features articles on research, practice, and behavioral disorders. This quarterly journal presents topics of interest to professionals from psychiatry, mental health, counseling, and many others.

• Journal of Learning Disabilities

Description: The Journal of Learning Disabilities (JLD) contains articles on practice, research, and theory. It is published bimonthly.

• Journal of Positive Behavior Interventions

Description: Journal of Positive Behavior Interventions (JPBI) deals exclusively with principles of positive behavioral support in school, home, and community settings for people with challenges in behavioral adaptation. JPBI, published quarterly, will include empirical research reports, commentaries, program descriptions, discussions of family supports, and coverage of timely issues.

• The Journal of Special Education

Description: The Journal of Special Education (JSE) offers quarterly research articles and scholarly reviews by experts in all subspecialties of special education for individuals with disabilities ranging from mild to severe.

- **Reclaiming Children and Youth: Journal of Emotional and Behavioral Problems**

Description: This quarterly journal brings practical solutions to the most pressing problems of troubled children and youth at risk. It presents research-validated strategies for use with youth in conflict with school, family, or community and reframes problems as opportunities for teaching pro-social behavior and values. Issues target timely subjects such as rage and aggression, courage for troubled girls, and teaching resilience and responsibility.

- **Remedial and Special Education**

Description: Remedial and Special Education (RASE) is a professional journal devoted to the discussion of issues involving the education of persons for whom typical instruction is not effective. Its emphasis is on the interpretation of research literature and recommendations for the practice of remedial and special education. RASE is published bimonthly.

- **Topics in Early Childhood Special Education**

Description: Topics in Early Childhood Special Education (TECSE) deals with issues and trends in early childhood special education. This quarterly publication translates theory and research into practice and presents articles by professionals in early childhood education, special education, and related fields.

RE:view
Rehabilitation and Education for Blindness and Visual Impairment
Publisher: Heldref Publications
1319 18th Street, NW
Washington, DC 20036-1802
Phone: (202) 296-6267
Fax: (202) 296-5149
E-mail: N/A
Description: RE:view, published quarterly, interests people concerned with services to individuals of all ages with visual disabilities.

L

Learning Disabilities

A definition of learning disabilities developed by the National Joint Committee on Learning Disabilities (NJCLD) reads as follows:

Learning disabilities is a generic term that refers to a heterogeneous group of disorders manifested by significant difficulties in the acquisition and use of listening, speaking, reading, writing, reasoning, or mathematical abilities. These disorders are intrinsic to the individual, presumed to be due to central nervous system dysfunction, and may occur across the life span. Problems in self-regulatory behaviors, social perception, and social interaction may exist with learning disabilities, but do not by themselves constitute a learning disability. Although learning disabilities may occur concomitantly with other handicapping conditions (for example, sensory impairment, mental retardation, serious emotional disturbance), or with extrinsic influences (such as cultural differences, inappropriate or insufficient instruction), they are not the result of those influences or conditions. (1990)

International Dyslexia Association (formerly The Orton Dyslexia Society)
Chester Building, Suite 382
8600 LaSalle Road
Baltimore, MD 21286-2044
Phone: (800) ABCD 123 or (410) 296-0232
Fax: (410) 321-5069
E-mail: info@interdys.org
Internet URL: http://www.interdys.org
Newsletters/Publications: Contact the organization for a list of publications.
Description: The society is an international scientific and educational association concerned with the widespread problem of the specific language disability of developmental dyslexia. Local and state chapters serve as literacy resources for dyslexic adults and those who teach or advise them.

Learning Disabilities Association of America, Inc. (LDA)
4156 Library Road
Pittsburgh, PA 15234
Phone: (412) 341-1515
Fax: (412) 344-0224
E-mail: ldanatl@usaor.net
Internet URL: http://www.ldanatl.org
Newsletters/Publications: The association also prints *LDA Newsbriefs*, a bi-monthly newsletter for parents, professionals, and adults with LD.
Description: LDA (formerly ACLD) is a non-profit volunteer advocacy organization providing information and referral for parents, professionals, and consumers involved with or in search of support groups. It also provides networking opportunities through local LDA Youth and Adult Section Chapters. A publication list is available.

Learning Resources Network
1550 Hayes Drive
Manhattan, KS 66502
Phone: (800) 678-5376
Fax: (785) 939-7766
E-mail: hq@lern.org
Internet URL: www.lern.org
Newsletters/Publications: This network publishes several monthly newsletters.
Description: Learning Resources Network provides information to practitioners of adult continuing education. It also gives consulting information, takes orders for publications, and provides phone numbers of associations and organizations that deal with learning disabilities.

National Center for Learning Disabilities (NCLD)
381 Park Avenue South, Suite 1401
New York, NY 10016

Phone: (888) 575-7373 or (212) 545-7510
Fax: (212) 545-9665
E-mail: none
Internet URL: http://www.ncld.org
Newsletters/Publications: *Their World,* an annual publication.
Description: NCLD is an organization committed to improving the lives of those affected by learning disabilities (LD). NCLD provides services and conducts programs nationwide, benefiting children and adults with LD, their families, teachers, and other professionals. NCLD has the latest information on learning disabilities and local resources for parents, professionals, employers, and others dealing with learning disabilities. Its Washington office advocates for federal legislation.

Recording for the Blind and Dyslexic (RFB)
20 Roszel Road
Princeton, NJ 20542
Phone: (800) 221-4792
Fax: (609) 987-8116
E-mail: webmaster@rfbd.org
Internet URL: http://www.rfbd.org
Newsletters/Publications: Contact the organization for a catalog.
Description: RFB is a national non-profit organization that provides taped educational books, called Talking Books, free on loan; books on diskette, library services, and other educational and professional resources to individuals who cannot read standard print because of a visual, physical, or perceptual disability. It has on-loan recorded books at all academic levels.

Learning Disabilities: Professional Organizations

Council for Learning Disabilities (CLD)
PO Box 40303
Overland Park, KS 62204
Phone: (913) 492-8755
Fax: (913) 492-2546
E-mail: N/A
Internet URL: http://www1.winthrop.edu/cld
Newsletters/Publications: *Learning Disability Quarterly*
Description: CLD is a national membership organization dedicated to assisting professionals who work in the field of learning disabilities.

Learning Disabilities Websites

LD ON-LINE
Internet URL: http://ldonline.org

Description: An extensive A-Z database on all aspects of LD, from primary to post-secondary concerns.

School Zone/Geocities
Internet URL: http:www.geocities.com/Heartland/Plains/6097/LD.html
Description: This site is part of the larger Geocities database which offers sites for numerous education and non-education areas. This particular site offers a wealth of information on Learning Disabilities.

Legal Resources

ADA Information Center On-Line
(See Americans with Disabilities Act)

Allsup Inc.–Disability Coordination Services
300 Allsup Place
Bellville, IL 62223
Phone: (800) 854-1418
Fax: (618) 236-5778
E-mail: N/A
Internet URL: http://www.allsupinc.com/index.html
Newsletters/Publications: N/A
Description: Allsup provides Social Security disability representational service, overpayment recovery service, Medicare benefits conversion and recovery, Medicare future entitlement, Medicare retroactive entitlement, disabled group identification/early retiree assessment, Medicare monitoring service, and Medigap.

American Association of People with Disabilities (AAPD)
1819 H Street NW, Suite 330
Washington, DC 20006
Phone: (800) 840-8844 or (800) 235-7125 (Voice/TTY)
Fax: (202) 457-0473
E-mail: N/A
Internet URL: http://.aapd-dc.org
Newsletters/Publications: N/A
Description: The purpose of AAPD is to:
- further the productivity, independence, full citizenship, and total integration of people with disabilities into all aspects of society and the natural environment.
- foster leadership among people with disabilities.
- support the full implementation and enforcement of disability non-discrimination laws, particularly the Americans with Disabilities Act of 1990 and the Rehabilitation Act of 1973.
- conduct programs to enhance the lives of people with disabilities, including programs to reduce poverty and unemployment, to assure that every disabled person has the right to his or her own living arrangement, and to assure that every child or adult with a disability has access to and funding for assistive technology.
- educate the public and government policy makers regarding issues affecting people with disabilities.

Bazelon Center for Mental Health Law
1101 15th Street NW, Suite 1212
Washington, DC 20005-5002
Phone: (202) 467-5730
Fax: (202) 223-0409
TDD: (202) 467-4232
E-mail: bazelon@nicom.com
Newsletters/Publications: N/A
Internet URL: http://www.bazelon.org
Description: The Judge David L. Bazelon Center for Mental Health Law is a non-profit legal advocacy organization. The name honors the federal appeals court judge whose landmark decisions pioneered the field of mental health law. Its advocacy is based on the principle that every individual is entitled to choice and dignity. For many people with mental disabilities, this means something as basic as having a decent place to live, supportive services, and equality of opportunity.

Child Care Law Center (CCLC)
973 Market Street, Suite 550
San Francisco, CA 94103
Phone: (415) 495-5498
E-mail: cclc@childcarelaw.com
Internet URL: http://ericps.ed.uiuc.edu/nccic/orgs/cclawctr.html
Newsletters/Publications: N/A
Description: CCLC is the only organization in the country working exclusively on the legal issues concerning the establishment and provision of child care. The center's major objective is to use legal tools to foster the development of quality, affordable child care programs. Since 1978, CCLC has served as a statewide legal support center offering free legal training and legal services to attorneys and others who work on child care issues for low-income families throughout California. The Child Care Law Center also provides legal assistance and information to non-profit centers, family day care providers, parents, policymakers, community and governmental agencies, unions, and employers throughout the country. In addition to its small legal staff, the center is able to call upon attorneys who contribute technical consultation and pro bono legal representation.

The Commission on Mental and Physical Disability Law
(See Advocacy)

Disability Rights Advocates
449 15th Street, Suite 303
Oakland, CA 94612
Phone: (510) 451-8644
Fax: (510) 451-8511
TTY: (510) 451-8716
E-mail: N/A
Newsletters/Publications: N/A
Internet URL: http://members.aol.com/dralegal
Description: **A non-profit civil rights organization for people with disabilities.**

Children's Defense Fund
(See Advocacy)

EDLAW, Inc.
PO Box 81-7327
Hollywood, FL 33081-0327
Phone: (954) 966-4489
Fax: (954) 966-8561
E-mail: edlawinc@access.digex.net
Internet URL: http://www.access.digex.net/~edlawinc
Newsletters/Publications: N/A
Description: EDLAW, Inc. is a full-service provider of information on education law of use to special educators, parents, and their advisors in meeting federal and state requirements for the education of students with disabilities. The texts of statutes and regulations referenced at EDLAW are public information and are posted to make them available at minimum cost and inconvenience.

Internet Legal Resource Guide
Internet: http://www.ilrg.com
Description: This site is a comprehensive national resource of information concerning law and the legal profession for scholars and lay persons alike. Quality is controlled to provide the most substantive legal resources online.

National Association of Protection and Advocacy Systems (NAPAS)
(See Advocacy)

National Association for Rights Protection and Advocacy (NARPA)
(See Advocacy)

US Department of Justice
(See Government Agencies–Federal)

United States Government Printing Office
(See Government Agencies–Federal)

Leukemia

Leukemia, lymphoma, Hodgkin's disease, and myeloma are cancers of the body's blood forming and immune systems, the bone marrow, AND lymph nodes. They are considered to be related cancers because they involve the uncontrolled growth of cells with similar functions.

Leukemia Society of America
600 3rd Avenue, 4th floor
New York, NY 10016
Phone: (800) 955-4654 or (212) 573-8484
Fax: (212) 856-9686

E-mail: bockf@leukemia.org
Internet URL: http://www.leukemia.org
Newsletters/Publications: The Leukemia Society of America publishes many educational brochures and pamphlets that are available to the public at no cost. The materials are designed to provide up-to-date information in language understandable by the layperson.
Description: The Leukemia Society of America is a national voluntary health agency dedicated to curing leukemia, lymphoma, Hodgkin's disease, and myeloma- and to improving the quality of life of victims and their families.

Lowe's Syndrome

Lowe's Syndrome, also known as oculo-cerebro-renal syndrome, is a rare inherited metabolic disease that affects males. This disorder is characterized by lack of muscle tone (hypotonia), multiple abnormalities of the eyes and bones, the presence at birth of clouding of the lenses of the eyes (cataracts), mental retardation, and kidney problems. Other findings may include eyeball protrusion from the eye socket (enophthalmos), failure to gain weight and grow at the expected rate, weak or absent deep tendon reflexes, and multiple kidney problems.

Lowe Syndrome Association
222 Lincoln Street
West Lafayette, IN 47906
Phone: (765) 743-3634
TTD: N/A
Fax: N/A
E-mail: lsa@medhelp.org
Internet URL: http://www.medhelp.org/lowesyndrome
Newsletters/Publications: Publications include brochures, a planned publications list, and a booklet entitled *Living with Lowe Syndrome*.
Description: The Lowe Syndrome Association is an international voluntary health organization composed of parents, health care professionals, and other interested individuals. It was formed to provide information to parents of children with Lowe Syndrome. Established in 1983, the organization fosters communication and networking among affected families for the purpose of mutual support and information exchange. The Lowe Syndrome Association also seeks to support medical research leading to prevention, and more effective treatments for the disease. Educational publications are designed to provide accurate and timely information to parents, teachers, and physicians world wide.

Lupus

Lupus is a chronic (long-lasting) auto-immune disease wherein the immune system, for unknown reasons, becomes hyperactive and attacks normal tissue. This attack results in inflammation and brings about symptoms.

Lupus Foundation of America, Inc.
130 Piccard, Suite 200
Rockville, MD 20850
Phone: (800) 558-0121 or (301) 670-9292 (Voice)
Fax: (301) 670-9486
E-mail: N/A
Internet URL: http://internet-plaza.net/lupus
Newsletters/Publications: *Lupus News* is published quarterly and includes 16 pages of the latest information on a variety of lupus-related topics.
Description: The mission of the Lupus Foundation of America is to improve the quality of life of people with lupus, their family, and friends through detection, alleviation of suffering, and eradication through research.

The "Living with Lupus" website strives to contribute to the accomplishment of this mission by providing those within the Internet community affected by lupus a source of up-to-date information and support.

M

Magazines/Newspapers: Disabilities

The following magazines represent a cross section of magazine resources available on disabilities. For a comprehensive list of disability magazines, use "Handilinks" noted below.

Able News
PO Box 395
Old Bethpage, NY 11804
Phone: (516) 939-2253
Fax: (516) 939-0540
E-mail: N/A
Internet URL: N/A
Description: This monthly newspaper focuses on resources, independent living, and daily life.

Accent on Living
Publisher: Cheever Publishing, Inc.
PO Box 700
Bloomington, IL 61702
Phone: (309) 378-2961
Fax: N/A

E-mail: N/A
Internet URL: N/A
Description: This quarterly magazine serves as a guide to services and information on daily living, and equipment for persons with disabilities.

Enable Magazine On-line
Publisher: American Association for People with Disabilities
3659 Cortea Road, Suite 110
Bradenton, FL 34205
Phone: (888) 436-2253
Fax: N/A
E-mail: N/A
Internet URL: http://www.enable-magazine.com
Description: Enable covers such subjects as home design, sports, medical updates, new product developments, recreation, employment opportunities, and so on.

Exceptional Children Magazine
(See Council for Exceptional Children in Professional Educational Organizations)

Exceptional Parent Magazine
120 State Street
Hackensack, NJ 07605
Phone: (800) E-Parent or (201) 489-0871
Fax: (201) 634-6099
E-mail: egmegiz@aol.com
Internet URL: http://www.eparent.com
Description: This magazine for parents of children with disabilities focuses on early childhood. It contains human interest stories, in-depth coverage of disability topics, personal features, book reviews, and more.

Handilinks
Internet URL: http://www.handilinks.com
Description: Handilinks is a comprehensive site in itself. For magazines dealing with disabilities click on "Magazines," then "Magazines Disabilities," then scroll down to choose a link to all disability magazines.

Mainstream Magazine
Publisher: Cyndi Jones
2973 Beech Street, Suite 1
San Diego, CA 92102
Phone: (619) 234-3138
Fax: (619) 234-3155
E-mail: N/A
Internet URL: http://www.mainstream-mag.com
Description: Published 10 times a year, this national magazine for people with disabilities features new products, technology, education, employment, housing, transportation, stories about people living independently, politics, advocacy, travel, and recreation.

Special Child Magazine
Publisher: kidABiLity (See Parent Resources)
Internet URL: http://ww.specialchild.com
Description: An online publication for parents of children with special needs.

We Magazine
Publisher: We Media Enterprises, Inc.
495 Broadway
New York, NY 10012
Phone: (800) WEMAG26 or (212) 941-9584
Fax: N/A
E-mail: info@wemagazine.com
Description: This lifestyle magazine for people with disabilities contains all kinds of information including sports, recreation, travel, politics, entertainment, and a whole lot more.

Math Assessment Measures

Enright Diagnostic Inventory of Basic Arithmetic Skills (Enright)
Author: Brian E. Enright
Publisher: Curriculum Associates, Inc.
5 Esquire Road, North
Billerica, MA 01862-2589
Phone: (800) 225-0248
Fax: (800) 366-1158
Type of Test: Criterion-referenced
Administration Time: 15-30 minutes
Type of Administration: Individual/group
Administrators: Special education teacher, classroom teacher
Age/Grade Level: Grades 1–6

Key Math Diagnostic Arithmetic Tests–Revised (Key Math–R)
Authors: Austin J. Connolly, William Nachtman, and E. Milo Pritchett
Publisher: American Guidance Service
4201 Woodland Road
Circle Pines, MN 55014-1796
Phone: (612) 786-4343 or (800) 328-2560
Fax: (612) 786-9077
Type of Test: Norm-referenced and domain-referenced
Administration Time: Approximately 30–45 minutes
Type of Administation: Individual
Administrators: Special education teacher, classroom teacher
Age/Grade Level: Preschool–grade 6

The Steenburgen Diagnostic-Prescriptive Math Program and Quick Math Screening Test

Author: Fran Steenburgen Gelb, MS
Publisher: Academic Therapy Publications
20 Commercial Boulevard
Novato, CA 94949-6191
Phone: (415) 883-3314 or (800) 422-7249
Fax: (415) 883-3720
Type of Test: Criterion-referenced
Administration Time: 10–20 minutes
Type of Administration: Group
Administrators: Special education teacher, classroom teacher
Age/Grade Level: Ages 6 to 11

Test of Early Mathematics Ability–2 (TEMA–2)
Authors: Herbert P. Ginsberg and Arthur J. Baroody
Publisher: PRO-ED, Inc.
8700 Shoal Creek Boulevard
Austin, TX 78758-6897
Phone: (512) 451-3246 or (800) 897-3202
Fax: (800) FXPROED
Type of Test: Criterion-referenced
Administration Time: With a few exceptions, the TEMA-2 is not a timed test; therefore, no precise time limits are imposed on the children being tested.
Type of Administration: Individual
Administrators: Special education teacher, classroom teacher
Age/Grade Level: Ages 3 to 9

Test of Mathematical Abilities–2 (TOMA–2)
Authors: Virginia L. Brown, Mary E. Cronin, and Elizabethn McEntire
Publisher: PRO-ED, Inc.
8700 Shoal Creek Boulevard
Austin, TX 78758-6897
Phone: (512) 451-3246 or (800) 897-3202
Fax: (800) FXPROED
Type of Test: Criterion-referenced
Administration Time: Varies
Type of Administration: TOMA-2 can be administered individually or in a group.
Administrators: Special education teacher, classroom teacher
Age/Grade Level: Ages 8.0 to 18.11

Medical Professional Associations

American Medical Association (AMA)
515 North State Street
Chicago, IL 60610

Phone: (312) 464-5000
Fax: (312) 464-4184
E-mail: N/A
Internet URL: http://www.ama-assn.org
Newsletters/Publications: *The Journal of the American Medical Association (JAMA)*, published weekly. For products, publications, and other information and services call (800) 621-8335.
Description: AMA is the largest medical professional membership organization.

Mental Health

American Academy of Child and Adolescent Psychiatry
(See Professional Organizations)

Center for Effective Collaboration and Practice
American Institute for Research
1000 Thomas Jefferson Street, SW, Suite 400
Washington, DC 20007
Phone: (888) 457-1551 or (202) 944-5400
Fax: (202) 944-5454
E-mail: center@air-dc.org
Internet URL: www.air-dc.org/cecp/links/mh.html
Newsletters/Publications: Contact agency for a list of publications.
Description: It is the mission of the center to foster the development and adjustment of children with or at-risk of developing serious emotional disturbance. The center collaborates at federal, state, and local levels to contribute to and facilitate the production, exchange and use of knowledge of effective practices. The center offers publications, teacher training, resources, and links to other mental health agencies and sites. The center deals with children K-12 and post-secondary education.

Center for Mental Health Services
(See Government Agencies–Federal)

Federation of Families for Children's Mental Health
1021 Prince Street
Alexandria, VA 22314
Phone: (703) 684-7710
Fax: (703) 836-1040
E-mail: ffcmh@crosslink.net
Internet URL: http://www.ffcmh.org
Newsletters/Publications: Call for a list of publications.
Description: The Federation of Families for Children's Mental Health is a not-for-profit, parent-run advocacy organization focused on the needs of children and youth with emotional, behavioral, or mental disorders. Its mission is to provide leadership in the field of children's mental health and develop necessary human and financial resources to meet its goals. The

federation addresses the unique needs of children and youth with emotional, behavioral, or mental disorders from birth through the transition to adulthood. It works to ensure the rights to full citizenship, support, and access to community-based services for all affected children and their families. The federation also seeks to provide information and engage in advocacy regarding research, prevention, early intervention, family support, education, transition services, and other services.

National Alliance for the Mentally Ill (NAMI)

200 North Glebe Road, Suite 1015
Arlington, VA 22203-3754
Phone: (800) 950-6264 or (703) 524-7600
Fax: (703) 524-9094
TDD: (703) 516-7991
E-mail: membership@nami.org
Internet URL: http://www.nami.org
Newsletters/Publications: The alliance publishes a bimonthly newsletter entitled *The Advocate*, and *The Decade of the Brain*.
Description: NAMI is a not-for-profit, voluntary health organization dedicated to providing mutual support, education, advocacy, and research funding for people affected by mental illness, their families, and friends. The organization also serves those who have been diagnosed with schizophrenic depression and other related disorders. Established in 1979, this self-help organization refers individuals to nationwide support groups, services, and outreach programs.

National Institute of Mental Health
(See Government Agencies)

National Mental Health Association

1021 Prince Street
Alexandria, VA 22314-2971
Phone: (800) 969-6642 or (703) 684-7722
Fax: (703) 684-5968
TDD: (800) 433-5959
E-mail: nmhainfo@aol.com
Internet URL: http://www.nmha.org
Newsletters/Publications: Educational materials distributed by the association include quarterly newsletters entitled *Prevention Update* and *The Bell*.
Description: Established in 1909, the National Mental Health Association (NMHA) is a not-for-profit voluntary organization that addresses the mental health needs of individuals throughout the United States. The association, with more than 300 affiliates in 35 states, has a network of volunteers that work to meet the mental health needs of their communities. Activities include support groups, community outreach and education, information and referral programs, patient advocacy, and a wide array of other services. Nationally, the association works with the media to keep the public informed about mental health and mental illness, and with the federal government to promote research and services for people with mental health problems. It also works with other major organizations to ensure that the nation's mental health needs are understood and addressed.

National Mental Health Services Knowledge Exchange Network (KEN)
(See Clearinghouses)

Mental Health: Professional Organizations

American Academy of Child and Adolescent Psychiatry (AACAP)
3615 Wisconsin Avenue, NW
Washington, DC 20016-3007
Phone: (202) 966-7300
Fax: (202) 966-2891
Internet URL: http:www.aacap.org
Newsletters/Publications: Call for a list of publications.
Description: AACAP is the leading national professional medical association dedicated to treating and improving the quality of life for children, adolescents, and families affected by mental, behavioral, and developmental disorders.

American Counseling Association (ACA)
5999 Stevenson Avenue
Alexandria, VA 22304-3300
Phone: (800) 347-6641 or (703) 823-9800
Fax: (703) 823-0252
E-mail: N/A
Internet URL: http://www.counseling.org
Newsletters/Publications: Call for a list of publications.
Description: The largest professional organization for guidance counselors.

American Psychiatric Association (APA)
1400 K Street, NW
Washington, DC 20005
Phone: (202) 682-6326
Fax: (202) 682-6114
E-mail: apa@psych.org
Internet URL: http://www.psych.org/main.html
Newsletters/Publications: Call for a list of publications.
Description: The largest professional association for psychiatric professionals.

American Psychological Association (APA)
750 First Street, NE
Washington, DC 20002
Phone: (202) 336-5500
Fax: N/A
E-mail: N/A
Internet URL: http://www.apa.org
Newsletter/Publications: Call for a list of publications.
Description: The APA is the largest scientific and professional association representing psychologists in the United States.

National Association of School Psychologists (NASP)
4340 East West Highway, Suite 402
Bethesda, MD 20814
Phone: (301) 657-0270
Fax: (301) 657-0275
E-mail: nasp8455@AOL.com
Internet URL: http://www.naspweb.org
Newsletters/Publications: Call for a list of publications.
Description: NASP is an international non-profit membership association of school psychologists. It provides videos, books, a newpaper, and a quarterly *School Psychology Review.*

National Association of Social Workers (NASW)
750 First Street NE, Suite 700
Washington, DC 2002-4241
Phone: (202) 408-8600
Fax: (202) 336-8311
TTD: (202) 408-8396
E-mail: N/A
Internet URL: http://www.naswdc.org
Newsletters/Publications: Call for a list of publications.
Description: NASW is the largest professional organization for social workers.

Mental Health Websites

Internet Mental Health
Internet URL: http://www.mentalhealth.com
Description: A free encyclopedia of mental health information including diagnosis, medications, disorders, and an online magazine.

Mental Health Resources on the Internet
Internet URL: http://www.techline.com/~ombuds/mhlinks.htm
Description: Provides numerous mental health links to other resources on this topic.

Mental Retardation/Developmental Disabilities

The essence of mental retardation is significantly subaverage general intellectual functioning that is accompanied by severe limitations in adaptive behavior in at least two of the following skill areas: communication, self care, home living, social/interpersonal skills, use of community resources, self direction, functional academic skills, work, leisure, health, and safety. The onset must occur before age 18.

American Association on Mental Retardation (AAMR)
444 North Capitol Street NW, Suite 846
Washington, DC 20001-1512
Phone: (800) 424-3688 or (202) 387-1968
Fax: (202) 387-2193
E-mail: info@aamr.org
Internet URL: http://www.aamr.org
Newsletters/Publications: Call for a list of publications.
Description: AAMR is a national membership organization that provides information and services, influences public policy, and advocates for mental retardation.

American Association of University Affiliated Programs for Persons with Developmental Disabilities (AAUAP)
8630 Fenton Street, Suite 410
Silver Spring, MD 20910
Phone: (301) 588-8252
TTD: (301) 588-3319
Fax: (301) 588-2842
E-mail: info@aauap.org
Internet URL: http://www.aauap.org
Newsletters/Publications: Call for a list of publications.
Description: AAUAP is a national association that represents three different affiliated programs. AAUAP has sites at major universities and teaching hospitals in all states. These sites target and engage in activities to support the independence, productivity, integration, and inclusion into the community of individuals with developmental disabilities and their families.

The Arc
500 East Border Street, Suite 300
Arlington, TX 76010
Phone: (800) 433-5255 or (817) 261-6003
Fax: (817) 277-3491
TDD: (817) 277-0553
E-mail: thearc@metronet.com
Newsletters/Publications: Contact the association for a publications catalog.
Internet URL: http://thearc.org/welcome.html
Description: The Arc (formerly The Association for Retarded Citizens) is a volunteer organization with more than 1,100 affiliated chapters and 140,000 members across the United States. The Arc is the country's largest voluntary organization committed to the welfare of all children and adults with mental retardation and their families.

The Arc is committed to securing the opportunity for all people with mental retardation to choose and realize their goals of where and how they learn, live, work, and play. The Arc is further committed to reducing the incidence and limiting the consequence of mental retardation through education, research, advocacy, and the support of families, friends, and community. Through the successful pursuit of quality and justice, The Arc will provide leadership in the field of mental retardation and develop necessary human and financial resources to attain its goals.

The Arc has a wide variety of publications on topics related to mental retardation including fact sheets, booklets, Q&As, and position papers. Additionally, the Arc hosts an annual conference.

International Resource Center for Down Syndrome
(Part of the Center for Mental Retardation)
Keith Building
1621 Euclid Avenue, Suite 514
Cleveland, OH 44115
Phone: (216) 621-5858 or (800) 899-3039 (toll-free in OH only)
Fax: (216) 621-0221
E-mail: hf854@cleveland.freenet.edu
Internet URL: N/A
Newsletters/Publications: *CMR News*, published quarterly.
Description: The center provides research, information, parent support, and education.

National Down Syndrome Congress
1605 Chantilly Drive NE, Suite 250
Atlanta, GA 30324-3269
Phone: (800) 232-NDSC or (404) 633-1555
Fax: (404) 633-2817
E-mail: mdsccenter@aol.com
Internet URL: http://members.carol.net/ndsc
Newsletters/Publications: *Down Syndrome News* is published 10 times a year
and is available through subscription.
Description: NDSC's mission is to be the national advocacy organization for Down Syndrome
and to provide leadership in all areas of concern related to persons with Down Syndrome. It
provides research, education, resources, advocacy, and more.

National Down Syndrome Society (NDSS)
666 Broadway, Suite 810
New York, NY 10012-2317
Phone: (800) 221-4602 or (212) 460-9330
Fax: (212) 979-2873
E-mail: info@ndss.org
Internet URL: http://www.ndss.org
Newsletters/Publications: *Update*, published quarterly.
Description: NDSS sponsors research, assists families, increases public awareness, and pro-
vides resources and information.

National Institute for People with Disabilities (YAI)
460 West 34th Street
New York, NY 10001-2382
Phone: (212) 563-7474
TDD: (212) 290-2787
FAX: (212) 268-1083
E-mail: link@yai.org
Internet URL: http://www.yai.org
Newsletters/Publications: Call for a list of publications.
Description: YAI is a not-for-profit agency serving children and adults with developmental
disabilities in the New York metropolitan area and surrounding counties. It offers information
and referral, early intervention and preschool, medical and rehabilitation services, crisis inter-

vention, respite programs, after school programs, service coordination, residential services, adult day services, home health care, clinical services, parent and family training, employment training and placement, and camping, recreation, and travel. While YAI provides local services to the New York and surrounding areas, it also encourages national involvement through staff and management training, development of systems and policies, training resources, and compliance consultations. It also has a network of educational videos.

Voice of the Retarded (VOR)
5005 Newport Drive, Suite 108
Rolling Meadows, Illinois, 60008
Phone: (847) 253-6020
Fax: (847) 253-6054
E-mail: vor@compuserve.com
Internet URL: N/A
Newsletters/Publications: VOR publishes *VOR Newsletter* quarterly, which is free to members and any interested parties.
Description: Voice of the Retarded provides information, support, and advocacy services according to individual and group needs, and keeps public officials, legislators, and the general public informed about issues that affect persons with mental retardation. It supports alternatives in residential living and rehabilitation systems most suitable to the individual needs of a person with mental retardation and his/her family. Voice of the Retarded supports research into causes, prevention, and treatment of mental retardation.

VOR maintains state coordinators and a data base of organizational members. It welcomes inquiries from parents regarding local parent groups, and has an extensive collection of research files to handle a variety of questions. Copies of material may be requested.

Mental Retardation/Developmental Disabilities Websites

Developmental Disability Resource Index
Internet URL: http://www.dfnears.com/library/mr.html
Description: This site provides information on all types of developmental disabilities.

Multiple Chemical Sensitivity/Environmental Illness

Multiple Chemical Sensitivity (MCS) is basically a subset of Environmental Illness (EI), which is caused by living in a toxic world. The chemicals that were synthesized after World War II (including, pesticides, synthetic fragrances, cleaning products, detergents, and so forth) are mostly "petro-chemicals" (petroleum based) and are quite toxic to humans. There have been virtually no studies done on the majority of these chemicals to see how they affect humans.

American Academy of Environmental Medicine (AAEM)
P. O. Box CN 1001-8001
New Hope, PA 18938
Phone: (215) 862-4544
Fax: (215) 862-4583
E-mail: 1055 30.3664@compuserve.com
Internet URL: http://www.aaem.com/index.html
Newsletters/Publications: Membership in the AAEM includes a subscription to the official journal, *Journal of Nutritional and Environmental Medicine*. This publication consists of clinical, experimental, historical, and research articles. The academy also publishes a quarterly newsletter, *Environmental Physician*.
Description: The organization can be helpful in locating an environmental medicine specialist in your area.

Chemical Injury Information Network (CIIN)
P.O. Box 301
White Sulphur Springs, MT 59645
Phone: (406) 547-2255
Fax: (406) 547-2455
E-mail: N/A
Internet URL: http://www.biz-comm.com/CIIN
Newsletter/Publications: CIIN's monthly newsletter is called *Our Toxic Times.*
Description: The Chemical Injury Information Network (CIIN) is a tax-exempt, non-profit charitable support and advocacy organization run by the chemically injured for the benefit of the chemically injured. It focuses primarily on education, credible research into Multiple Chemical Sensitivities (MCS), and the empowerment of the chemically injured. CIIN provides its members:

- Expert witness/Doctor referrals
- Attorney referrals
- A list of organization(s) in the state where the member resides
- A list of CIIN members for the state where the member resides
- Referrals to experts in the fields of electro-magnetic fields (EMFs), less-toxic pesticide, and weed control
- Peer counseling
- Materials for educational events, such as Earth Day booths
- Resource materials

H.E.A.L. (Human Ecology Action League, Inc.)
(See Rare Disorders)

National Center for Environmental Health Strategies
1100 Rural Avenue
Voorhees, NJ 08043
Phone: (609) 429-5358
E-mail: wjrd37A@prodigy.com
Internet URL:
http://www.parentsoup.com/library/organizations/bpd00606.html
Description: The National Center for Environmental Health Strategies is a non-profit organization fostering the development of creative solutions to environmental health problems. The

center provides a clearinghouse for chemical and environmental danger in the home, at school, at work, and in the community.

Of particular interest to parents are their projects on indoor pollution, e.g. "sick" schools and buildings; problematic products such as new carpet installation; and pesticide-induced illnesses. The center publishes *The Delicate Balances* newsletter and offers information packages, educational materials, and technical assistance. A one-year membership costs $15.

National Foundation for the Chemically Hypersensitive

4407 Swinson-Newman Road
Rhodes, MI 48652
Phone: (517) 689-6369
Fax: N/A
E-mail: 4woman@soza.com
Internet URL:
http://www.4woman.org/nwhic/references/mdreferrals/nfch.htm
Newsletters/Publications: Call for a complete list of publications.
Description: The National Foundation for the Chemically Hypersensitive is a non-profit, tax exempt volunteer organization devoted to research; education; dissemination of information; patient to doctor referrals; patient to attorney referrals and information; social security disability information; workers compensation information; advice and resource assistance for the chemically injured and their relatives; assistance with low cost housing resources; compilation of thousands of case histories; development of epidemiological studies; and a network to help the patient with referrals for safe living, food, and clothing.

Muscular Dystrophy

The term muscular dystrophy refers to a group of genetic diseases marked by progressive weakness and degeneration of the skeletal or voluntary muscles that control movement. The muscles of the heart and some other involuntary muscles are also affected in some forms of muscular dystrophy, and a few forms involve other organs as well.

Muscular Dystrophy Association (MDA)

3300 East Sunrise Drive
Tucson, AZ 85718
Phone: (800) 572-1717 or (520) 529-2000
Fax: (602) 529-5300
E-mail: mda@mdausa.org
Internet URL: http://www.mdausa.org
Newsletters/Publications: MDA publishes *Quest Magazine* and the *ALS Newsletter.*
Description: The Muscular Dystrophy Association is a source for news and information about 40 neuromuscular diseases, and MDA research and services available to adults and children. This site includes a searchable database with 230 MDA clinics across the country.

Multiple Sclerosis

Multiple sclerosis is a chronic, often disabling disease of the central nervous system. Symptoms may be mild, such as numbness in the limbs, or severe, paralysis or loss of vision.

Most people with MS are diagnosed between the ages of 20 and 40 but the unpredictable physical and emotional effects can be lifelong. The progress, severity, and specific symptoms of MS in any one person cannot yet be predicted, but advances in research and treatment are giving hope to those affected by the disease.

National Multiple Sclerosis Society
733-3rd Avenue
New York, NY 10017
Phone: (800) 344-4867 or (212) 986-3240
Fax: (212) 986-7981
E-mail: info@nmss.org
Internet URL: http://www.nmss.org
Newsletters/Publications: Contact the agency for a list of publications.
Description: The National Multiple Sclerosis Society is dedicated to ending the devastating effects of multiple sclerosis. The society provides up-to-date information on the diagnosis, causes, and treatment of MS.

N

Neurofibromatosis

Neurofibromatosis Type 1 (NF-1) is a rare inherited disorder of the nervous system and is characterized by the development of tumors on the covering of nerves. The symptoms of Neurofibromatosis Type 1 include brown spots (cafe-au-lait) and freckles on the skin, as well as multiple benign tumors on the covering of nerves. These tumors can grow on any nerve and may appear at any time, including childhood, adolescence, or adulthood. Neurofibromatosis Type 1 is inherited as an autosomal dominant genetic trait. Approximately 50 percent of individuals with NF-1 do not have a family history of Neurofibromatosis; these cases represent spontaneous genetic changes (mutations).

The term "Neurofibromatosis" is also used in a general way to describe two genetically distinct disorders: Neurofibromatosis Type 1 (NF-1) and Neurofibromatosis Type 2 (NF-2). Neurofibromatosis Type 2 is characterized by benign tumors on both auditory nerves (acoustic neuromas of 8th cranial nerves) and tumors primarily on the central nervous system (brain and spine). Acoustic Neuromas generally cause a loss of hearing.

National Neurofibromatosis Foundation
95 Pine Street, 16th Floor
New York, NY 10005
Phone: (800) 323-7938 or (212) 344-6633
TDD: (212) 344-6633
Fax: (212) 747-0004
E-mail: nnff@aol.com
Internet URL: http://www.nf.org
Newsletters/Publications: Call for a list of publications.
Description: Since 1978, the foundation has been dedicated to sponsoring scientific research aimed at finding the causes and cures for the neurofibromatoses, promoting the development of clinical activities, creating public awareness, and providing patient support services. In addition, NNF promotes education of health care professionals, offers patient advocacy, and provides referrals to genetic counseling and support groups. The National Neurofibromatosis Foundation offers educational and supportive information through its directory, database, pamphlets, newsletters, handbooks, and audio-visual aids.

Neurofibromatosis, Inc.
8855 Annapolis Road, Suite 110
Lanham, MD 20706-2924
Phone: (800) 942-6825 or (301) 577-8984
TDD: (410) 461-5213
Fax: (301) 577-0016
E-mail: nfinc1@aol.com
Internet URL: http://members.aol.com/NFInc1/index.htm
Newsletters/Publications: Call for a list of publications.
Description: Established in 1988, Neurofibromatosis, Inc. services the needs of affected individuals through coordinated educational, support, clinical, and research programs. The organization provides information about NF1 and NF2 to affected individuals, family members, health care and other professionals, and the general public; offers referrals to local medical resources; and assists in identifying community support services. Neurofibromatosis, Inc. also encourages and supports medical, clinical, educational, and sociological research into the prevention, treatment, cure, and/or effects of the Neurofibromatoses.

O

Obsessive Compulsive Disorder

OCD is characterized by obsessions and compulsions, or both. Obsessions are unwanted thoughts or images that repetitively intrude into awareness, while compulsions are seemingly unstoppable repetitive habits or behaviors in which an individual engages in order to reduce discomfort and anxiety. Both the obsessive thoughts and compulsive behaviors are usually recognized as unrealistic or irrational by OCD sufferers, but typically they feel powerless to stop either.

Obsessive Compulsive Disorder
Internet URL: http://www.fairlite.com/ocd
Description: Provides information, personal contact sites, bulletin boards, treatment, medical information and so on.

Obsessive Compulsive Disorder Internet Mental Health (See Mental Health Websites)
Internet URL: http://www.mentalhealth.com/dis/p20-an05.html
Description: An extensive discussion of OCD with other resources and links.

OC Foundation (OCF)
PO Box 70
Milford, CT 06460-0070
Phone: (203) 878-5669
Fax: (203) 874-2826
E-mail: jphs28a@Prodigy.com
Internet URL: http://pages.prodigy.com/alwillen/ocf.html
Newsletters/Publications: *OCF Newsletter*, published six times a year.
Description: OCF is a community of individuals with an interest in Obsessive Compulsive Disorder or related neurobiological disorders. The goals of the organization are to educate the public and professional communities about the disorder, to support afflicted individuals and their family members, and to promote research.

Occupational Therapy Assessment Measures

Several tests already described in other sections are frequently used by ocuupational thera-pists during their evaluation. These include:

- Bruninks-Oseretsky Test of Motor Proficiency (See Comprehensive Measures of Perceptual Abilities)
- Degangi-Berk Test of Sensory Integration (See Early Childhood Measures)
- Denver Development Screening Test-Revised (See Early Childhood Mearures)
- McCarthy Scales of Children's Abilities (See Intelligence Tests)
- Motor Free Visual Perception Test (See Perceptual Measures)

Milani-Comparetti Motor Development Test
Authors: Wayne Stuberg, Pam Dehne, Jim Miedaner and Penni White
Publisher of the Test: Meyer Rehabilitation Institute
University of Nebraska Medical Center
600 South 42nd Street, Box 985450
Omaha, NE 68198
Phone: (402) 559-6430
Fax: (402) 559-5737
Type of Test: Standardized
Administration Time: 10–15 minutes
Type of Adminstration: Individual
Age/Grade Level: 1 to 16 months

Miller Assessment for Preschoolers (MAP)
Author: Lucy Jane Miller
Publisher: The Psychological Corporation
555 Academic Court
San Antonio, TX 78204-2498
Phone: (800) 211-8378
Fax: (800) 232-1223
TDD: (800) 723-1318
Type of Test: Standardized
Administration Time: 20–30 minutes
Type of Administration: Individual
Age/Grade Level: Ages 2.9 to 5.8

Quick Neurological Screening Test (QNST)
Authors: Margaret Motti, Harold M. Steling, Norma V. Spalding, and C. Slade Crawfold
Publisher: Academic Therapy Publications
20 Commercial Boulevard
Novato, CA 94949-6191
Phone: (415) 883-3314 or (800) 422-7249

Fax: (415) 883-3720
Type of Test: Criterion-referenced
Administration Time: Untimed
Type of Administration: Individual
Age/Grade Level: Ages 5 to 18

Sensory Integration and Praxis Test (SIPT)
Author: Jean Ayres
Publisher: Western Psychological Services
12031 Wilshire Boulevard
Los Angeles, CA 90025
Phone: (310) 478-2061 or (800) 648-8857
Fax: (310) 478-7838
Type of Test: Norm-referenced
Administration Time: The entire battery can be given in two hours.
Type of Administration: Individual
Age/Grade Level: Ages 4 to 9

Purdue Perceptual Motor Survey (PPM)
Authors: Eugene G. Roach and Newell C. Kephart
Publisher: The Psychological Corporation
555 Academic Court
San Antonio, TX 78204-2498
Phone: (800) 211-8378
Fax: (800) 232-1223
TDD: (800) 723-1318
Type of Test: Criterion-referenced
Administration Time: 30–40 minutes
Type of Administration: Individual
Age/Grade Level: Preschool–Grade 8

Occupational Therapy: Professional Organizations

Occupational therapists evaluate and treat individuals with injuries, illnesses, cognitive impairments, psychosocial dysfunction, mental illness, developmental or learning disabilities, physical disabilities, or other disorders or conditions. Evaluation and intervention focuses on an individual's level of function and involves assessment of performance areas, performance components, and performance contexts. Intervention involves the use of purposeful activity for developing, improving, sustaining, or restoring function in performance areas including, but not limited to, daily living skills, work performance, educational performance skills, and leisure capacities.

The performance components (sensorimotor, cognitive, psychosocial, and psychological) are the elements of performance in which occupational therapists intervene for the purpose of attaining an individual's highest level of functional independence. Services of an occupational therapist also include design, development, adaptation, application, or training in the use of assistive technology devices; design, fabrication, or application of orthotic devices; training in the use of orthotic or prosthetic devices; application of physical agent modalities; and the adaptation of environments and processes to enhance functional performance.

American Occupational Therapy Association Inc. (AOTA)
4720 Montgomery Lane
PO Box 31220
Bethesda, MD 20824-1220
Phone: (301) 652-2682
Fax: (301) 652-7711
E-mail: N/A
Internet URL: http://www.aota.org
Newsletters/Publications: AOTA publishes *The American Journal of Occupational Therapy, OT Practice Magazine,* and *The Journal of Occupational Therapy Students.*
Description: The mission of the American Occupational Therapy Association is to support a professional community for members and to develop and preserve the viability and relevance of the profession. The organization serves the interests of its members, represents the profession to the public, and promotes access to occupational therapy services.

Organizations: General Disabilities

Alliance of Genetic Support Groups
4301 Connecticut Avenue, NW, Suite 404
Washington, DC 20008-2304
Phone: (800) 336-4363 or (202) 966-5557
E-mail: info@geneticalliance.org
Internet URL: http://www.geneticalliance.org
Newsletters/Publications: *ALERT* is the group's monthly newsletter.
Description: The Alliance of Genetic Support Groups is a non-profit organization dedicated to helping individuals and families who have genetic disorders. Its toll-free helpline is a resource for consumers and professionals looking for genetic support groups and genetic services.

American Council on Rural Special Education (ACRES)
Department of Special Education
Kansas State University
2323 Anderson Avenue, Suite 226
Manhattan, KS 66502
Phone: (785) 53 ACRES
Fax: (785) 532-7732
E-mail: acres@ksu.edu
Internet URL: http://www.ksu.edu/acres
Newsletters/Publications: *The Rural Special Education Quarterly*

Description: ACRES is a national organization devoted entirely to special education issues that affect rural America. The mission of the organization is to provide leadership and support for children with exceptional needs, their families, and the professionals who work with them.

Association for the Care of Children's Health (ACCH)

19 Mantua Road
Mount Royal, NJ 08061
Phone: (609) 224-1742
Fax: (609) 423-3420
E-mail: amkent@smarthub.com
Internet URL: http://www.acch.org
Newsletter/Publications: Call for a list of publications.
Description: ACCH is a multi-disciplinary membership organization of health care providers, family members, facility designers, teachers, child life specialists, chaplains, hospitals, and others committed to improving the quality of health care for children and their families through educational materials and informational meetings.

Association for Persons with Severe Handicaps (TASH)

(See Advocacy)

Association of Birth Defect Children, Inc. (ABDC)

930 Woodcock Road, Suite 225
Orlando, FL 32803
Phone: (800) 313-2232 or (407) 245-7035
Fax: (407) 245-7087
E-mail: abdc@marketweb.com
Internet URL: http://www.birthdefects.org
Newsletters/Publications: *ABDC News*
Description: ABDC was started by parents after the Gulf War. It has a birth defect registry and a parent matching service.

Beach Center on Families and Disability
Bureau of Child Research

University of Kansas
3111 Haworth Hall
Lawrence, KS 66045
Phone: (913) 864-7600
Fax: (913) 864-7605
E-mail: beach@dole.lsi.ukans.edu
Internet URL: http://www.lsi.ukans.edu/beach/BEACH.htm
Newsletters/Publications: Call for a list of publications.
Description: The center focuses on family support, family empowerment, and family quality of life as influenced by public policy and professional practice. It also has a national program that provides training for fathers and their children with chronic illness and disabilities.

Center for Children with Chronic Illness and Disabilities

University of Minnesota
#D-115, Box 721
420 Delaware Street, SE

Minneapolis, MN 55455
Phone: (612) 626-3939
Fax: (612) 626-2134
E-mail: instihd@tc.umn.edu
Internet URL: http://www.peds.umn.edu
Newsletters/Publications: Call for a list of publications.
Description: The organization provides interdisciplinary rehabilitation, research, and a training center committed to increasing and applying knowledge that fosters the physical, psychological, and social development and competence of children and adolescents with chronic illness and disabilities and their families.

Council for Exceptional Children (CEC)
(See Professional Organizations)

Easter Seals
230 West, Monroe, Suite 1800
Chicago, IL 60606
Phone: (800) 221-6827 or (312) 726-6200
TTD: (312) 726-4258
Fax: (312) 726-1494
E-mail: info@easter-seals.org
Internet URL: http://www.easter-seals.orgf
Newsletters/Publications: Call for a complete list of publications. Easter Seals also provides informational packets on disability awareness.
Description: This organziation helps children and adults with disabilities gain independence through a variety of services.

Educational Equity Concepts (EEC)
114 East 32nd Street
New York, NY 10016
Phone (V/TTD): (212) 725-0947
Fax: (212) 725-0947
E-mail: 75507.1306@compuserve.com
Internet URL: http://www.onisland.com/eec
Newsletters/Publications: Contact the organization for a list of publications.
Description: Educational Equity Concepts is a national non-profit organization founded in 1982. EEC creates programs and materials that help educators provide bias-free learning environments and activities. Its mission is to decrease discrimination in education based on gender, race/ethnicity, and disability.

Elwyn Inc.
111 Elwyn Road
Elwyn, PA 19063
Phone: (610) 891-2000
Fax: (610) 891-2458
E-mail: N/A
Internet URL: http://www.elwyn.org
Newsletters/Publications: Call for a list of publications.

Description: Elwyn Inc. is a human services organization that serves a wide variety of disabilities. It offers programs in education, rehabilitation, vocational/employment services, and residential supports for living. It has satellite offices in various locations across the country.

Family Resource Center on Disabilities
(See Parent Resources)

March of Dimes Birth Defects Foundation
1275 Mamaroneck Avenue
White Plains, NY 10605
Phone: (888) 663-4637 or (914) 428-7100
Fax: (914) 997-4763
TDD: (914) 997-4764
E-mail: resourcecenter@modimes.org
Internet URL: http://www.modimes.org
Newsletters/Publications: Call for a complete list of publications.
Description: The foundation provides information research on pre-pregnancy, pregnancy, and birth defects.

National Center for Disability Services
201 IU Willits Road
Albertson, NY 11507
Phone: (516) 747-5400
Fax: (516) 465-1466
E-mail: N/A
Internet URL: http://www.business-disability.com
Newsletters/Publications: Call for a list of publications and resources.
Description: The National Center for Disability Services is an internationally known non-profit facility that is dedicated to empowering people with disabilities to be active, independent, and self-sufficient participants in society. Besides operating a tuition-free school, the agency also provides infant assessment, parent training, recreation programs, employment evaluations, placement services, technology services and evaluations, and other services.

National Organization on Disability
910 16th Street NW, Suite 600
Washington, DC 20006
Phone: (202) 293-5960
TTD: (202) 293-5968
Fax: (202) 293-7999
E-mail: ability@nod.org
Internet URL: http://www.nod.org
Newsletters/Publications: Call for a list of publications.
Description: The National Organization on Disability promotes the full and equal participation of America's 54 million men, women, and children with disabilities in all aspects of life. NOD was founded in 1982 at the conclusion of the United Nations International Year of Disabled Persons and is the only national disability network organization concerned with all disabilities, all age groups, and all disability issues.

Rehabilitation Research and Training Center (RRTC)

Rancho Los Amigos Medical Center
7601 East Imperial Highway
Downey, CA 90242
Phone: (310) 401-7402
Fax: (310) 401-7011
E-mail: N/A
Internet URL: http://www.usc.edu/go/awd/index.html
Newsletters/Publications: Call for a list of publications.
Description: The Rehabilitation Research and Training Center (RRTC) on Aging With a Disability is funded by the National Institute on Disability and Rehabilitation Research (NIDRR), a part of the US Department of Education. There are about 40 centers, all of which focus on a specific problem affecting people who have a disability. This RRTC is a collaborative effort of Rancho Los Amigos Medical Center and the University of Southern California. The purposes of the centers are to conduct research in its problem area, to train others about findings in this area as well as how to conduct rehabilitation research, and to disseminate information to consumers and professionals.

Special Olympics International

1325 G Street NW, Suite 500
Washington, DC 20005
Phone: (202) 628-3630
Fax: (202) 824-0200
E-mail: specialolympics@msn.com
Internet URL: http://www.specialolympics.org
Newsletters/Publications: Call for a list of publications.
Description: The first Special Olympics Games held at Soldier Field in Chicago, Illinois, on July 20, 1968, were the beginning of a worldwide movement to demonstrate that people with mental retardation are capable of remarkable achievements in sports, education, employment, and beyond.

World Institute on Disability (WID)

510 16th Street, Suite 100
Oakland, CA 94612
Phone: (510) 763-4100
TTD: (510) 208-9493
Fax: (510) 763-4109
E-mail: webmail@wid.org.
Internet URL: http://www.wid.org
Newsletters/Publications: Call the agency for a list of publications.
Description: The World Institute on Disability is a non-profit public policy center dedicated to the promotion of independence and full inclusion in society of people with disabilities. Founded in 1983 by leaders of the Independent Living/Civil Rights Movement for people with disabilities, WID is committed to bringing policy into action.

Osteogenesis Imperfecta

This genetic disorder is characterized by bones that break easily, often from little or no apparent cause.

Osteogenesis Imperfecta Foundation, Inc. (OIF)
804 West Diamond Avenue, Suite 204
Gaithersburg, MD 20878
Phone: (301) 947-0083
Fax: (301) 947-0456
E-mail: N/A
Internet URL: http://www.oif.org
Newsletters/Publications: *Breakthrough*, a quarterly newsletter.
Description: OIF is a voluntary national health organization dedicated to helping people cope with the problems associated with this disorder. It provides education, awareness, mutual support, and research into the treatment and cure of ostenogenesis imperfecta.

P

Panic Disorder and Agoraphobia Websites

Panic disorder is a serious condition for approximately 1 out of every 75 people. It usually appears during the teens or early adulthood. While the exact causes are unclear, there does seem to be a connection with major life transitions that are potentially stressful: graduating from college, getting married, having a first child, and so on. There is also some evidence for a genetic predisposition. If a family member has suffered from panic disorder, one has an increased risk of suffering from it, especially during a time that is particularly stressful.

A panic attack is a sudden surge of overwhelming fear that comes without warning and without any obvious reason. It is far more intense than the feeling of being "stressed out" that most people experience. Symptoms of a panic attack include:
• raging heartbeat
• difficulty breathing
• terror that is almost paralyzing
• dizziness, lightheadedness, or nausea
• trembling, sweating, shaking
• choking, chest pains
• hot flashes or sudden chills

- tingling in fingers or toes
- fear of "going crazy" or about to die

(From The American Psychological Association)

American Psychiatric Association
(See Mental Health–Professional Organizations)

American Psychological Association
(See Mental Health–Professional Organizations)

Panic Disorder
Mining Company (See Websites–General)
Internet URL: http://panicdisorder.miningco.com
Description: The Mining Company panic disorder site provides information for families and individuals.

Panic Disorder
Internal Mental Health (See Mental Health Websites)

Parent Resources

American Academy of Child And Adolescent Psychiatry (AACAP)
Facts for Family
(See Professional Organizations)
Internet URL: http://www.aacap.org/web/aacap/factsFam
Description: AACAP developed Facts for Families to provide concise and up-to-date information on issues that affect children, teenagers, and their families. AACAP provides this important information as a public service. Facts for Families materials may be duplicated and distributed free of charge as long as the American Academy of Child and Adolescent Psychiatry is properly credited and no profit is gained from their use.

Directory of Parenting Organizations
From **Parent Soup**
Internet URL: http://www.parentsoup.com//resources/organizations.html
Newsletters/Publications: Call the agency for a list of publications.
Description: This site offers an extensive database of parenting organizations under the following areas: activities, childcare, education, fathers, health, politics, pregnancy, sports, and volunteer.

Family Resource Center on Disabilities
20 East Jackson Boulevard, Room 300
Chicago, IL 60604
Phone: (800) 952-4199 or (312) 939-3513
TTD: (312) 939-3159
Fax: (312) 939-7297
E-mail: N/A

Internet URL: N/A
Newsletters/Publications: *Family Resource Center,* published monthly. The center also provides training manuals, pamphlets, and other information. Call for a complete list of publications.
Description: The center has a coalition of parents, professionals, and volunteers, seeking to improve services for all children with disabilities. This is a federally funded parent center that provides referral services, family support services, transition services, special education rights training, and training for parent leaders.
NOTE: This parent center is one of more than 70 federally funded agencies throughout the US. Contact this agency for information on the particular parent center in your area.

Family Village
(See Websites–General)

Federation for Children with Special Needs
95 Berkeley Street, Suite 104
Boston, MA 02116
Voice/TTD: (617) 482-2915
Fax: (617) 695-2939
E-mail: fcsninfo@fcsn.org
Internet URL: http://www.fcsn.org
Newsletters/Publications: Call the agency for a list of publications.
Description: The Federation contributes expertise in family-centered policies, programs, and practices and provides special linkages to Parent Training and Information Centers (PTIs), parent leaders, and advocates.

Kid Ability
Phone: (800) 333-8087
Fax: N/A
E-mail: kidability@aol.com
Internet URL: http://www.kidability.com
Newsletters/Publications: *Special Child Magazine*
(See Magazines Disabilities)
Description: This organization provides products including books, clothing, daily living aids, computer products, toys, and games.

Kids Source ON-LINE
1066 Kelly Drive, Suite 113
San Jose, CA 95129
Phone: (408) 253-0246
Fax: (408) 253-7391
Internet URL: http://www.kidsource.com
Newsletters/Publications: Call for a list of publications.
Description: Kids Source is an online community that provides information and advice in the areas of health and education.

Kids Together, Inc.
(See Individuals with Disabilities Act/Idea–Information)

Description: This site is a comprehensive database for information on inclusion. The site under Idea is a starting point. Go to Home Page of Kids Together for other informational areas.

National Organization of Parents of Blind Children (NOPBC)

1800 Johnson Street
Baltimore, MD 21230
Phone: (410) 659-9314
Fax: (410) 685-5653
E-mail: nfb@access.digex.net
Internet URL: http://www.nfb.org
Newsletters/Publications: The organization offers *Future Reflections,* a magazine for parents and educators of blind children; an annual Braille Readers are Leaders contest for Braille students; a Braille pen-pal service; Slate Mates and other networking services; special summer activities; and national, state and local seminars. NOPBC distributes free literature, helps to establish cane banks, and provides assistance to parents and blind children whose rights have been denied.
Description: The National Organization of Parents of Blind Children is a division of The National Federation of the Blind. It is a national organization of parents of blind and visually impaired children whose purpose is to facilitate the sharing of experience and concerns among parents of blind children, to provide information and support, to develop and expand resources for parents and their children, and to help parents gain understanding of blindness through contact with blind adults. Its ultimate goal is to create a climate of opportunity for blind children in home and society environments; to eliminate discrimination and prejudice against the blind; and to achieve for the blind security, equality, and opportunity.

National Parent Information Network

(See ERIC Resources–Clearinghouses)

National Parent Network on Disabilities

(See Advocacy)

Our-Kids

Randy Ryan
Our-Kids Administrator
Phone: N/A
Fax: N/A
E-mail: randy@opid.littondsd.com
Internet URL: http://rdz.stjohns.edu/lists/our-kids
Newsletters/Publications: N/A
Description: Our-Kids is a "family" of parents, caregivers, and others who are working with children with physical and/or mental disabilities and delays. The list is called "Our-Kids." While it isn't exactly descriptive, it avoids the pitfalls of labeling kids anything but what they most certainly are: the wonderful little people in our lives.

The Our-Kids list consists of more than 800 people representing children of varying diagnoses: everything from indefinite developmental delays and sensory integration problems, to cerebral palsy, to rare genetic disorders. Over 35 countries are represented on the list now. Our-Kids is part of the St. Johns University ~ATHENAEUM~ project.

Parent to Parent
National Parent to Parent Support and Information System
PO Box 907
Blue Ridge, GA 30513
Phone: (800) 651-1151
Fax: (706) 632-8830
E-mail: judd103w@wonder.em.cdc.gov
Internet URL: http://www.nppsis.org
Newsletters/Publications: Call for a list of publications.
Description: Parent to Parent is a networking program that matches parents with other parents based on the disabilities of their children.

Parent Advocacy Coalition for Educational Rights(PACER)
(See Advocacy)

Parents Helping Parents:
The Parent-Directed Family Resource Center for Children with Special Needs
3041 Olcott Street
Santa Clara, CA 95054
Phone: (408) 727-5775
Fax: N/A
E-mail: info@php.com
Internet URL: http://www.php.com
Newsletters/Publications: Call for a list of publications.
Description: Parents Helping Parents is a parent-directed family resource center serving children with special needs, their families, and the professionals who serve them.

Parent Training and Information Project (PTI)
Federation for Children with Special Needs
95 Berkeley Street, Suite 104
Boston, MA 02116
Phone: (617) 482-2915
Fax: (617) 695-2939
E-mail: fcsninfo@bitwise.net
Internet URL: http://www.fcsn.org
Newsletter/Publications: Call for a list of publications.
Description: PTI has a federally funded program that provides local resources and advocacy training for disability and special education issues.

The Sibling Support Project
Children's Hospital and Medical Center
PO Box 5371, CL-09
Seattle, WA 98105-0371
Phone: (206) 368-4911
Fax: (206) 368-4816
E-mail: dmeyer@chmc.org

Internet URL: http://www.chmc.org/departmt/sibsupp/default.htm
Newsletters/Publications: NASP (National Association of Sibling Programs).
Books include *Living with a Brother or Sister with Special Needs!* Resources
include videos and movies related to brothers' and sisters' experiences.
Description: The Sibling Support Project is a national program dedicated to the interests of
brothers and sisters of people with special health and developmental needs.

Perceptual Assessment Measures

These tests are used by special educators, psychologists, and other professionals to identify
specific processing difficulties that may be hindering a child's ability to process information
and learn. Tests that specifically measure areas of visual perception are:

Bender Visual Motor Gestalt Test (BVMGT)
Author: Lauretta Bender
Publisher: The American Orthopsychiatric Association Inc.
19 West 44th Street, Suite 1616
New York, NY 10036
Phone: (212) 564-5930
Fax: (212) 564-6180
Type of Test: Standardized
Administration Time: 10 minutes for an individual, 15–25 minutes for group
administration
Type of Administration: Individual or group
Age/Grade Level: 4 to 12 years using the Koppitz Scoring System, 5 to 14
years using the Watkins Scoring System, and 15 to 50 years using the Pascal and
Suttell Scoring System

Marianne Frostig Developmental Test of Visual Perception (DTVP)
Author: Marianne Frostig, in collaboration with Welty Lefever and John R.B.
Whittlessey
Publisher: PRO-ED, Inc.
8700 Shoal Creek Boulevard
Austin, TX 78758-6897
Phone: (512) 451-3246 or (800) 897-3202
Fax: (800) FXPROED
Type of Test: Standardized
Administration Time: 30–45 minutes for an individual, 40–60 minutes for
group administration
Type of Administration: Individual or group
Age/Grade Level: Ages 3 to 8

Developmental Test of Visual Motor Integration–Fourth Edition (VMI-4)
Author: Keith E. Beery

Publisher: PRO-ED, Inc.
8700 Shoal Creek Boulevard
Austin, TX 78758-6897
Phone: (512) 451-3246 or (800) 897-3202
Fax: (800) FXPROED
Type of Test: Standardized
Administration Time: 10–15 minutes
Type of Administration: Individual or group
Age/Grade Level: Ages 3 to 18; grades preschool-12

Motor Free Perceptual Test–Revised (MVPT-R)
Authors: Ronald Colarusso and Donald D. Hammill
Publisher: Academic Therapy Publications
20 Commercial Boulevard
Novato, CA 94949-6191
Phone: (415) 883-3314 or (800) 422-7249
Fax: (415) 883-3720
Type of Test: Standardized, Norm-referenced
Administration Time: 10–15 minutes
Type of Administration: Individual
Age/Grade Level: Ages 4.0 to 11.11

Tests that specifically measure areas of auditory peception are:

Goldman–Fristoe–Woodcock Test of Auditory Discrimination
Authors: Ronald Goldman, Macalyne Fristoe, and Richard W. Woodcock
Publisher: American Guidance Service
4201 Woodland Road
Circle Pines, MN 55014-1796
Phone: (612) 786-4343 or (800) 328-2560
Fax: (612) 786-9077
Type of Test: Norm-referenced
Administration Time: 20–30 minutes
Type of Administration: Individual
Age/Grade Level: Ages 4 to 70

Lindamood Auditory Conceptualization Test (LACT)
Authors: Charles Lindamood and Patricia Lindamood
Publisher: The Riverside Publishing Company
8420 Bryn Mawr Avenue
Chicago, IL 60631
Phone: (800) 323-9540
Fax of Publisher: (630) 467-7192
Type of Test: Criterion-referenced
Administration Time: 10 minutes
Type of Administration: Individual
Age/Grade Level: Pre-school-adult

Tests of Auditory Perceptual Skills–Revised (TAPS-R)
Author: Morrison F. Gardner
Publisher: Psychological and Educational Publications
PO Box 520
Hydesville, CA 95547-0520
Phone: (800) 523-5775
Fax: (800) 447-0907
Type of Test: Standardized
Administration Time: Approximately 5–10 minutes
Type of Administration: Individual
Age/Grade Level: Ages 4 to 13

Wepman Test of Auditory Discrimination–2nd Edition (ADT-2)
Authors: Joseph M. Wepman and William M. Reynolds
Publisher: Western Psychological Services
12031 Wilshire Boulevard
Los Angeles, CA 90025
Phone: (310) 478-2061 or (800) 648-8857
Fax: (310) 478-7838
Type of Test: Standardized
Administration Time: 15–20 minutes
Type of Administration: Individual
Age/Grade Level: Ages 4 to 8

Phobias

According to the American Psychiatric Association, phobia is an uncontrollable, irrational, and persistent fear of a specific object, situation, or activity. Every year, approximately 5–9 percent of Americans experience one or more phobias that range from mild to severe. There are three types of phobias: specific phobia, social phobia, and agoraphobia.

American Psychiatric Association
(See Mental Health)

National Institute of Mental Health
(See Government Agencies–Federal)

Internet Mental Health
(See Mental Health Websites)

Internet Mental Health Resource
(See Mental Health Websites)

Physical Disabilities

Information on a specific physical disability is found under separate sections including:
- Cerebral Palsy
- Spina Bifida
- Spinal Cord Injury
- Muscular Dystrophy
- Osteogenesis Imperfecta

Physical Therapy Professional Organizations

A physical therapist is a professional trained to help disabled individuals maintain and develop muscular and orthopedic capability and to make correct and useful movements.

American Physical Therapy Association
1111 North Fairfax Street
Alexandria, VA 22314
Phone: (800) 999-2782 or (703) 684-2782
TTD: (703) 683-6748
Fax: (703) 684-7343
E-mail: N/A
Internet URL: http://www.apta.org
Newsletters/Publications: *Physical Therapy;* a monthly journal magazine called *PT;* and a weekly newsletter, *PT Bulletin.*
Description: The association is a national professional organization whose goal is to foster advancement in physical therapy practice, research, and education.

Post-Secondary Education Resources

Association on Higher Education and Disability (AHEAD)
(See Professional Organizations–General)

College Board On-line
Internet URL: http://www.collegeboard.org
Description: This is a comprehensive website containing complete information for parents, students, counselors, and other professionals on all aspects of college boards.

College and Career Programs for Deaf Students
Internet URL: http://www.gallaudet.edu/~cadsweb/colleges.html
E-mail: N/A
Description: The ninth edition is published by Gallaudet University and National Technical Institute for the Deaf.

College Planning for Students with Learning Disabilities
(See ERIC–Clearinghouses)
Description: Topics pertaining to college planning for students with learning disabilities can be found in the ERIC clearinghouse on Handicapped and gifted children. Articles pertaining to learning disabilities and college planning include Developing An Appropriate Individualized Educational Program, Special Skills For College-Bound Students, Potential Areas of Interpersonal Problems, Characteristics of the Postsecondary Institution, The Learning Disabilities Program, Making the Final Selection, References and Selected College Guides.

Community Colleges and Students with Learning Disabilities.
(See Heath Resource Center–Clearinghouses)

Directory of College Facilities and Services for People with Disabilities (Fourth Edition)
Publisher: Oryx Press
(See Publishers)
Description: The directory profiles of more than 1500 campus facilities including a description of the institution, its campus and facilities (accessibility), and the services provided.

HEATH Resource Center, The National Clearinghouse on Post Secondary Education for Individuals with Disabilities
One Dupont Circle NW, Suite 800
Washington, DC 20036-1110
Phone: (800) 544-3284
Voice/TTD: (202) 939-9320
Fax: (202) 833-4760
E-mail: heath@ace.nche.edu
Internet URL: http://www.acenet.edu/programs/heath
Newsletters/Publications: For a listing of HEATH's numerous publications on a variety of topics worth exploring, use the following Internet URL: http://www.acenet.edu/Programs/HEATH/HEATHpubs.html
Description: HEATH provides information on educational support services, policies, procedures, adaptations, transition, and opportunities at American campuses, vocational training schools, adult education programs, independent living centers, and other training entities after high school for individuals with disabilities.

How College Students with Learning Disabilities Can Advocate for Themselves
Author: Linda Tesslet, Learning Disabilities Association (LDA), September/October 1997
Description: (Included are some suggestions for easing the transition from depending on others to being one's own advocate.)

(See Learning Disabilities Association in Learning Disabilities)

Post-secondary Education
From LD ONLINE
Internet URL: http://www.ldonline.org/ld_indepth/postsecondary/index.html
E-mail: N/A
Description: This site assembles information to assist in the planning and selection process, plus lots of advice on creating a successful post-secondary education experience.

Post-traumatic Stress Syndrome

Post-traumatic Stress Disorder affects people differently. Some of the common symptoms are recurrent nightmares of the traumatic event, sudden panic, hypervigilance, exaggerated startle reflexes, irritability, difficulty in concentrating, and difficulty in establishing emotional relationships.

Any severely traumatic event can trigger post-traumatic stress syndrome. The two most common causes of severe post-traumatic stress disorder seem to be rape and war-time military service.

Post-Traumatic Stress Resources Web Page
Internet URL: http://www.long-beach.va.gov/ptsd/stress.html
Description: The Post-traumatic Stress Resources Web Page is created and maintained by the PTSD Program of the Department of Psychiatry, Carl T. Hayden VAMC, Phoenix Arizona. This site contains links to numerous sites on post-traumatic stress.

Internet Mental Health
(See Mental Health Websites)

Internet Mental Health Resource
(See Mental Health-Websites)

Prader-Willi Syndrome Organizations

Prader-Willi Syndrome is a disorder that is sometimes associated with, but not a subtype of, autism. The classical features of this disorder include an obsession with food which is often associated with impulsive eating, compact body build, underdeveloped sexual characteristics, and poor muscle tone. Most individuals afflicted with Prader-Willi Syndrome have mild mental retardation.

Some of the behaviors common to both Prader-Willi Syndrome and autism are delays in language and motor development, learning disabilities, feeding problems in infancy, sleep disturbances, skin picking, temper tantrums, and a high pain threshold.

Prader-Willi Syndrome Association
5700 Midnight Pass Road, Suite 6
Sarasota, FL 34242

Phone: (800) 926-4797 or (941) 312-0400
Fax: (941) 312-0142
E-mail: pwsausa@aol.com
Internet URL: http://www.pwsausa.org
Newsletters/Publications: *The Gathered View*, a newsletter, is published bi-monthly.
Description: PWSA provides information, education, and support services to members in its state and regional chapters.

Private Schools Placement for Exceptional Children

National Association for Private Schools for Exceptional Children (NAPSEC)
1522 K Street NW, Suite 1032
Washington, DC 20005
Phone: (202) 408-3338
Fax: (202) 408-3340
E-mail: napsec@AOL.com
Internet URL: http://www.spedschools.com/napsec.html
Newsletters/Publications: *NAPSEC News* is published quarterly. Call for a list of publications.
Description: NAPSEC provides referral service for persons interested in private special education placements throughout the country. It also offers publications and sponsors conferences.

Professional Educational Organizations: General

The following organizations are primarily for professional membership.
American Association of School Administrators (AASA)
1801 North Moore Street
Arlington, VA 22209
Phone: (703) 528-0700
Fax: (703) 841-1543
E-mail: N/A
Internet URL: http://www.aasa.org
Newsletters/Publications: *Leadership News* is a monthly newsletter. Call for a list of other publications.
Description: AASA is the professional organization for more than 165,000 educational leaders. The focus of AASA is to improve the condition of children and youth, prepare schools and

school systems for the 21st century, connect schools and communities, and enhance the quality and effectiveness of school leaders.

American Federation of Teachers (AFT)
555 New Jersey Ave NW, 10th Floor
Washington, DC 20001
Phone: (202) 879-4400
Fax: N/A
E-mail: N/A
Internet URL: http://www.aft.org
Newsletters/Publications: Call for a list of publications.
Description: AFT is a 984,000-member union of public and professional employees, including public and private school teachers, paraprofessionals and school-related personnel (PSRPs), higher education faculty and professionals, employees of state and local governments, and nurses and health professionals.

American Therapeutic Recreation Association
PO Box 15215
Hattiesburg, MS 39404-5215
Phone: (601) 264-3413
Fax: (601) 264-3337
E-mail: atta@accessnet.com
Internet URL: http://www.atra-tr.org
Newsletters/Publications can be accessed by members over the Internet only.
Description: Therapeutic recreation is the provision of treatment services and the provision of recreation services to persons with illnesses or disabling conditions. The primary purposes of treatment services, which are often referred to as recreational therapy, are to restore, remediate, or rehabilitate to improve functioning and independence as well as reduce or eliminate the effects of illness or disability. This is a professional organization that provides newletters, publications, conferences, and workshops.

Association for Childhood Education International (ACEI)
17904 Georgia Avenue, Suite 215
Olney, MD 20832
Phone: (800) 423-3563
Fax:: (301) 570-2212
E-mail: aceimemb@aol.com
Internet URL: http://www.udel.edu/bateman/ace
Newsletters/Publications: *Journal of Research in Childhood Education* is published bi-annually, *Journal of Childhood Education* is published six times a year, and an extensive catalog of materials, videos, booklets for educators is available by contacting the organization.
Description: This organization is dedicated to the dual mission of promoting the inherent rights, education, and well being of children from infancy through early adolescence; and high standards of preparation and growth for educators.

Association on Higher Education and Disability (AHEAD)
PO Box 21192
Columbus, OH 43221-0192
Phone: (614) 488-4972
Fax: (614) 488-1174
E-mail: ahead@postbox.acs.ohio-state.edu
Internet URL: http://www.ahead.org
Newsletters/Publications: Contact the agency for a publications catalog.
Description: The Association on Higher Education and Disability (AHEAD) is an international, multi-cultural organization of professionals committed to full participation in higher education for persons with disabilities. The association is a vital resource, promoting excellence through education, communication, and training. Its numerous training programs, workshops, publications, and conferences are planned and developed by its elected officials and governing board and carried out by the full-time executive vice president and staff.

AHEAD was founded in 1977 to address the need and concern for upgrading the quality of services and support available to persons with disabilities in higher education.

Association of Teacher Educators
1900 Association Drive, Suite ATE
Reston, VA 22091-1502
Phone: (703) 620-3110
Fax: (703) 620-9530
E-mail: ATE1@aol.com
Internet URL: http://www.siu.edu/departments/coe/ate
Newsletters/Publications: Call for a list of publications.
Description: The Association of Teacher Educators was founded in 1920 and is the only national individual membership organization devoted solely to the improvement of teacher education for both school and campus-based teacher educators. ATE members represent more than 650 colleges and universities, 500 major school systems, and the majority of the state departments of education.

Council for Exceptional Children (CEC)
Educational Resources Information Center (ERIC)
1920 Association Drive
Reston, VA 22091
Phone: (888) 232-7733 or (703) 620-3660
Fax: (703) 264-9494
E-mail: servive@cec.sped.org
Internet URL: http://www.cec.sped.org
Newsletters/Publications: Call for a list of publications.
Description: CEC, with its ERIC resources center, is the largest international professional organization dedicated to improving educational outcomes for individuals with exceptionalities, students with disabilities, and/or the gifted. CEC accomplishes its worldwide mission on behalf of educators and others working with individuals with exceptionalities by advocating for appropriate government policies, setting professional standards, providing continuing professional development, and assisting to obtain conditions and resources necessary for effective professional practice.

National Association of State Directors of Special Education (NASDSE)
1800 Diagonal Road, Suite 320
King Street Station 1
Alexandria, VA 22314
Voice: (703) 519-3800
TDD: (703) 519-7008
Fax: (703) 519-3808
E-mail: luzanne@nasdse.org
Internet URL: http://www.lrp.com/ed/inasdse.htm
Newsletters/Publications: Call for a list of publications.
Description: NASDSE contributes expertise in state policy development, management, and operation, and provides special linkages to state education agencies.

National Education Association (NEA)
1201 16th Street, NW
Washington, DC 20036
Phone: (202) 833-4000
Fax: N/A
E-mail: N/A
Internet URL: http://www.nea.org
Newsletters/Publications: *NEA Today*
Description: NEA is the country's oldest and largest organization committed to advancing the cause of public education. It has more than 2.3 million members who work at every level of education, and affiliates in every state. The association is open to anyone who works for a public school district, a college or university, or any other public institution devoted primarily to education. It also provides resources, information, publications, and free materials for educators.

Publishers and Distributors of Special Education Curriculum Materials, Professional Books, and Media Materials

The following is a list of approximately 100 publishers of materials for teachers of students with special needs. While hundreds of publishers and distributors exist, we have chosen what we believe is an adequate cross-section of these companies. The chart has been broken into categories to facilitate your search. When a company has an asterisk (*) next to its name, it means that it also provides materials that may appear in another category as well. All the information about that company can be found in the alphabetical list that follows the category.

Publishers by Category

Assessment/Evaluation
- Academic Therapy*
- American Guidance Service-AGS*

- C.H. Stoelting*
- Council for Exceptional Children*
- CTB/McGraw-Hill
- Curriculum Associates*
- Hawthorne Educational Services*
- MultiHealth Systems
- PRO-ED*
- Psychological Assessment Resources
- Psychological Corporation
- Psychological and Educational Publications, Inc.
- Riverside Publishing
- Slosson*
- Western Psychological Services*
- Wide Range Inc.

Assistive Technology

- Ablenet
- Crestwood Company

Curriculum

- Academic Communication Associates
- Academic Therapy*
- Addison Wesley Longman Publishers*
- A.D.D. Warehouse*
- American Guidance Service–AGS*
- Attainment Company
- Bureau for AT-Risk Youth
- Childswork ChildsPLAY
- C.H. Stoelting*
- Curriculum Associates*
- EBSCO Curriculum Materials
- Educators Publishing Service, Inc.
- Funtastic Therapy
- Gallaudet University Press*
- Glencoe/McGraw-Hill
- Globe Fearon Publishers
- J. Weston Walch Publishers
- Kapable Kids*
- Kaplan Concepts for Exceptional Children
- Lakeshore Learning Materials
- PCI Educational Publishing
- Prufrock Press
- Remedia Publications
- Research Press*
- Resources for Educators*
- Saddleback Educational, Inc.

- Scholostic
- Scott Foresman/Addison Wesley
- Slosson*
- SRA/McGraw-Hill
- Teacher Ideas Press
- Things for Learning
- Training Resource Network
- Western Psychological Services*
- Wintergreen Orchard House

Curriculum Software

- Cambridge Development Laboratory
- Don Johnston
- National School Products
- Scantron Quality Computers
- Sunburst Communications*

Professional Texts/College Texts and Specialty Titles

- Academic Press
- Addison Wesley Longman Publishers*
- Allyn & Bacon
- Aspen Publishers
- Brooks/Cole Publishing Co.
- Brunner/Mazel
- Charles C Thomas Publisher
- Greenwood Publishing Group, Inc.
- Guilford Publishing
- Health Source Bookstore
- Jossey-Bass Publishers
- Love Publishing
- Merrill Education Publishers
- Prentice Hall*
- Professional Books Inc.*
- Singular Press
- Springer Publishing
- Technomic Publishing Company, Inc.

Reference Books

- Grey House Publishing
- Porter Sargent Publishing
- Princeton Review Publishing (College Guides for Special Ed)

Self-help Materials/Books/Classroom Management for Children and Adolescents

- Accelerated Development
- Boulden Publishing

- Cognitive Therapeutics
- CompCare Publishers
- Council for Exceptional Children*

Teacher Guides/Staff Development

- Academic Therapy Publications*
- A.D.D. WareHouse
- Brookes
- Brookline Books
- Center For Applied Research in Education
- C.H. Stoelting*
- Council for Exceptional Children*
- Free Spirit Publishing
- Gallaudet University Press*
- Hawthorne Educational Services, Inc.*
- Haworth Press
- J.E. Stewart Teaching Tools
- National Professional Resources, Inc.
- Oryx Press
- Plenum Publishing Corporation
- Prentice Hall*
- PRO-ED*
- Professional Books, Inc.*
- Resources for Educators*
- Spring Books
- Teachers College Press
- Woodbine House

Toys/Games

- Kapable Kids*

Videos/Audios/Films

- Aquarius Health Care Videos
- Child Development Media
- Films for the Humanities and Sciences
- HRM Video
- Insight Media
- Recorded Books, Inc.
- Research Press*
- Stanfield
- Sunburst Communications*

Ablenet, Inc.
1081 10th Avenue SE
Minneapolis, MN 55414
Phone: (612) 379-0956 or (800) 322-0956

Fax: (612) 379-9143
E-mail: N/A
Internet URL: www.ablenetinc.com

Academic Communication Associates
Publication Center, Dept. 698
4149 Avenieda Dela Plata
PO Box 586249
Oceanside, CA 92058-6249
Phone: (760) 758-9593
Fax: (760) 758-1604
E-mail: acom@acadcom.com
Internet URL: http://www.acadcom.com

Academic Press
525 B Street, Suite 1900
San Diego, CA 92101
Phone: (619) 699-6400
Fax: (619) 699-6580
E-mail: textbook@acad.com
Internet URL: www.apnet.com

Academic Therapy Publications
20 Commercial Boulevard
Novato, CA 94949-6191
Phone: (415) 883-3314 or (800) 422-7249
Fax: (415) 883-3720
E-mail: atpub@aol.com
Internet URL: http://www.atpub.com

Accelerated Development/A Division of Taylor & Francis Group
1900 Frost Road, Suite 1010
Bristol, PA 19007-1598
Phone: (800) 821-8312
Fax: (215) 785-5515
E-mail: pfalcone@tandfpa.com
Internet URL: http://www.tandfpa.com

Aquarius Health Care Videos
5 Powderhouse Lane
PO Box 1159
Sherborn, MA 01770
Phone: (508) 651-2963
Fax: (508) 650-4216
E-mail: aqvideo@tiac.net
Internet URL: http://www.acquariusproductions.com

A.D.D. WareHouse
A Publication of C.H.A.D.D.
300 NW 70th Avenue, Suite 102
Plantation, FL 33317
Phone: (954) 792-8944 or (800) 233-9273
Fax: (954) 792-8545
E-mail: N/A
Internet URL: www.addwarehouse.com

Addison Wesley Longman Publishing Co.
1 Jacob Way
Reading, MA 01867
Phone: (800) 552-2499 or (781) 944-3700
Fax: (800) 284-8292
E-mail: N/A
Internet URL: http://www.awl.com

Allyn & Bacon
160 Gould Street
Needham Heights, MA 02194
Phone: (781) 455-1200
Fax: N/A
E-mail: ab_webmaster@abacon.com
Internet URL: http://www.abacon.com/index.html

American Guidance Service
4201 Woodland Road
Circle Pines, MN 55014-1796
Phone: (612) 786-4343 or (800) 328-2560
Fax: (612) 786-9077
E-mail: agsmail@agsnet.com
Internet URL: www.agsnet.com

Aspen Publishers Inc.
7201 McKinney Circle
PO Box 990
Fredrick, MD 21701
Phone: (800) 234-1660
Fax: (800) 901-9075
E-mail: N/A
Internet URL: www.aspenpub.com

Attainment Company
PO Box 930160
Verona, WI 53593-0160
Phone: (800) 327-4269
Fax: (800) 942-3865

E-mail: info@attainment-inc.com
Internet URL: http://www.attainment-inc.com

Boulden Publishing
PO Box 1186
Weaverville, CA 96093-1186
Phone: (800) 238-8433
Fax: (916) 623-5525
E-mail: N/A
Internet URL: http://www.bouldenpub.com

Brookline Books
PO Box 1047
Cambridge, MA 02238-1047
Phone: (617) 868-0360 or (800) 666-BOOK
Fax: (617) 868-1772
E-mail: brooklinebks@delphi.com
Internet URL: http://PEOPLE.DELPHI.com/BROOKLINE.bks

Brookes Publishing Company
PO Box 10624
Baltimore, MD 21285-0624
Phone: (410) 337-9580
Fax: (410) 337-8539
E-mail: custserve@pbrooks.com
Internet URL: http://www.pbrooks.com

Brooks/Cole Publishing Co.
511 Forest Lodge Road
Pacific Grove, CA 93950
Phone: (408) 373-0728
Fax: (408) 375-2222
E-mail: N/A
Internet URL: http://www.thomson.com/brookscole/default.html

Brunner/Mazel
47 Runway Road, Suite G
Levittown, PA 19057
Phone: (800) 821-8312 or (215) 269-0400
Fax: (215) 269-0363
E-mail: bkorders@pandfpa.com
Internet URL: http://www.tandfpa.com

Bureau for At Risk Youth
135 Dupont Street
PO Box 760
Plainview, NY 11803-0760

Phone: (800) 999-6884
Fax: (516) 349-5521
E-mail: info@at-risk.com
Internet URL: www.at-risk.com

Cambridge Development Laboratory
86 West Street
Waltham, MA 02154
Phone: (800) 637-0047 or (781) 890-4640
Fax: (781) 890-2894
E-mail: N/A
Internet URL: N/A

Charles C Thomas
2600 South First Street
Springfield, IL 62794
Phone: (217) 789-8980 or (800) 258-8980
Fax: (217) 789-9130
E-mail: books@ccthomas.com
Internet URL: www.ccthomas.co

Child Development Media
5632 Van Nuys Boulevard, Suite 286
Van Nuys, CA 91401
Phone: (800) 405-8942
Fax: (818) 994-0153
E-mail:cdmi@ix.netcom.com
Internet URL: http://www.childdevmedia.com

Child's Work Child's Play
Genesis Direct Inc.
100 Plaza Drive
Secaucus, NJ 07094-3613
Phone: (800) 962-1141
Fax: (201) 583-3644
E-mail: care@genesisDirect.com
Internet URL: www.childsplay.com

C.H. Stoelting Co.
620 Wheat Lane
Wood Dale, IL 60191
Phone: (630) 860-9700
Fax: (630) 860-9775
E-mail: psychtest@stoeltingco.com
Internet URL: http://www.stoeltingco.com/tests

Cognitive Therapeutics
3430 South Dixie, Suite 104
Dayton, OH 45439
Phone: (800) 444-9482
Fax: (513) 293-5362
E-mail: cognitivet@aol.com
Internet URL: http://www.innergames.com

CompCare Publishers
2415 Annapolis Lane
Minneapolis, MN 55441
Phone: (800) 328-3330 or (612) 559-4800
Fax: N/A
E-mail: N/A
Internet URL: N/A

Council for Exceptional Children
(See Professional Organizations)

Crestwood Company
6625 North Sidney Place
Milwaukee, WI 53209-3259
Phone: (414) 352-5678
Fax: (414) 352-5679
E-mail: crestcomm@AOL.com
Internet URL: http://www.communicationaids.com

CTB/McGraw-Hill
20 Ryan Ranch Road
Monterey, CA 93940-5703
Phone: (800) 538-9547
Fax: (800) 282-0266
E-mail: N/A
Internet URL: www.ctb.com

Curriculum Associates, Inc.
5 Esquire Road, N
Billerica, MA 01862-2589
Phone: (800) 225 0248
Fax: (800) 366-1158
E-mail: cainfo@curriculumassociates.com
Internet URL: www.curriculumassociates.com

Don Johnston Inc.
1000 North Rand Road, Building 115
Wauconda, IL 60084
Phone: (847) 526-2682 or (800) 999-4660

Fax: (847) 526-4117
E-mail: djde@aol.com
Internet URL: http://www.donjohnston.com

EBSCO Curriculum Materials
Box 11521
Birmingham, AL 35202-1521
Phone: (800) 633-8623
Fax: (205) 991-1482
E-mail: ECM@EBSCO.com
Internet URL: http://www.ecmtest.com

Educators Publishing Service, Inc.
31 Smith Place
Cambridge, MA 02138
Phone: (800) 225-5750
Fax: (617) 547-0412
E-mail: epsbooks@epsbooks.com
Internet URL: www.epsbooks.com

Films for the Humanities and Sciences
PO Box 2053
Princeton, NJ 08543-2053
Phone: (609) 275-1400 or (800) 257-5126
Fax: (609) 275-3767
E-mail: custserv@films.com
Internet URL: http://www.films.com

Free Spirit Publishing Inc.
400 First Avenue N, Suite 616
Minneapolis, MN 55401-1724
Phone: (800) 735-7323
Fax: (612) 337-5050
E-mail: help#4kids@freespirit.com
Internet URL: http://www.freespirit.com

Funtastic Therapy
RD 4 Box 14, John White Road
Cranberry, NJ 08512
Phone: (800) 531-3176 or (609) 275-4393
Fax: (609) 275-0488
E-mail: N/A
Internet URL: N/A

Gallaudet University Press
800 Florida Avenue, NE
Washington, DC 20002-3695

Phone: (800) 621-2736
TTY: (888) 630-9347
Fax: (800) 621-8476
E-mail: N/A
Internet URL: http://gupress.gallaudet.edu/

Glencoe/McGraw-Hill
A Division of McGraw-Hill
PO Box 508
Columbus, OH 43216
Phone: (800) 334-7344
Fax: (614) 860-1877
E-mail: N/A
Internet URL: http://www.glencoe.com

Globe Fearon Educational Publishers
4350 Equity Drive
PO Box 2649
Columbus, OH 43216
Phone: (800) 848-9500
Fax: (614) 771-7361
E-mail: N/A
Internet URL: http://www.globefearon.com

Greenwood Publishing Group, Inc.
88 Post Road West
Westport, CT 06881
Phone: (203) 226-3571
Fax: (203) 222-1502
E-mail: N/A
Internet URL: http://www.greenwood.com

Grey House Publishing
Pocket Knife Square
Lakeville, CT 06039
Phone: (860) 435-0868 or (800) 562-2139
Fax: (860) 435-0867
E-mail: books@greyhouse.com
Internet URL: http://www.greyhouse.com

Guilford Publishing Co.
72 Spring Street, Dept L6
New York, NY 10012-4019
Phone: (212) 431-9800 or (800) 365-7006
Fax: (212) 966-6708
E-mail: info@guilford.com
Internet URL: http://www.guilford.com

Haworth Press
10 Alice Street
Binghamton, NY 13904
Phone: (607) 722-5857 or (800) 342-9678
Fax: (607) 722-6362
E-mail: getinfo@haworth.com
Internet URL: http://www.haworth.com

Hawthorne Educational Services
800 Gray Oak Drive
Columbia, MO 65201
Phone: (800) 542-1673
Fax: (800) 442-9509
E-mail: N/A
Internet URL: N/A

Health Source Bookstore
1404 K Street
Washington, DC 20005
Phone: (800) 713-7122
Fax: (202) 789-7899
E-mail: healthsource@appio.org
Internet URL: http://www.appi.org/healthsource

HRM Video
175 Tompkins Avenue, (Dept. NG22)
Pleasantville, NY 10570-3156
Phone: (800) 431-2050
Fax: (914) 747-1744
E-mail: N/A
Internet URL: http://www.hrmvideo.com

Insight Media
2162 Broadway
PO Box 621
New York, NY 10024-0261
Phone: (800) 233-9910
Fax: (212) 721-6316
E-mail: cs@insight-media.com
Internet URL: http://www.insight-media.com

James Stanfield Publishing Co.
Drawer 93
PO Box 41058
Santa Barbara, CA 93140
Phone: (800) 421-6534

Fax: (805) 897-1187
E-mail: N/A
Internet URL: http://www.stanfield.com

J.E. Stewart Teaching Tools
18518 Kenlake Place NE
Seattle, WA 98155
Phone: (206) 486-4510
Fax: N/A
E-mail: N/A
Internet URL: N/A

Jossey-Bass Publishers
350 Sansome Street
San Francisco, CA 94104
Phone: (800) 956-7339 or (415) 433-1767
Fax: (800) 605-2665
E-mail: N/A
Internet URL: http://www.josseybass.com

J. Weston Walch Publishers
321 Valley Street
PO Box 658
Portland, ME 04104-0658
Phone: (800) 341-6094
Fax: (207) 772-3105
E-mail: N/A
Internet URL: http://www.walch.com

Kapable Kids
PQ Box 250
Bohemia, NY 11716
Phone: (800) 356-1564
Fax: (516) 563-7179
E-mail: N/A
Internet URL: N/A

Kaplan Concepts for Exceptional Children
PO Box 609
1310 Lewisville-Clemmons Road
Lewisville, NC 27023-0609
Phone: (800) 334-2014
Fax: (800) 452-7526
E-mail: cec@kaplanco.com
Internet URL: http://www.kaplanco.com

Lakeshore Learning Materials
2695 East Dominquez Street
PO Box 6261
Carson, CA 90749
Phone: (800) 421-5354 or (310) 537-8600
Fax: (310) 537-5403
E-mail: N/A
Internet URL: http://www.lakeshorelearning.com

Love Publishing Company
9101 East Canyon Avenue, Suite 2200
Denver, CO 80237
Phone: (303) 757-2579
Fax: (303) 221-7444
E-mail: lovepublishing@compuserve.com
Internet URL: N/A

Merrill Education Publishing Co.
A Division of Prentice Hall/Pearson Education
445 Hutchison Avenue
Columbus, OH 43235-5677
Phone: (800) 526-0485
Fax: N/A
E-mail: info@merrilleducation.com
Internet URL: http://www.merrilleducation.com/

MultiHealth Systems
908 Niagara Falls Boulevard
North Tonawanda, NY 14120-2060
Phone: (800) 456-3003
Fax: (888) 540-4484
E-mail: customer_service@mhs.com
Internet URL: http://www.mhs.com

National Professional Resources
25 South Regent Street
Port Chester, NY 10573
Phone: (800) 453-7461
Fax: (914) 937-9327
E-mail: N/A
Internet URL: http://www.nprinc.com

National School Products
101 East Broadway
Maryville, TN 37804-5751
Phone: (800) 627-9393
Fax: (800) 289-3960
E-mail: N/A

Internet URL: http:www.ier.com

Oryx Press
4041 North Central Avenue, Suite 700
Phoenix, AZ 85012
Phone: (800) 279-6799
Fax: (800) 279-4663
E-mail: info@oryxpress.com
Internet URL: http://www.oryx.com

PCI Educational Publishing
2800 NE Loop 410, Suite 105
San Antonio, TX 78218-1525
Phone: (210) 824-5949 or (800) 594-4263
Fax: (210) 824-8055
E-mail: N/A
Internet URL: http://www.pcicatalog.com

Plenum Publishing Corporation
233 Spring Street
New York, NY 10013-1578
Phone: (800) 221-9369 or (212) 620-8000
Fax: (212) 463-0742
E-mail: info@plenum.com
Internet URL: http://www.plenum.com

Porter Sargent Publishers, Inc.
11 Beacon Street, Suite 1400
Boston, MA 02108
Phone: (617) 523-1670
Fax: (617) 523-1021
E-mail: psargent@massshore.net
Internet URL: N/A

Prentice Hall/Center for Applied Research in Education
A Division of Pearson Education
240 Frisch Boulevard
Paramus, NJ
Phone: (800) 288-4745
Fax: (201) 909-6361
E-mail: N/A
Internet URL: http://www.phdirect.com

Princeton Review
A Division of Random House
2315 Broadway
New York, NY 10024
Phone: (212) 362-6900

Fax: (212) 874-8282
E-mail: N/A
Internet URL: http://www.review.com

PRO-ED, Inc.
8700 Shoal Creek Boulevard
Austin, TX 78758-6897
Phone: (800) 897-3202 or (512) 451-3246
Fax: (800) FXPROED
E-mail: N/A
Internet URL: http://www.proedinc.com

Professional Books, Inc.
215 California Street
Newton, MA 02458
Phone: (800) 210-7323 or (617) 630-9393
Fax: (617) 630-9396
E-mail: READ9books@aol.com
Internet URL: http://www.psychbooks.com

Prufrock Press
PO Box 8813
Waco, TX 76714-8813
Phone: (800) 998-2208
Fax: (800) 240-0333
E-mail: N/A
Internet URL: http://www.prufrock.com/

Psychological Assessment Resources
PO Box 998
Odessa, FL 33556
Phone: (800) 331-8378
Fax: (800) 727-9329
E-mail: N/A
Internet URL: http://www.parinc.com

Psychological Corporation
555 Academic Court
San Antonio, TX 78204-2498
Phone: (800) 211-8378
TDD: (800) 723-1318
Fax: (800) 232-1223
E-mail: N/A
Internet URL: http://www.hbtpc.com/

Psychological and Educational Publications
PO Box 520
Hydesville, CA 95547-0520

Phone: (800) 523-5775
Fax: (800) 447-0907
E-mail: N/A
Internet URL: http://www.pep1.com

Recorded Books, Inc.
270 Skipjack Road
Prince Frederick, MD 20678
Phone: (800) 638-1304
Fax: (410) 535-5499
E-mail: N/A
Internet URL: www.recordedbooks.com

Remedia Publications
10135 East Via Linda, Suite D124
Scottsdale, AZ 85258-5312
Phone: (800) 826-4740
Fax: (602) 661-9901
E-mail: N/A
Internet URL: http://www.rempub.com

Research Press
PO Box 9177
Champaign, IL 61826
Phone: (217) 352-3273 or (800) 510-2707
Fax: (217) 252-1221
E-mail: rp@researchpress.com
Internet URL: http://www.researchpress.com

Resources for Educators
Prentice Hall
PO Box 362916
Des Moines, IA 50336-2916
Phone: (800) 491-0551
Fax: (800) 835-5327
E-mail: N/A
Internet URL: http://www.phdirect.com

Riverside Publishing Company
425 Spring Lake Drive
Itasca, IL 60143-2079
Phone: (800) 323-9540
Fax: (630) 467-7192
E-mail: N/A
Internet URL: http://www.riverpub.com

Saddleback Educational, Inc.
3505 Cadillac Avenue, Building F-9
Costa Mesa, CA 92626-1443
Phone: (888) SDL-BACK
Fax: (714) 545-1108
E-mail: info@sdlback.com
Internet URL: N/A

Scholastic, Inc.
PO Box 7502
Jefferson City, MO 65102
Phone: (800) 724-6527
Fax: (573) 635-7630
E-mail: N/A
Internet URL: http://www.scholostic.com

Scantron Quality Computers
20200 Nine Mile Road
St. Clair Shores, MI 48080
Phone: (800) 777-3642
Fax: (810) 774-2698
E-mail: sales@sqc.com
Internet URL: http://www.sqc.com

Scott Foresman/Addison Wesley
School Services
1 Jacob Way
Reading, MA 01867
(*Note:* Regional offices throughout the US)
Phone: (800) 552-2259
Fax: (800) 333-3328
E-mail: N/A
Internet URL: http://www.sf.aw.com

Singular Publishing Group Inc.
401 West A Street, Suite 325
San Diego, CA 92101
Phone: (800) 521-8545
Fax: (619) 238-6789
E-mail: singpub@mail.cerfnet.com
Internet URL: http://www.singpub.com

Slosson Educational Publications
PO Box 280
East Aurora, NY 14052-0280
Phone: (888) SLOSSON
Fax: (800) 655-3840

E-mail: slosson@slosson.com
Internet URL: http://www.slosson.com

Spring Books
Gallaudet University Press
800 Florida Avenue, NE
Washington, DC 20002
Phone: (800) 621-2736
Voice/TTY: (888) 630-9347
Fax: (800) 621-8476
E-mail: N/A
Internet URL: http://gupress.gallaudet.edu

Springer Publishing Co.
536 Broadway
New York, NY 10012
Phone: (212) 431-4370
Fax: (212) 941-7842
E-mail: springer@springerpub.com
Internet URL: http://www.springerpub.com

SRA/McGraw-Hill
A Division of McGraw-Hill
220 East Danieldale Road
DeSoto, TX 75115-2490
Phone: (800) 843-8855
Fax: (214) 228-1982
E-mail: N/A
Internet URL: http://www.sra-4kids.com

Sunburst Communications
101 Castleton Street
PO Box 40
Pleasantville, NY 10570
Phone: (800) 431-1934
Fax: (914) 769-2109
E-mail: N/A
Internet URL: http://www.sunburst.com

Teachers College Press
1234 Amsterdam Avenue
New York, NY 10027
Phone: (212) 678-3929 or (800) 488-BOOK
Fax: (212) 678-4149
E-mail: N/A
Internet URL: http://www.tc.columbia.edu/~tcpress/

Teacher Ideas Press
A Division of Libraries Unlimited, Inc.
PO Box 6633
Englewood, CO 80155-6633
Phone: (800) 237-6124 or (303) 770-1220
Fax: (303) 220-8843
E-mail: lu-books@lu.com
Internet URL: http://www.lu.com

Technomic Publishers
851 New Holland Avenue
Box 3535
Lancaster, PA 17604
Phone: (800) 233-9936 or (717) 291-5609
Fax: (717) 295-4538
E-mail: customer@techpub.com
Internet URL: http://www.techpub.com

Things For Learning
PO Box 908
Rutherfordton, NC 28139
Phone: (800) 228-6178 or (704) 287-7536
Fax: (704) 287-9506
E-mail: N/A
Internet URL: N/A

Training Resource Network
PO Box 439
St. Augustine, FL 32085-0439
Phone: (904) 823-9800
Fax: (904) 823-3554
E-mail: trninc@AOL.com
Internet URL: http://www.trninc.com

Western Psychological Services
Creative Therapy Store
12031 Wilshire Boulevard
Los Angeles, CA 90025
Phone: (800) 648-8857 or (310) 478-2061
Fax: (310) 478-7838
E-mail: N/A
Internet URL: N/A

Wide Range Inc.
P.O. Box 3410
Wilmington, DE 19804-0250
Phone: (800) 221-9728

Fax: (302) 652-1644
E-mail: wr@widerange.com
Internet URL: N/A

Wintergreen Orchard House
An Imprint of Riverside Publicating
Guidance Customer Service
425 Spring Lake Drive
Itasca, IL 60143-2079
Phone: (800) 323-9540
Fax: (630) 467-6069
E-mail: N/A
Internet URL: http://www.riverpub.com

Woodbine House
6510 Bells Mill Road
Bethesda, MD 20817
Phone: (800) 843-7323 or (301) 897-3570
Fax: (301) 897-5838
E-mail: info@Woodbinehouse.com
Internet URL: http://ww.woodbinehouse.com

R

Rare Disorders

A rare or "orphan" disease affects fewer than 200,000 people in the United States. There are more than 5000 rare disorders that, taken together, affect approximately 20 million Americans. One in every twelve individuals in this country has received a diagnosis of a rare disease.

Human Ecology Action League (HEAL)
PO Box 49126
Atlanta, GA 30359-1126
(for persons with environmental illnesses)
Phone: (404) 248-1898
Fax: N/A
E-mail: HEALNatnl@aol.com

Internet URL: http://members.aol.com/HEALNatnl
Newsletters/Publications: *The Human Ecologist,* published quarterly; and *The Supplement,* an online newsletter published bi-monthly.
Description: HEAL is a national non-profit education and information organization founded by physicians and citizens concerned about the health effects of environmental exposures. It provides current information on the health effects of environmental and chemical exposures.

National Organization for Rare Disorders (NORD)

PO Box 8923
New Fairfield, CT 06812-8923
Phone: (800) 999 NORD or (203) 746-6518
TTD: (203) 746-6927
Fax: (203) 746-6481
E-mail: orphan@nord-rbd.com
Internet URL: http://NORD-RDB.com/~orphan
Newsletters/Publications: *Orphan Disease Update* and *NORD Online*
Description: The National Organization for Rare Disorders (NORD) is a unique federation of voluntary health organizations dedicated to helping people with rare "orphan" diseases and assisting the organizations that serve them. NORD is committed to the identification, treatment, and cure of rare disorders through programs of education, advocacy, research, and service. NORD has chapters throughout the country.

Reading Assessment Measures

Decoding Skills Test (DST)
Authors: Ellis Richardson and Barbara DiBenedetto
Publisher: Western Psychological Services
12031 Wilshire Boulevard
Los Angeles, CA 90025
Phone: (310) 478-2061 or (800) 648-8857
Fax: (310) 478-7838
Type of Test: Criterion-referenced
Administration Time: 15–30 minutes
Type of Administration: Individual
Administrator: Special education teacher, reading specialist, psychologist, and classroom teacher
Age/Grade Level: Children and adults who are reading at first- through fifth-grade levels

Durrell Analysis of Reading Difficulty (DARD)
Authors: Donald O. Durrell and Jane H. Catterson
Publisher: The Psychological Corporation
555 Academic Court
San Antonio, TX 78204-2498

Phone: (800) 211-8378
Fax: (800) 232-1223
Type of Test: Standardized
Administration Time: 30–90 minutes
Type of Administration: Individual
Administrator: Special education teacher, reading specialist, psychologist, and classroom teacher
Age/Grade Level: Grades 1–6

Gates-MacGinitie Silent Reading Tests–Third Edition
Authors: Walter MacGinite and Ruth MacGinite
Publisher: The Riverside Publishing Company
8420 Spring Lake Drive
Itasca, IL 60143-2079
Phone: (800) 323-9540
Fax: (630) 467-7192
Type of Test: Standardized
Administration Time: 40–60 minutes
Type of Administration: Individual
Administrator: Special education teacher, reading specialist, psychologist, and classroom teacher
Age/Grade Level: Grades 1–6

Gates-McKillop-Horowitz Reading Diagnostic Tests
Authors: Arthur I. Gates, Anne S. McKillop, and Elizabeth Horowitz
Publisher: Teachers College Press
1234 Amsterdam Avenue
New York, NY 10027
Phone: (212) 678-3929
Fax: (212) 678-4149
Type of Test: Standardized
Administration Time: 40–60 minutes
Type of Administration: Individual
Administrator: Special education teacher, reading specialist, psychologist, and classroom teacher
Age/Grade Level: Grades 1–6

Gilmore Oral Reading Test
Authors: John V. Gilmore and Eunice C. Gilmore
Publisher: The Psychological Corporation
555 Academic Court
San Antonio, TX 78204-2498
Phone: (800) 211-8378
Fax: (800) 232-1223
TDD: (800) 723-1318
Type of Test: Standardized
Administration Time: 15–20 minutes.

Type of Administration: Individual
Administrator: Special education teacher, reading specialist, psychologist, and classroom teacher
Age/Grade Level: Grades 1–8

Gray Oral Reading Test–3 (GORT–3)
Authors: J. Lee Wiederholt and Brian R. Byrant
Publisher: PRO-ED
8700 Shoal Creek Boulevard
Austin, TX 78757-6897
Phone: (512) 451-3246
Fax: (800) 397-7633
Type of Test: Standardized
Administration Time: 15–20 minutes
Type of Administration: Individual
Administrator: Special education teacher, reading specialist, psychologist, and classroom teacher
Age/Grade Level: Grades 1–8

Nelson-Denny Reading Test (NDRT)
Authors: James T. Brown, Vivian Vick Fishco, and Gerald Hanna
Publisher: The Riverside Publishing Company
8420 Spring Lake Drive
Itasca, IL 60143-2079
Phone: (800) 323-9540
Fax: (630) 467-7192
Type of Test: Standardized, Norm-referenced
Administration Time: 35–45 minutes
Type of Administration: Individual or group
Administrator: Special education teacher, reading specialist, psychologist, and classroom teacher
Age/Grade Level: Grades 9–college

Slosson Oral Reading Test–Revised
Authors: Richard L. Slosson; revised by Charles L. Nicholson
Publisher: Slosson Educational Publication Inc.
PO Box 280
East Aurora, NY 14052-0280
Phone: (716) 652-0930
Fax: (800) 655-3840
Type of Test: Standardized
Administration Time: Untimed (approx. 3–5 minutes)
Type of Administration: Individual
Administrator: Special education teacher, reading specialist, psychologist, and classroom teacher
Age/Grade Level: Pre-school–adult

Spache Diagnostic Reading Scales
Author: George D. Spache
Publisher: CTB MacMillan/McGraw-Hill
Del Monte Research Park
Garden Road
Montery, CA 93940
Phone: (800) 538-9547
Fax: (800) 282-0266
Type of Test: Standardized
Administration Time: 60 minutes
Type of Administration: Individual
Administrator: Special education teacher, reading specialist, psychologist, and classroom teacher
Age/Grade Level: Grades 1–7 and poor readers in grades 8–12.

Test of Reading Comprehension–Third Edition (TORC-3)
Authors: Virginia L. Brown, Donald D. Hammill, and J. Lee Wiederholt
Publisher: PRO-ED, Inc.
8700 Shoal Creek Boulevard
Austin, TX 78758-6897
Phone: (512) 451-3246 or (800) 897-3202
Fax: (800) FXPROED
Type of Test: Norm-referenced
Administration Time: 30 minutes
Type of Administration: Individual/group
Administrator: Special education teacher, reading specialist, psychologist, and classroom teacher
Age/Grade Level: Ages 7 to 18

Woodcock Reading Mastery Tests–Revised (WRMT-R)
Author: Richard W. Woodcock
Publisher: American Guidance Service
4201 Woodland Road
Circle Pines, MN 55014-1796
Phone: (612) 786-4343 or (800) 328-2560
Fax of Publisher: (612) 786-9077
Type of Test: Standardized
Administration Time: 40–45 minutes
Type of Administration: Individual
Administrator: Special education teacher, reading specialist, psychologist, and classroom teacher
Age/Grade Level: Grades K–12

Resource Room

A resource room is a special education support "pull out" program provided by schools to service certain classified special education students. The room provides support services taught by a special education teacher. The minimum time required if this service is part of a child's IEP is 3 hours a week, which can be divided as needed. The maximum weekly time is up to 60 percent of the child's day. No more than five classified children can be educated in a resource room at one time.

Resource Room Teacher–Program Policy and Implementation
Lakehead Public Schools
Ontario, Canada
Board of Education Policies
Internet URL: http://www.lhbe.edu.on.ca/policy/policies/sert.htm
Newsletters/Publications: N/A
Description: This is a very good starting place for new and experienced resource room teachers. This district seems to have a thoroughly outlined policy, program, implementation and responsibilities for resource room teachers, and is very well organized.
Note: When you reach the bottom of the page, continue to "Go To Corresponding Procedure." The first site deals with policy, while the following sites deal with program procedures and intervention models.

Rett Syndrome

Rett Syndrome, a rare congenital neurological disorder that affects only females, is characterized by progressive degeneration of certain tissues of the brain, resulting in loss of previously acquired mental and motor skills, impaired control of voluntary movements (ataxia), episodes of uncontrolled electrical disturbances of the brain (seizures), autistic behavior, and/or other abnormalities and physical features.

International Rett Syndrome Association
9121 Piscataway Road, Suite 2B
Clinton, MD 20735
Phone: (800) 818-7388 or (301) 856-3334
Fax: (301) 856-3336
E-mail: irsa@paltech.com
Internet URL: http://www2.paltech.com/irsa/irsa.htm
Newsletters/Publications: The association also provides a variety of educational and support information through its directory, quarterly newsletter, books, audiovisual materials, brochures, and flyers.
Description: The association's mission includes supporting and promoting research into the prevention, control, and cure of the disorder; increasing public awareness; and providing emotional support for affected families. The International Rett Syndrome Association engages in

patient advocacy; promotes family and professional education; provides referrals to support groups, genetic counseling, and other services; and promotes legislation beneficial to affected individuals and families.

S

Section 504

Students with disabilities are protected by an additional source, Section 504 of the Rehabilitation Act of 1973. Even students whose disabilities are not recognized by the Individuals with Disabilities Education Act (IDEA) are covered under the civil rights of Section 504.

Section 504 states that no individual with a disability can be denied access to any program or activity that receives federal funds because of his/her disability. Programs that receive federal funds must be accessible to people with disabilities. They must be barrier free. "Reasonable accommodations" such as interpreters, assistive devices, transportation, etc., must be provided when needed. (Office of Civil Rights)

Educational Accommodations Under Section 504 of The Rehabilitation Act of 1973
Author: Ellen L. Wristen, Attorney-at-Law
7315 East Main Street
(PO Box 710)
Reynoldsburg, OH 43068-0710
Phone: (614) 856-9920
Fax: (614) 856-9605
E-mail: ReyWristen@aol.com
Internet URL: http://home.webmonster.net/sped.oh
Newsletters/Publications: N/A
Description: This is a well-organized and thorough site for information on Section 504, ADA information, and school law for parents.

Rehabilitation Act of 1973
Boston University
Center for Psychiatric Rehabilitation
930 Commonwealth Avenue
Boston, MA 02215
Phone: (V) (617) 353-3549
Fax: (617) 353-7700

E-mail: N/A
Internet URL: http://software.bu.edu/SARPSYCH/whatlaws-rehaba.html
Newsletters/Publications: N/A
Description: This site offers a very good explanation of the Rehabilitation Act, with other links, and an explanation of other sections affecting special educators.

Sexuality and Disability

There are many sites that offer guidelines, information, and links on this topic. We have listed several important sites, some of which are cross-referenced elsewhere in this book.

Arc of the United States, The
(See Mental Retardation/Developmentally Disabled)

Center for Disability Information and Referral
(See University-Based Sites)

National Clearinghouse on Women and Girls with Disabilities
(See Clearinghouses)

National Information for Children and Youth with Disabilities (NICHCY)
(See Clearinghouses)

Sexuality Information and Education Council of the United States (SIECUS)
130 West 42nd Street, Suite 2500
New York, NY 10036
Phone: (212) 819-9770
Fax: (212) 819-9776
E-mail: Siecus@siecus.org
Internet UL: http://www.siecus.org
Newsletters/Publications: Call for a complete list of publications.
Description: A national non-profit organization that affirms that sexuality is a natural and healthy part of living. SIECUS develops, collects, and disseminates information, promotes comprehensive education about sexuality, and advocates the rights of individuals to make responsible sexual choices. SIECUS publishes the guidelines for comprehensive sexuality education, grades K–12, and provides information on sexuality and disabilities.

Short Stature

Constitutional Growth Delay is a term describing a temporary delay in the skeletal growth and height of a child with no other physical abnormalities causing the delay. Short stature may be the result of a growth pattern inherited from a parent (familial) or occur for no apparent reason (sporadic). Typically there is a period during childhood in which growth slows down, eventually resuming at a normal rate. (From NORD)

Little People of America
PO Box 745
Lubbock, TX 79408
Phone: (888) LPA-2001 (English and Spanish)
Fax: N/A
E-mail: lpadatabase@juno.com
Internet URL: http://www.lpaonline.org
Newsletters/Publications: *LPA Today*, published bi-monthly. Call for a list of publications.
Description: Little People of America, Inc. (LPA) will assist dwarfs with their physical and developmental concerns resulting from short stature. By providing medical, environmental, educational, vocational, and parental guidance, short-statured individuals and their families may enhance their lives and lifestyles with minimal limitations. LPA Foundation, Inc. provides educational scholarships, medical assistance grants, assistance in adoption, and funds for publications and other projects.

Social Maturity Scales

Developmental Assessment for the Severely Handicapped (DASH)
Author: Mary Kay Dykes
Publisher: PRO-ED, Inc.
8700 Shoal Creek Boulevard
Austin, TX 78758-6897
Phone: (512) 451-3246 or (800) 897-3202
Fax: (800) FXPROED
Type of Test: Performance rating
Administration Time: 120–180 minutes
Type of Administration: Individual
Age/Grade Level: Individuals functioning within the developmental range of birth to 8 years

Light's Retention Scale (LRS)
Author: H. Wayne Light
Publisher: Academic Therapy Publications
20 Commercial Boulevard
Novato, CA 94949-6191
Phone: (415) 883-3314 or (800) 422-7249
Fax: (415) 883-3720
Type of Test: Survey
Administration Time: 10–15 minutes

Type of Administration: Individual
Age/Grade Level: Grades K–12

Vineland Adaptive Behavior Scale (VABS)
Authors: Sara S. Sparrow, David A. Balla, and Domenie V. Cicchetti
Publisher: American Guidance Service
4201 Woodland Road
Circle Pines, MN 55014-1796
Phone: (612) 786-4343 or (800) 328-2560
Fax: (612) 786-9077
Type of Test: Norm-referenced
Administration Time: 20–60 minutes
Type of Administration: Individual
Age/Grade Level: Birth to 18.11, and low functioning adults ages 3 through 12.11

Speech/Language Assessment Measures

Boehm Test of Basic Concepts–Revised (BTBC–R)
Author: Ann E. Boehm
Publisher: The Psychological Corporation
555 Academic Court
San Antonio, TX 78204-2498
Phone: (800)-211-8378
Fax: (800) 232-1223
TDD: (800) 723-1318
Type of Test: Norm-referenced
Administration Time: 30–40 minutes
Type of Administration: Group
Age/Grade Level: Grades K–2

Comprehensive Receptive and Expressive Vocabulary Test (CREVT)
Author: Gerald Wallace and Donald D. Hammill
Publisher: PRO-ED, Inc.
8700 Shoal Creek Boulevard
Austin, TX 78758-6897
Phone: (512) 451-3246 or (800) 897-3202
Fax: (800) FXPROED
Type of Test: Standardized
Administration Time: 20–30 minutes
Type of Administration: Individual
Age/Grade Level: Ages 4.0 to 17.11

Goldman-Fristoe Test of Articulation
Authors: Ronald Goldman and Macalyne Fristoe

Publisher: American Guidance Service
4201 Woodland Road
Circle Pines, MN 55014-1796
Phone: (612) 786-4343 or (800) 328-2560
Fax: (612) 786-9077
Type of Test: Norm-referenced
Administration Time: 10–20 minutes
Type of Administration: Individual
Age/Grade Level: Ages 2 and over

Kaufman Survey of Early Academic and Language Skills (K-SEALS)
Authors: Alan S. Kaufman and Nadeen L. Kaufman
Publisher: American Guidance Service
4201 Woodland Road
Circle Pines, MN 55014-1796
Phone: (612) 786-4343 or (800) 328-2560
Fax: (612) 786-9077
Type of Test: Norm-referenced
Administration Time: 15–25 minutes
Type of Administration: Individual
Age/Grade Level: Ages 3.0 to 6.11

Peabody Picture Vocabulary Test–3 (PPVT–III)
Authors: Lloyd M. Dunn and Leota M. Dunn, with Kathleen T. Williams
Publisher: American Guidance Service
4201 Woodland Road
Circle Pines, MN 55014-1796
Phone: (612) 786-4343 or (800) 328-2560
Fax: (612) 786-9077
Type of Test: Norm-referenced
Administration Time: 10–12 minutes
Type of Administration: Individual
Age/Grade Level: Ages 2 to 90+

Test for Auditory Comprehension of Language–Revised (TACL–R)
Author: Elizabeth Carrow Woolfolk
Publisher: The Riverside Publishing Company
8420 Bryn Mawr Avenue
Chicago, IL 60631
Phone: (800) 323-9540
Fax: (630) 467-7192
Type of Test: Norm-referenced
Administration Time: 10–20 minutes
Type of Administration: Individual
Age/Grade Level: Ages 3.9 to 11

Test of Adolescent and Adult Language–Third Edition (TOAL–3)
Authors: Virginia Brown, Donald Hammill, Stephen Larson, J. Lee Wiederholt
Publisher: PRO-ED, Inc.
8700 Shoal Creek Boulevard
Austin, TX 78758-6897
Phone: (512) 451-3246 or (800) 897-3202
Fax: (800) FXPROED
Type of Test: Standardized
Administration Time: 60–180 minutes
Type of Administration: Individual and group
Age/Grade Level: Ages 12 to 25

Test of Language Development–Intermediate 2 (TOLD–I:2)
Authors: Phyllis L. Newcomer, Donald D. Hammill
Publisher: PRO-ED, Inc.
8700 Shoal Creek Boulevard
Austin, TX 78758-6897
Number of Publisher Phone: (512) 451-3246 or (800) 897-3202
Fax: (800) FXPROED
Type of Test: Norm-referenced
Administration Time: 40 minutes
Type of Administration: Individual
Age/Grade Level: Ages 8.6 to 12.11

Test of Language Development–Primary 2 (TOLD–P:2)
Authors: Phyllis L. Newcomer, Donald D. Hammill
Publisher: PRO-ED, Inc.
8700 Shoal Creek Boulevard
Austin, TX 78758-6897
Phone: (512) 451-3246 or (800) 897-3202
Fax: (800) FXPROED
Type of Test: Norm-referenced
Administration Time: 30–60 minutes
Type of Administration: Individual
Age/Grade Level: Ages 4.0 to 8.11

Test of Early Language Development–Second Edition (TELD–2)
Authors: Wayne P. Iliesko, D. Kim Reid, Donald D. Hammill
Publisher: PRO-ED, Inc.
8700 Shoal Creek Boulevard
Austin, TX 78758-6897
Phone: (512) 451-3246 or (800) 897-3202
Fax: (800) FXPROED
Type of Test: Norm-referenced
Administration Time: 20 minutes
Type of Administration: Individual
Age/Grade Level: Ages 2.0 to 7.11

Spelling Assessment Measures

Test of Written Spelling–3 (TWS–3)
Authors: Stephen C. Larsen, Donald D. Hammill
Publisher: PRO-ED, Inc.
8700 Shoal Creek Boulevard
Austin, TX 78758-6897
Phone: (512) 451-3246 or (800) 897-3202
Fax: (800) FXPROED
Type of Test: Standardized
Administration Time: 15 to 25 minutes
Type of Administration: Group or individual
Administrators: Special education teacher, reading specialist, psychologist, and classroom teacher
Age/Grade Level: Ages 6.0 to 18.11

Spina Bifida

Spina bifida is a birth defect in the backbone and sometimes in the spinal cord. It is the most frequently occurring permanent disabling birth defect, and about one out of every 1,000 babies is born with spina bifida. Spina bifida occurs within the first four weeks of pregnancy, and is one of the most devastating birth defects. It results from the spine not forming properly. (In a severe case,) the spinal cord may protrude through the back. People born with spina bifida may need surgery and other extensive care throughout their lives because of the paralysis resulting from damage to the spinal cord. Most of the children born with spina bifida also have hydro-cephalus, which is the accumulation of fluid in the brain. This is controlled by shunting, the process of relieving the fluid in the brain by redirecting it to the abdominal area. Living well into adulthood is common for people with spina bifida due to today's medical techniques.

Spina Bifida Association of America (SBAA)
4590 MacArthur Boulevard NW, Suite 250
Washington, DC 20007-4226
Phone: (800) 621-3141 or (202) 944-3285
Fax: (202) 944-3295
E-mail: N/A
Internet URL: http://www.sbaa.org
Newsletters/Publications: SBAA publishes a number of informational brochures and reports about spina bifida for both children and adults, and edu-cational videotape programs for parents and health professionals. SBAA also has produced a 35mm slide presentation on the abilities and potential of people with spina bifida. *Insights,* a bimonthly newsletter, offers helpful ideas for living with spina bifida.

Description: The Spina Bifida Association of America (SBAA), founded in 1972, is a non-profit organization dedicated to making the public, professionals, and governmental agencies more aware of worldwide health efforts concerned with spina bifida. The association is a network of chapters across the United States. In addition to its information functions, SBAA conveys developments in the fields of medicine, education, and legislation that offer assistance; supports research into the causes and prevention of spina bifida; promotes the comprehensive treatment of persons with spina bifida; and encourages the training of competent professionals dealing with the care of people with spina bifida.

Spinal Cord Injury

Spinal Cord Injury (SCI) is damage to the spinal cord that results in a loss of function such as mobility or feeling. Frequent causes of damage are trauma (e.g., car accident, gunshot, falls) or disease (e.g., polio, spina bifida, Friedreich's Ataxia). The spinal cord does not have to be severed for a loss of functioning to occur. In most people with SCI, the spinal cord is intact but the damage to it results in loss of functioning. SCI is very different from back injuries such as ruptured disks, spinal stenosis, or pinched nerves. (From The National Spinal Cord Injury Association)

National Spinal Cord Injury Association
8300 Colesville Road, Suite 5515
Silver Spring, MD 20910
Phone: (800) 962-9629 or (301) 588-6959
Fax: (301) 588-9414
E-mail: nscia2@aol.com
Internet URL: http://www.spinalcord.org
Newsletters/Publications: *SCI Life*, published quarterly
Description: The mission of the National Spinal Cord Injury Association is to enable people with SCI to make choices and take actions to achieve their highest level of independence and personal fulfillment.

National Spinal Cord Injury Hotline
(800) 424-8200
Description: The hotline offers reference and referral service for spinal cord injury information.

Spinal Cord Injury Network
UAB Spain Rehabilitation Center
1717 6th Avenue, South
Birmingham, AL 35233-7330
Phone: (205) 934-4011
Fax: N/A
E-mail: sciweb@uab.edu
Internet URL: http://www.spinalcord.uab.edu
Newsletters/Publications: Call for a list of publications.
Description: The center provides comprehensive and organized information, and resources from recognized organizations, researchers, and educators on (Spinal Cord Injury).

Spinal Cord Society (SCS)
Wendell Road
Fergus Falls, MN 56537
Phone: (218) 739-5252
Fax: (218) 739-5262
E-mail: N/A
Internet URL: http://members.aol.com/scsweb/private/scshome.htm
Newsletters/Publications: *Spinal Cord Society Newsletter* offers monthly news of SCS activities, research, meetings, and services.
Description: SCS is an advocacy organization that works to seek a cure for spinal cord injuries. Founded in 1978, it has over 180 volunteer chapters in the United States and other countries. SCS supports a research program, a clinical center, and a computerized data and referral service. It coordinates with other medical facilities to establish a cure for spinal cord injury paralysis. The society is supported by membership fees and contributions.

Spinal Muscular Atrophy

Spinal Muscular Atrophy (SMA) is a disease of the anterior horn cells. Anterior horn cells are located in the spinal cord. SMA affects the voluntary muscles for activities such as crawling, walking, head and neck control, and swallowing. It mainly affects the proximal muscles, which are those closest to the point of origin or, in this case, those closest to the trunk of one's body. Weakness in the legs is generally greater than weakness in the arms. Some abnormal movements of the tongue, called tongue fasciculations, may be present in patients with Type I and some patients with Type II. The senses/feelings are normal, as is intellectual activity. It is often observed that patients with SMA are unusually bright and sociable.

Families of Spinal Muscular Atrophy
PO Box 196
Libertyville, IL 60048
Phone: (800) 886-1762
Fax: N/A
E-mail: membership@fsma.org
Internet URL: http://www.abacus96.com/fsma/home.htm
Newsletters/Publications: *Directions*, published quarterly.
Description: Families of Spinal Muscular Atrophy is a volunteer non-profit organization founded in 1984 by a group of concerned parents. Families of SMA supports research, offers education, and provides public awareness concerning the Spinal Muscular Atrophy diseases.

State Education Agencies

For a complete listing of special education state agencies, we suggest you use the following source from NICHCY (See Clearinghouses).

State Resource Sheets
Internet URL: http://www.nichcy.org/states.htm
Description: This NICHCY site provides a complete listing of every state's senators, governors, agencies serving children and youth with disabilities, state chapters of disability organizations and parent groups, and parent training and information projects.

Statistics on Disabilities

Disability Resources Inc.
Internet URL: http://www.abilityinfo.com/category/current.html
Note: This section of the Disability Resources website is called Keeping Current and provides access to various statitical websites. Browse through the list to Statistics.

Disability Statistics Rehabilitation Research and Training Center
Institute for Health & Aging, UCSF
3333 California Street, Room 340
San Francisco, CA 94118
Phone: (415) 502-5210
Fax: (415) 502-5208
Voice/TTY: (415) 502-5217
E-mail: Information_Specialist@quickmail.ucsf.edu
Internet URL: http://dsc.ucsf.edu
Newsletters/Publications: Call for a list of publications.
Description: The purpose of the Disability Statistics Center is to produce and disseminate statistical information on disability and the status of people with disabilities in American society, and to establish and monitor indicators of how conditions are changing over time to meet their health, housing, economic, and social needs.

International Center for Disability Information
Richard T. Walls, Ph.D.
(West Virginia University)
PO Box 6122
Morgantown, WV 26506-6122
Phone: (304) 293-5313
Fax: N/A
E-mail: walls@rtc1.icdi.wvu.edu
Internet URL: http://web.icdi.wvu.edu/disability/tables.html
Newsletters/Publications: Call for a list of publications.
Description: This site has a vast library of statistical tables and information pertaining to a variety of health and disability issues.

The Research Archive on Disability in the U.S. (RADIUS)
170 State Street, Suite 260
Los Altos, CA 94022
Phone: (800) 846-3475

Fax: (415) 949-3299
E-mail: socio@socio.com
Internet URL: http://www.socio.com
Newsletters/Publications: Call for a list of publications.
Description: The Research Archive on Disability in the U.S. (RADIUS) has been established with the guidance of a national advisory panel of experts. It is funded by the National Center for Medical Rehabilitation Research (NCMRR) within the National Institute for Child Health and Human Development (NICHD). The purpose of the project is to facilitate access to the best data sets on the prevalence, incidence, correlates, and consequences of disability in the United States.

United States Census Bureau
Internet URL: http://www.census.gov/hhes/www/disable.html
(See Government Agencies–Federal)

Stuttering

Stuttering is a developmental disorder. Some experts believe that stuttering develops from the normal mistakes all children make when learning to talk (called "normal disfluencies"). While most children can pick themselves up after a stumble, some children get into a vicious cycle of trying harder to talk, tensing their speech-production muscles too much, and getting more stuck.

Other experts have found that severe stuttering can develop almost overnight in young children. They believe that stuttering may not develop gradually from normal disfluencies. Genes have been found associated with stuttering, so these experts believe that a genetic defect causes something in the child's brain to trigger stuttering.

Although the cause of stuttering is not clear, everyone agrees that childhood stuttering can develop into a severe physical and psychological disability. (Stuttering FAQ, Thomas David Kehoe)

National Center for Stuttering
200 East 33rd Street, Suite 17C
New York, NY 10016
Phone: (800) 221-2483
Fax: (212) 683-1372
E-mail: N/A
Internet URL: http://www.stuttering.com
Newsletters/Publications: Call for a list of publications.
Description: The National Center For Stuttering was established in 1976. Its purposes are:
- to provide up-to-date factual information about stuttering.
- to provide a National Stutterer's Hotline.
- to treat small groups of selected individuals who stutter.
- to provide continuing education for speech pathologists.
- to conduct research into the causes and treatment of stuttering.
  The center conducts its therapeutic, research, and training activities in various cities across the United States and Europe.

(Also see Communication Disorders)

Suicide Resources

National Center for Injury Prevention and Center for Disease Control
(See Government Agencies)
Internet URL: http://www.cdc.gov
Description: The center has a comprehensive list of prevention guidelines.

Summer Camps and Recreational Information

GENERAL

Annual Special Camp Guide
Resources for Children with Special Needs
200 Park Avenue South, Suite 816
New York, NY 10003
Phone: (212) 677-4650

Directories of Summer Camps for Children with Disabilities
(See NICHCY in Clearinghouses)

Easter Seals Resident Camps, 1998
National Easter Seals Society
230 West Monroe Street, Suite 1800
Chicago, IL 60606
Phone: (312) 726-6200
Internet URL: http://www.seals.com

Guide to Summer Camps and Summer Schools
1995-1996 Edition
Porter Sargent Publishers, Inc. (See Publishers)
Description: The guide lists current facts from 1300 camps and schools as well as programs for those with special needs and learning disabilities.

Parents' Guide to Accredited Camps, 1998
American Camping Association, Inc.
5000 State Road 67, North
Martinsville, IN 46151-7902
Phone: (800) 428-2267 or (765) 342-8456
Internet URL: http://www.aca-camps.org/search.html

DISABILITY SPECIFIC

Camp List for Children with Cancer
The Candlelighters Childhood Cancer Foundation
7910 Woodmont Avenue, Suite 460
Bethesda, MD 20814
Phone: (301) 657-8401

Camps for Children and Adults with Attention Deficit Disorder
499 NW 70th Avenue, Suite 101
Plantation, FL 33317
Phone: (954) 587-3700
Call for a state-by-state listing.

Camps for Children with Spina Bifida
Spina Bifida Association of America
4590 MacArthur Boulevard NW, Suite 250
Washington, DC 20007
Phone: (202) 944-3285 or (800) 621-3141
Call for a state-by-state listing.

Directory of Summer Camps for Children with Learning Disabilities
Learning Disabilities Association (LDA)
4156 Library Road
Pittsburgh, PA 15234
Phone: (412) 341-1515
Internet URL: http://www.ldanatl.org/store/LD_Directories.html

Summer Camps for Children Who Are Deaf or Hard of Hearing
National Information Center on Deafness
Gallaudet University
800 Florida Avenue, NE
Washington, DC 20002
Phone: (202) 651-5051
Internet URL: http://www.gallaudet.edu/~nicd/142.html

WEBSITES

Courage Camps
Internet URL: http://www.ccourage.cz
Description: Courage Camps offer safe, accessible, and natural environments for children and adults with a wide range of disabilities.

Kids Camps
Internet URL: http://www.kidscamps.com
Description: This is a comprehensive site with pictures that describe all types of camps across the country. It also provides lists of special needs camps.

T

Teacher Guides and Directories

Complete Learning Disabilities Directory
Publisher: Grey House Publishing (See Publishers)
Internet URL: http://www.greyhouse.com/LearningDisabilities/index.html
Description: The directory covers the wide range of learning disabilities resources available nationwide.

The Complete Directory for People with Disabilities
Publisher: Grey House Publishing (See Publishers)
Internet URL: http://www.greyhouse.com/Dis abilities/index.html
Description: Important and useful information for and about people with disabilities and professionals is provided in one comprehensive guidebook.

The Complete Directory for People with Chronic Illnesses
Publisher: Grey House Publishing (See Publishers)
Internet URL: http://www.greyhouse.com/ChronicIllness/index.html
Description: This site offers comprehensive overview of the support services and information resources available for people diagnosed with chronic illnesses. The directory organizations, educational materials, books, newsletters, databases, and periodicals.

The Complete Directory for People with Rare Disorders
Publisher: Grey House Publishers (See Publishers)
Internet URL: http://www.greyhouse.com/RareDisorders/index.html
Description: This site provides comprehensive and needed access to important information on more than 1000 rare disorders.

Dictionary of Special Education and Rehabilitation—4th Edition
Publisher: Love Publishing (See Publishers)
Internet URL: N/A
Description: This comprehensive book of terms and their definitions relates to all aspects of special education.

Directory for Exceptional Children (13th Ed.)
Publisher: Porter Sargent Publishers, Inc. (See Publishers)
Internet URL: N/A
Description: Three thousand schools, facilities, and organizations nationwide serving children and adults were surveyed to cover a complete range of disabilities.

Disability in the United States
Publisher: Springer Publishing Co. (See Publishers)
Internet URL: http://www.springerpub.com

Encyclopedia of Education Information for Elementary and Secondary School Professionals
Publisher: Grey House Publishing (See Publishers)
Internet URL: http://www.greyhouse.com/LearningDisabilities/index.html
Description: This site lists suppliers of special materials, foundations to contact for grants, magazines to submit articles to, schools to teach in abroad, trade shows and conferences, and lots more.

The New Teacher's Guide to The U.S. Department of Education
Internet URL: http://www.ed.gov/pubs/TeachersGuide
Description: This online guide is also available in alternate formats upon request from the US Department of Education at (800) USA-LEARN. The guide provides information on grants, field services, resources, clearinghouses, publications, and more.

Tinnitus

Tinnitus is the medical term for the perception of sound when no external sound is present; it is often referred to as "ringing in the ears." It can also take the form of hissing, roaring, whittling, chirping, or clicking. The noise can be intermittent or constant, with single or multiple tones. It can strike people of all ages.

American Tinnitus Association
PO Box 5
Portland, OR 97207-0005
Phone: (503) 248-9985
Fax: (503) 248-0024
E-mail: N/A
Internet URL: http://www.ata.org
Newsletters/Publication: *Tinnitus Today*, published quarterly
Description: The association provides information about tinnitus and referrals to local hearing professionals/support groups nationwide. It also provides a bibliography service, funds scientific research related to tinnitus, offers workshops for professionals, and works to promote public education about tinnitus.

Tourette's Syndrome

Tourette's Syndrome is an inherited, neurological disorder characterized by repeated and involuntary body movements (tics) and uncontrollable vocal sounds. In a minority of cases, the vocalizations can include socially inappropriate words and phrases—called coprolalia. These outbursts are neither intentional nor purposeful. Involuntary symptoms can included eye blinking, repeated throat clearing or sniffing, arm thrusting, kicking movements, shoulder shrugging, or jumping.

These and other symptoms typically appear before the age of 18 and the condition occurs in all ethnic groups, with males affected three to four times more often than females. Although the symptoms of TS vary from person to person and range from very mild to severe, the majority of cases fall into the mild category. Associated conditions can include obsessivity, attentional problems, and impulsiveness. (From the Tourette's Syndrome Foundation)

Tourette's Syndrome Association
4240 Bell Boulevard, Suite 205
Bayside, NY 11361
Phone: (718) 224-2999 (800) 237-0717
Fax: (718) 279-9596
E-mail: tourette@ix.netcom.com
Internet URL: http://tsa.mgh.harvard.edu
Newsletters/Publications: *Tourette's Syndrome Association Newsletter* is published 4 times a year.
Description: The association develops and disseminates educational material to individuals, professionals, and agencies in the fields of health care, education, and government; coordinates support services to help people and their families cope with the problems that occur with TS; and funds research. Various brochures, flyers, publications, and videos are available.

Transition Services Resources

Transition services means a coordinated set of activities for a student with a disability, designed to promote movement from school to post-school activities including, but not limited to, post-secondary education, vocational training, integrated competitive employment (including supportive employment), continuing and adult education, adult services, independent living, or community participation.

Foundation on Employment and Disability
3820 Del Amo Boulevard, Suite 201
Torrance, CA 90503
Phone: (213) 214-3430

Internet Resources for Special Children (IRSC) Employment Resources
(See Websites–Genetral)

National Center on Employment for the Deaf
Part of the National Technical Institute for the Deaf (NTID)
52 Lomb Memorial Drive Building
Rochester, NY 14623
Phone: (716) 475-6834

Fax: (716) 475-7570
E-mail: N/A
Internet URL: http://www.rit.edu/NTID/co/ce
Newsletters/Publications: Call for a list of publications.
Description: The institute's services include job search, guide sheets, résumé review, and training for supervisors and co-workers.

National Center for Research in Vocational Education (NCRVE)
University of California, Berkeley
203 Addison Street, Suite 500
Berkeley, CA 94720-1674
Phone: (510) 642-3175
Fax: N/A
E-mail: N/A
Internet URL: http://vocserve.berkley.edu
Newsletters/Publications: Call for a comprehensive list of publications.
Description: NCRVE is the nation's largest center engaged in research, development, dissemination, and outreach in work-related education. NCRVE is an eight-member consortium, with Berkleley assisted in its efforts by University of Illinois; MPR Associates; University of Minnesota; RAND; Teacher's College, Columbia University; University of Wisconsin; and Virginia Polytechnic Institute and State University. The wide range of NCRVE puts it in contact with the enormous diversity of educational institutions and labor markets in the US. The center's mission is to strengthen school-based and work-based learning to prepare all individuals for employment, further education, and life-long learning.

National Clearinghouse of Rehabilitation Training Materials
Oklahoma State University
5202 Richmond Hill Drive
Stillwater, OK 74078-4080
Phone: (800) 223-5219 or 405-624-7650
Fax: (405) 624-0695
E-mail: ftanya @ okway.okstate.edu
Internet URL: http://www.nchrtm.okstate.edu/index_3.html
Newsletters/Publications: Call for a list of publications.
Description: The National Clearinghouse of Rehabilitation Training Materials (NCRTM) exists to provide a wide variety of disability-related training resources to those who serve persons with disabilities. NCRTM locates and distributes training materials in a wide variety of content areas for rehabilitation practitioners in state, federal, and private agencies nationwide. These materials are not generally found in a traditional library.

National Transition Alliance for Youth with Disabilities (NTA)
Transition Research Institute
University of Illinois
117 Children's Research Center
51 Gerty Drive
Champaign, IL 61820
Phone: (217) 333-2325
Internet URL: http://www.dssc.org/nta/html/index_2.htm

Newsletters/Publications: Contact the organization for a list of publications.
Description: The National Transition Alliance for Youth with Disabilities (NTA) seeks the formation of one education system that benefits from the lessons learned from special education, regular education, and vocational education. NTA is working to create a brighter future for all youth transitioning from school to employment, post-secondary experiences, and independent living. It serves to bridge agencies responsible for providing transition services and the lessons learned from people in the disabilities field.

National Transition Network (NTN)

103 U-Tech Center
1313 SE 5th Street
Minneapolis, MN 55414
Phone: (612) 627-4008
Fax: (612) 627-1998
E-mail: N/A
Internet URL: http://www.ici.coled.umn.edu/ntn
Newsletters/Publications: *Network News* newsletter and a variety of publications.
Description: NTN provides technical assitance and evaluation services to states with grants for Transition Systems Change, School to Work, and Implementation and Development. The general mission of NTN is to strengthen the capacity of individual states to effectively improve transition and school-to-work policies, programs, and other policies.

President's Committee
Job Accommodation Network

West Virginia University
918 Chestnut Ridge Road, Suite 1
PO Box 6080
Morgantown, WV 26506-6080
Phone: (800) 526-7234
Voice/TTD information only: (800) 232-9675
Fax: N/A
E-mail: jan@.iedi.wvu.edu
Internet URL: http://janweb.icdi.wvu.edu
Newsletters/Publications: Call the agency for a list of publications.
Description: The Job Accommodation Network (JAN) is not a job placement service, but an international toll-free consulting service that provides information about job accommodation and employability of people with disabilities. JAN also provides information regarding the Americans with Disabilities Act.

Rehabilitation Services Administration

(See Government Agencies–Federal)

Supported Employment Parents Transition & Technical Assistance (SEPT/TA)

(See Pacer–Parent Resources)

Traumatic Brain Injury

Traumatic Brain Injury (TBI) is defined within the IDEA as an acquired injury to the brain caused by an external physical force, resulting in total or partial functional disability or psychosocial impairment, or both, that adversely affects a child's educational performance. The term applies to open and closed head injuries resulting in impairments in one or more areas, such as cognition; language; memory; attention; reasoning; abstract thinking; judgment; problem-solving; sensory, perceptual, and motor abilities; psychosocial behavior; physical functions; information processing; and speech. The term does not apply to brain injuries that are congenital or degenerative, or brain injuries induced by birth trauma. (U.S. Federal Register, 57(189), September 29, 1992, p. 44802)

Brain Injury Association
(Formerly the National Head Injury Foundation)
105 North Alfred Street
Alexandria, VA 22314
Phone: (703) 236-6000
Fax: (703) 236-6001
E-mail: N/A
Newsletters/Publications: *Brain Injury Source* is published quarterly.
Description: The mission of the Brain Injury Association is to advocate for and with people with brain injury, to secure and develop community-based services for individuals with brain injury and their families, to support research leading to better outcomes that enhance the life of people who sustain a brain injury, and to promote prevention of brain injury through public awareness, education, and legislation. The site provides a kids corner, national directory, and database.

Travelers with Disabilities Resources

Resources for Travelers with Disabilities

Access-Able Travel Source
Internet URL: http://www.access-able.com
Description: Access provides information on:
- Travel Tips are our most frequently asked questions about travel information.
- Cruise lines and what ships are accessible.
- Relay and voice phone numbers for hotels, car rental, airlines, and states.
- Travel agencies that have tours or can plan trips for special needs.
- Forums and Bulletin Boards to speak out.

Accessible Adventures
Internet URL: http://www.Accessible Adventures.com
Description: Accessible Adventures is a new charter and tour company based in Burlington, Vermont. Tours are designed for groups, but a few friends or family may constitute a group.

With flexible scheduling, the company can pick up at the airport or Amtrak station, or at home if it is within a day's drive of Burlington.

Additionally, several sporting opportunities are available through the activities of Vermont Adaptive Ski and Sport, and others. Summer and winter, Vermont Adaptive Ski and Sport is able to help travelers enjoy their activity of choice. Programs of instruction and participation are available in snow skiing, sailing, canoeing, horseback riding, or driving, tandem or hand-cycling, and more.

Global Access: A Network for Disabled Travelers
Internet URL: http://www.geocities.com/Paris/1502
Description: Global Access provides a site that can facilitate travel planning with a place for disabled travelers to share their experiences. It also provides links to other travel sites.

Travel Turtle Tours
240 Main Street
Danbury, CT 06810
Phone: (800) 453-9195
Fax: (203) 830-4049
E-mail: tourturtle @ aol.com
Internet URL:
http://www.accessable.com/tours/turtle/featours.htm#about.htm
Description: The agency provides information on accessible tours, cruises, and day trips. It also offers a unique rating system for travelers that indicates such things as:
- Requires or does not require assistance to push wheelchair over rough terrain
- Can or cannot transfer independently
- Has or does not have full trunk independence
- Has high, adequate, or low endurance
- Is capable, requires minimal or no assistance of ADL (Activities of Daily Living)

Tuberous Sclerosis

Tuberous Sclerosis is a rare genetic multisystem disorder characterized by the appearance of characteristic benign tumors in various areas of the body, seizures, and mental retardation. Other findings and symptoms may include developmental delays, characteristic skin lesions (e.g., adenoma sebaceum), lesions in the eyes (ocular), uncontrollable involuntary muscle spasms (myoclonic jerking), and/or learning disabilities. The range and severity of associated symptoms and findings may vary greatly from case to case.

National Tuberous Sclerosis Association
8181 Professional Place, Suite 110
Landover, MD 20785
Phone: (800) 225-6872 or (301) 459-9888
Fax: (301) 459-0394
E-mail: ntsa@ntsa.org
Internet URL: http://www.ntsa.org

Newsletters/Publications: The association provides a variety of educational and supportive information through its database, directory, regular newsletter, reports, audio-visual materials, and brochures.

Description: The National Tuberous Sclerosis Association is a voluntary not-for-profit organization dedicated to improving the quality of life of individuals and families affected by Tuberous Sclerosis. Established in 1974, the association is committed to promoting and sponsoring medical research studies into the diagnosis, cause, management, and cure of Tuberous Sclerosis and ensuring that affected individuals and families have access to appropriate medical services, support services, and resource information. The organization is involved in the development of public and professional educational programs aimed at increasing awareness of Tuberous Sclerosis and prompting early diagnosis and effective treatment. The National Tuberous Sclerosis Association also provides referrals to genetic counseling, support groups, and other services; promotes patient advocacy and legislation beneficial to affected individuals; and conducts international symposia on Tuberous Sclerosis.

Turner Syndrome

Turner Syndrome is a chromosomal condition causing short stature and infertility in women and girls. It is caused by the complete or partial absence of one of the two X chromosomes normally found in women.

Turner Syndrome Society of the United States
1313 Southeast 5th Street, Suite 327
Minneapolis, MN 55414
Phone: (800) 365-9944
Fax: (612) 379-3619
E-mail: N/A
Internet URL: http://www.turner-syndrome-us.org
Newsletters/Publications: *Turner's Syndrome News* is the organization's newsletter sent automatically to members. Call for a list of other publications.
Description: Turner's Syndrome Society of the United States is a non-profit membership organization whose mission is to increase public awareness, increase the understanding of those affected, provide a forum for interaction between those affected, and monitor research by working together with health-care professionals.

U

University-Based Information Sites

Center for Disability Information and Referral, Institute for the Study of the Developmentally Disabled
University of Indiana
2853 East 10th Street
Bloomington, IN 47408-2601
Phone (Voice/TTD): (812) 855-9396
Fax: N/A
E-mail: CeDir@indiana.edu
Internet URL: http://www.isdd.indiana.edu/~cedir
Newsletters/Publications: Call for a list of publications.
Description: The center provides access to information to meet individuals' related needs through print, non-print, and human resources. It also provides disability-related information, develops products, provides training and technical assistance, and conducts research.

Center for Research on Learning
University of Kansas
3061 Dole
Lawrence, KS 66045
Phone: (785) 864-4780
Fax: N/A
E-mail: jtollefson@ukans.edu
Internet URL: http://www.ku-crl.org
Newsletters/Publications: Call for a list of publications.
Description: This is an umbrella research organization dedicated to research in learning disabilities, adult literacy, advanced technology in education, and organizational learning. A series of products are also offered at this site including instructional materials, teacher training and support tools, video tapes, publications, and an extensive bibliography.

Family Village
Waisman Center,
University of Wisconsin-Madison
(See Websites–General)

Gallaudet University
800 Florida Avenue, NE
Washington, DC 20002-3695
Phone (Voice/TTD): (202) 651-5000
Fax: N/A
E-mail: publicrel@gallua.gallaudet.edu
Internet URL: http://www.gallaudet.edu
Newsletters/Publications: *Gallaudet Today*
Description: Established in 1864 by an act of Congress, Gallaudet offers more than 50 under-
graduate and graduate degree programs and numerous continuing education and summer
courses. The university disseminates information through such units as the Gallaudet University
Bookstore, Gallaudet University Press, Gallaudet Research Institute, Pre-College National Mission
Programs, College for Continuing Education, and the National Information Center on Deafness.

National Center for Youth with Disabilities
University of Minnesota
Box 721-UMHC
420 Delaware Street, SE
Minneapolis, MN 55455
Phone: (612) 626-2825
Fax: N/A
E-mail: ncyd@gold.tc.umn.edu
Internet URL: http://www.coled.umn.edu/EdPsy/SchPsy/NYCD.html
Newsletters/Publications: Call for a list of publications.
Description: NCYD is an information, resource, and policy center focusing on adolescents
with chronic illnesses and disabilities and the issues surrounding their transition to adult life.
NCYD is affiliated with the Society for Adolescent Medicine and is located in the Division of
General Pediatrics, Adolescent Health Program. The center's mission is to raise awareness of
the needs of youth with disabilities and foster coordination and collaboration among agencies, professionals, parents, and youth in planning and providing services to address those
needs. NCYD maintains the National Resource Library of information about youth with disabilities. This comprehensive computerized database includes up-to-date expertise programs and
literature of all relevant disciplines.

National Technical Institute for the Deaf
Rochester Institute of Technology
Marketing Communications Department
52 Lomb Memorial Drive, LBJ Building
Rochester, NY 14623-5604
Phone (Voice/TTD): (716) 475-6906
Fax: (716) 475-5623 or (716) 475-6500
E-mail: N/A
Internet URL: http://www.rit.edu
Newsletters/Publications: Call for a list of publications.
Description: The institute provides technological post-secondary education to deaf and hard
of hearing students. It also disseminates informational materials and instructional videotapes
on issues related to deaf people and deaf culture.

Special Education Resources from the Curry School of Education at the University of Virginia
Phone: N/A
Fax: N/A
E-mail: Curry@curry.edschool.virginia.edu
Internet URL: http://teach.virginia.edu/go/cise/ose/home.html
Newsletters/Publications: Call for a list of publications.
Description: This university site provides a wealth of information in the following areas:

- Special Education Information—Information about special education history, events, interventions, and more.
- Resources on the Internet—Internet resources about special education and disability.
- Categorical Information—Links to information and resources arranged by professionals in special education, and pictures and email addresses for some professionals in special education.
- Parents—Information for parents of students who need special education.

V

Visually Impaired

American Council of the Blind (ACB)
1155 15th Street NW, Suite 720
Washington, DC 20005
Phone: (202) 467-5081 or (800) 424-8666 Available 3:00–5:30PM Eastern Time only
Fax: (202) 467-5085
E-mail: ncrabb@access.digex.net
Internet URL: http://acb.org/
Newsletters/Publications: ACB publishes a monthly magazine, the *Braille Forum*, subscriptions to which are available free in braille, large print, cassettes, and DOS diskettes.
Description: American Council of the Blind (ACB) is a national organization established to promote the independence, dignity, and well-being of blind and visually impaired people. Members are blind, visually impaired, or fully sighted people from all walks of life. The council helps to improve the lives of the blind by working to enhance civil rights, employment, rehabilitation services, safe and expanded transportation, travel and recreation, Social Security benefits, accessibility, and works in coalition with other disability groups. The concerns of various professions and special populations are addressed by ACB's many national special interest affiliates and committees. These affiliates help the council address the special interests and concerns of women, minorities, students, families, guide dog users, braille readers, and many others.

American Foundation for the Blind (AFB)
11 Penn Plaza, Suite 300
New York, NY 10001
Phone: (800) 232-5463 or(212) 502-7600
TTD: (212) 502-7662
Fax: N/A
E-mail: afbinfo@afb.org
Internet URL: http://www.afb.org/afb
Newsletters/Publications: Call for a list of publications.
Description: AFB is a non-profit organization founded in 1921 and recognized as Helen Keller's cause in the United States. The American Foundation for the Blind (AFB) is a leading national resource for people who are blind or visually impaired, the organizations that serve them, and the general public. The mission of the American Foundation for the Blind is to enable people who are blind or visually impaired to achieve equality of access and opportunity that will ensure freedom of choice in their lives.

American Printing House for the Blind, Inc. (APH)
1839 Frankfort Avenue
PO Box 6085
Louisville, KY 40206-0085
Phone: (800) 223-1839 or (502) 895-2405
Fax: (502) 899-2274
E-mail: aph@iglou.com
Internet URL: http://www.aph.org
Newsletters/Publications: AHP publishes two newsletters, *APH Slate,* and *Micro Materials Update,* both semiannual and both free. It also has brochures, including "Wings for the Future," product brochures, catalogs, and a video/brochure package that explores ways that parents and teachers of children with visual impairment can make reading aloud an enjoyable learning experience.
Description: The American Printing House for the Blind promotes independence of blind and visually impaired persons by providing special media, tools, and materials needed for education and life. Its focus is primarily for people who are visually impaired, secondarily learning disabled people, and those who are multiply handicapped.

APH manufactures books and magazines in braille, large type, recorded, and computer disk form. It also manufactures a wide range of educational and daily living aids, such as braille paper and styluses, talking book equipment, and synthetic speech computer products. In addition, APH offers CARL ET AL, an electronic database that lists accessible books in braille, large type, recorded, computer disk, and tactile graphic formats.

Blind Children's Fund
4740 Okemos Road
Okemos MI 48864-1637
Phone: (517) 347-1357
Fax: (517) 347-1459
E-mail: blindchfnd@aol.com
Internet URL: http://www.blindchildrensfund.org
Newsletters/Publications: Call for a list of publications.

Description: The Blind Children's Fund, formerly known as the International Institute for the Visually Impaired, is an international not-for-profit organization that was established in 1978. The organization was incorporated to respond to the special educational and emotional needs of blind children and their families. The Blind Children's Fund represents a network of parents, professionals, and volunteers throughout the United States and the world who are committed to developing, organizing, and disseminating information and materials for affected families. It develops and distributes educational materials and literature, publishes a quarterly newsletter, and distributes national position papers relative to advocacy and program development for affected children. The fund organizes international symposia, conducts workshops and conferences, offers in-service and consultant services, and provides a slide and tape show for UNESCO in four languages that helps train professionals and paraprofessionals who work with infants and young children with blindness.

Foundation Fighting Blindness
Executive Plaza I, Suite 800
11350 McCormick Road
Hunt Valley, MD 21031-1014
Phone:(888) 394-3937 or (410) 785-1414
TDD: (800) 683-5551
Local TDD: (410) 785-9687
Fax: N/A
E-mail: N/A
Internet URL: http://www.blindness.org
Newsletter/Publications: Call for a list of publications.
Description: Foundation Fighting Blindness is a national eye research organization that funds laboratory and clinical research at more than 40 prominent institutions in the United States and foreign countries. It serves as a source of information for eye care specialists, professionals, and affected families.

The Lighthouse Inc.
111 East 59th Street
New York, NY 10022
Phone: (212) 821-9200
TTD: (212) 821-9713
Fax: (212) 821-9707
Publications and referrals: (800) 334-5497
E-mail: NA
Internet URL: http://www.lighthouse.org
Newsletters/Publications: The Lighthouse publishes a newsletter, *EnVision*, and a variety of other publications.
Description: The Lighthouse works with the families of children who are visually impaired and blind, professionals, and the general public. Its main purpose is to establish connections among the many people who can enhance the early development of the children with these conditions, work with families, the vision care system, special education programs, and the health and education networks to develop coordinated programs. The Lighthouse staff conducts applied and theoretical research and collaborates with other professionals to develop and share research findings.

National Association for Visually Handicapped (NAVH)
NAVH New York
22 West 21st Street
New York, NY 10010
Phone: (212) 889-3141
Fax: (212) 727-2931
E-mail: staff@navh.org
NAVH San Francisco
3201 Balboa Street
San Francisco, CA 94121
Phone: (415) 221 3201
Fax: (415) 221 8754
E-mail: staffca@navh.org
Internet URL: http://www.navh.org
Newsletters/Publications: *UPDATE* is the quarterly Newsletter available to Members and just for the asking.
Description: NAVH is a national voluntary health agency. It has supplied services to children and adults in 50 states and 91 foreign countries. Aside from large print, the agency program offers information, referral, visual aids and, most importantly, emotional support. NAVH is an agency not for the blind but for the "hard of seeing."

National Federation of the Blind (NFB)
1800 Johnson Street
Baltimore, MD 21230
Phone: (410) 659-9314
Fax: (410) 685-5653
E-mail: epc@roudley.com
Internet URL: http://www.nfb.org/
Newsletters/Publications: *The Braille Monitor* is the leading publication of the National Federation of the Blind (NFB). It is produced monthly and is available in large print, in braille, on cassette tape, or in e-mail formats.
Description: The purpose of the National Federation of the Blind is two-fold: to help blind persons achieve self-confidence and self-respect, and to act as a vehicle for collective self-expression by the blind. By providing public education about blindness, information and referral services, scholarships, literature and publications about blindness, aids and appliances and other adaptive equipment for the blind, advocacy services and protection of civil rights, Job Opportunities for the Blind, development and evaluation of technology, and support for blind persons and their families, members of the NFB strive to educate the public that the blind are normal individuals who can compete on terms of equality.

National Organization of Parents of Blind Children (NOPBC)
(See Parent Resources)

Recording for the Blind and Dyslexic (RFB)
20 Roszel Road
Princeton, NJ 20542
Phone: (800) 221-4792 or (609) 452-0606
Fax: (609) 987-8116

E-mail: N/A
Internet URL: http://www.rfbd.org
Newsletters/Publications: N/A
Description: RFB is a national non-profit organization that provides taped educational books, Talking Books free on loan, books on diskette, library services, and other educational and professional resources to individuals who cannot read standard print because of a visual, physical, or perceptual disability.

Note: **This site also exists in the section on Learning Disabilities.**

Visually Impaired-Websites

Blind Children's Center
Internet URL: http://www.blindcntr.org/
Description: The Blind Childrens Center is a family-centered agency that serves children with visual impairments from birth to school age. The center-based programs and services help the children acquire skills and build their independence. The center uses its expertise and experience to serve families and professionals worldwide through support services, education, and research.

Blind Links Web Page
Internet URL: http://seidata.com/~marriage/rblind.html
Description: This is one of the best links for this disability area.

Blindness Resource Center
The New York Institute for Special Education
Office of Development
999 Pelham Parkway
Bronx, NY 10469
Phone: (718) 519-7000 Ext. 315
Fax: (718) 231-9314
E-mail: N/A
Internet URL: http://www.nyise.org/blind.htm
Description: This is a very thorough site for resources dealing with visual impairments, and a good source for other disabilities as well.

National Library Service for the Blind and Physically Handicapped
Internet URL: http://lcweb.loc.gov/nls/nls.html
(See Government Agencies–Federal)

W

Web Sites: All Disabilities

Ability OnLine Support Network
Internet URL: http:www.ablelink.org
Description: Ability OnLine is an electronic mail system that connects young people with disabilities or chronic illness to disabled and non-disabled peers and mentors. This network site helps adolescents by removing the social barriers that can come with having a disability and illness, and by providing opportunities to form friendships, build self-confidence, exchange information, and share hope and encouragement through e-mail messages.

Ability OnLine is also a valuable resource for families and friends anxious to know more about an illness and to help manage it. The network provides disabled youngsters and their families with up-to-date information on medical treatments, educational strategies, and employment opportunities through peer support. Access to the network is available through the use of a computer, modem, and the telephone system either by dialing directly into the system or by telnet via the Internet.

disABILITY Information and Resources
Internet URL: http://www.eskimo.com/~jlubin/disabled.html
Description: This site has extensive resources, assistive technology sites, databases, and much more.

Disability Links by Douglas Zachary
Internet URL: http://www.acun.com/~dzack/link.html
Description: For advocacy, support, resources, defense, law, research, and more.

Disability Resources for Students and Professionals
Internet URL: http://www.abilityinfo.com/index.html
E-mail: webmaster@abilityinfo.com
Description: Disability Resources Inc. is a non-profit organization established to promote and improve awareness, and availability and accessibility of information for independent living. *Disability Resources Monthly* is an award-winning newsletter that monitors, reviews, and reports on resources for independent living.

Disability-Specific Web Sites

disABILITY Information and Resources
Internet URL: http://www.eskimo.com/~jlubin/disabled.html

Description: An extensive source of resources, assistive technology sites, databases and much more.

EASI (Equal Access to Software and Information)
Internet URL: http://www.isc.rit.edu/~easi
Description: An affiliate of the American Association for Higher Education (AAHE), EASI's mission is to make information technology accessible to persons with disabilities with the use of adaptive technology. EASI provides informative publications, on-site seminars, and a series of e-mail delivered workshops to assist colleges, schools, and businesses in making their information technology resources more accessible.

Family Village
Waisman Center,
University of Wisconsin–Madison
1500 Highland Avenue
Madison, WI 53705-2280
Phone: (608) 263-5973
TDD: (608) 263-0802
E-mail: rowley@waisman.wisc.edu
Internet URL: http://www.familyvillage.wisc.edu
Newsletters/Publications: None
Description: The Family Village is a global community that integrates information, resources, and communication opportunities on the Internet for persons with mental retardation and other disabilities, their families, and those who provide them services and supports. Family Village Web Site is an attempt to bring together valuable information for parents of individuals who have disabilities.

1400 Disability Links
Internet URL: http://www.best.com/~reed/1472criplinks.htmlption
Description: More than 1300 sites containing the word "disability."

Internet Resources for Special Children (IRSC)
Internet URL: http://www.irsc.org
E-mail: julio_c@one.net
Description: IRSC is a non-profit website that has been providing parents, educators, medical professionals, and caregivers with information regarding children with disABILITIES.

Internet Special Education Resources (ISER)
Internet URL: http://www.iser.com
Description: ISER is a nationwide directory of professionals who serve the learning disabled and special education communities.

Jerome and Deborah's BIG PAGE of Special Education Links
Internet URL: http://www.mts.net/~jgreenco/jerdeb.html
E-mail: dfalk1@meat.minet.gov.mb.ca
Description: This BIG PAGE is a well-organized site for special education sources for teachers, parents, professionals, and students.

Marc Sheehan's Special Education Page
Internet URL: http://www.halcyon.com/marcs/sped.html
Description: An extensive page of special education links.

Mining Company
Internet URL: http://www.miningco.com
Description: Mining Company provides thorough information on thousands of topics under 500 categories. Check out the education, family, and health sites for information on special education topics.

National Center to Improve Practice (NCIP)
Internet URL: http://www.edc.org/FSC/NCIP
Description: This site promotes the effective use of technology to enhance educational outcomes for students with sensory, cognitive, physical, and social/emotional disabilities. NCIP-net houses a series of facilitated discussion conferences focusing on technology and special education. NCIPnet enables communication with other members of NCIPnet—technology coordinators, staff developers, teachers, specialists, clinicians, administrators, university faculty, parents, advocates, and consumers—who share a common desire to improve the use of technology with students who have disabilities.

Pitsco's Launch to Special Education Resources
Phone: (800) 835-0686
Fax: (316) 231-3406
Internet URL: http://www.pitsco.com/p/resource.html
E-mail: pitsco@pitsco.com
Description: A vast database of educational resources. Be sure to click on the "Special Needs" site.

Pursuit–Disability Resources on the Internet
Internet URL: http://primes6.rehab.uiuc.edu/pursuit/homepage.html
E-mail: webmaster@pursuit.rehab.uiuc.edu
Description: Here's a wealth of resources including disability information; education accommodation resources; lessons on assistive technology and funding available for this technology; descriptions of careers in science, engineering, and mathematics; high school preparations for these careers; access to countless other disability information servers; and much more.

This site now has more than 400 pages of information to offer, plus a search system.

Solutions
Evan Kemp Associates
Internet URL: http://www.eka.com
E-mail: Solutions@eka.com
Description: Solutions is a web site that links people with disabilities and chronic health conditions to resources, products, and services that promote active, healthy, independent living.

Special Education Resources on the Internet (SERI)
Internet URL: www.hood.edu/seri/serihome.htm
Description: SERI is a collection of Internet-accessible information resources of interest to those involved in the fields related to special education. This collection exists to make online

special education resources more easily and readily available in one location. This site will continually modify, update, and add additional informative links. If you know of other resources that should be included here, please send the Internet URL to horner2@ix.netcom.com

Sympatico/Healthway
Internet URL: http://www.nt.sympatico.ca/healthway/health.html
Description: An extensive databased site containing information on a variety of health and disability topics.

Teacher Magazine on the Web
Organizations
Internet URL: http://www.teachermag.org/context/orgs/orgshtm
Description: This particular section site of Teacher Magazine on the Web contains a comprehensive A-Z listing of organizations involved in education policy or education reform. There are other sections on this website to explore.

Teacher's Special Ed Web Page (Jeni Turgeon)
Internet URL: http://www.zianet.com/sage/sped.htm
E-mail: sage@zianet.com
Description: This site includes lesson plans and resources for teachers to use in the classroom and in planning. It also provides interactive sites for kids in the classroom.

Williams Syndrome

Williams Syndrome is a rare congenital disorder characterized by heart and blood vessel abnormalities, high blood calcium levels, developmental delays, characteristic facial features, and/or additional abnormalities.

Williams Syndrome Association (WSA)
PO Box 297
Clawson, MI 48017-0297
Phone: (248) 541-3630
Fax: (248) 541-3631
E-mail: TMonkaba@aol.com
Internet URL: http://www.williams-syndrome.org
Newsletters/Publications: *Heart To Heart* is the national newsletter of the Williams Syndrome Association. The publication is distributed quarterly to all WS families as well as professional, national, and international paying members of the WSA.
Description: The association, established in 1983, is committed to locating affected individuals and their families and disseminating current medical and educational information to families, professionals, and the public. In addition, the organization seeks to increase professional awareness of and interest in Williams Syndrome and supports ongoing research into the educational, behavioral, social, and medical aspects of the disorder. The Williams Syndrome Association engages in patient and family advocacy; provides appropriate referrals to support groups; and holds annual regional conferences, social gatherings, and biennial conventions.

The association also provides a variety of informational materials to families, health care professionals, teachers, and others through its database, directory, quarterly newsletter, reports, medical monitoring guidelines for physicians, brochures, pamphlets, and audiovisual aids.

Writing Assessment Measures

Denver Handwriting Analysis (DHA)
Author: Peggy L. Anderson
Publisher: Academic Therapy Publications
20 Commercial Boulevard
Novato, CA 94949-6191
Phone: (415) 883-3314 or (800) 422-7249
Fax: (415) 883-3720
Type of Test: Criterion-referenced
Administration Time: 20–60 minutes
Type of Administration: Individual or group
Age/Grade Level: Ages 8 to 13

The Picture Story Language Test (PSLT)
Author: Helmer R. Myklebust
Publisher: The Psychological Corporation
555 Academic Court
San Antonio, TX 78204-2498
Phone: (800) 211-8378
Fax: (800) 232-1223
TDD: (800) 723-1318
Type of Test: Norm-referenced
Administration Time: 20–30 minutes
Type of Administration: Individual or group
Administrator: Special education teacher, classroom teacher
Age/Grade Level: Ages 7 to 17

Test of Early Written Language–2 (TEWL–2)
Author: Wayne P. Hresko
Publisher: PRO-ED, Inc.
8700 Shoal Creek Boulevard
Austin, TX 78758-6897
Phone: (512) 451-3246 or (800) 897-3202
Fax: (800) FXPROED
Type of Test: Standardized
Administration Time: 10–30 minutes
Type of Administration: Individual or group
Administrator: Special education teacher, reading specialist, psychologist, and classroom teacher

Age/Grade Level: Ages 3 to 7

Test of Written Language—2 (TOWL–2)
Authors: Donald D. Hammill and Stephen C. Larsen
Publisher: PRO-ED, Inc.
8700 Shoal Creek Boulevard
Austin, TX 78758-6897
Phone: (512) 451-3246 or (800) 897-3202
Fax: (800) FXPROED
Type of Test: Standardized, norm-referenced
Administration Time: 40–60 minutes
Type of Administration: Group or individual
Administrator: Special education teacher, classroom teacher
Age/Grade Level: Grades 2 to 12

Test of Written Language–3 (TOWL–3)
Authors: Donald D. Hammill and Stephen C. Larsen
Publisher: PRO-ED, Inc.
8700 Shoal Creek Boulevard
Austin, TX 78758-6897
Phone: (512) 451-3246 or (800) 897-3202
Fax: (800) FXPROED
Type of Test: Standardized, norm-referenced
Administration Time: Untimed
Type of Administration: Group or individual
Administrator: Special education teacher, classroom teacher
Age/Grade Level: Grades 2 to 12

Written Language Assessment (WLA)
Authors: J. Jeffrey Grill and Margaret M. Kirwin
Publisher: Academic Therapy Publications
20 Commercial Boulevard
Novato, CA 94949-6191
Phone: (415) 883-3314 or (800) 422-7249
Fax: (415) 883-3720
Type of Test: Norm-referenced
Administration Time: One hour
Type of Administration: Group
Administrator: Special education teacher, classroom teacher
Age/Grade Level: Ages 8.18 and older

Appendix A
Disability Books

There is extensive literature available on every topic. We have selected three to four titles on selected topics to provide a general idea of the available literature. It is not intended to be a complete list of special education books in the market today. We have included a brief, random selection on several topics.

Abuse and Neglect

Abuse and Neglect of Exceptional Children (Exceptional Children at Risk Series)(1991)
Author: Cynthia L. Warger
Publisher: Council of Exceptional Children

*Handbook for Understanding Child Abuse and Neglect,*1990 (3rd ed.)
Author: Bavolek
Publisher: Family Developments Resources

*Preventing Child Abuse and Neglect Through Parent Education,*1997
Author: N. Dickon Reppucci, et al.
Publisher: Paul H. Brooks

The Effects of Child Abuse and Neglect: Issues and Research, 1991
Author: Raymond H. Starr (Ed.), et al.
Publisher: Guilford Press

Understanding Child Abuse and Neglect, 1998 (4th ed.)
Author: Cynthia Crosson-Tower
Publisher: Allyn & Bacon

ADA

Americans with Disabilities Handbook: Basic Resource Document, 1993
Publisher: U.S. Equal Opportunity Employment Staff

Adaptive Technology

Adapting PCs for Disabilities, 1995
Author: Joseph J. Lazzaro
Publisher: Addison Wesley

Computer Resources for People with Disabilities: A Guide to Exploring Today's Assistive Technology, 1996 (2nd ed.)
Author: Steven Hawking, et al.
Publisher: Hunter House

ADD/ADHD

All About ADHD: The Complete Practical Guide for Classroom Teachers (Teaching Strategies), 1996
Author: Linda Pfiffner
Publisher: Scholastic Books

Attention Deficit Disorder and Learning Disabilities: Reality, Myths, and Controversial Treatments, 1993
Author: Barbara Ingersoll, et al.
Publisher: Mainstreet Books

Attention Deficit Hyperactivity Disorder: What Every Parent Wants To Know, 1994
Author: David L. Wodrich (Ed.)
Publisher: Paul H. Brooks

The Attention Zone: Parent's Guide to Attention Deficit/Hyperactivity Disorder, 1997
Author: Michael Cohen
Publisher: Brunner/Mazel

The A.D.D. Hyperactivity Workbook for Parents, Teachers, and Kids, 1996 (2nd ed.)
Author: Harvey C. Parket, et al.
Publisher: Specialty Press

Assessment

Assessment of Individuals with Mental Retardation, 1997
Author: Ronald L. Taylor
Publisher: Singular Publishing Group

Assessing Reading and Writing Difficulties, 1997
Author: Thomas G. Gunning
Publisher: Allyn & Bacon

The Special Educator's Complete Guide to 109 Diagnostic Tests, 1998
Author: Roger Pierangelo, Ph.D. & George Giuliani, Psy. D., J.D.
Publisher: Prentice Hall

Autism

Autism and Pervasive Developmental Disorders, 1998
Author: Fred R. Bolkmar (Ed.)
Publisher: Cambridge

Autism: Understanding the Disorder, 1997
Author: Gary B. Mesibov, et al.
Publisher: Plenum Publishing Corp.

Autism: Identification, Education and Treatment, 1992
Author: Dianne E. Berkell (Ed.)
Publisher: L. Erebaum

Autism and Learning: A Guide to Good Practice, 1997
Author: Stuart Powell (Ed.)
Publisher: Taylor

Autism and the Family: Problems, Prospects and Coping with the Disorder, 1998
Author: David E. Gray
Publisher: Charles C Thomas

Behavior Management

Anger Management in Schools: Alternatives to Student Violence, 1995
Author: Jerry Wilde
Publisher: Technomic Pub. Co.

Antisocial Behavior in School: Strategies and Best Practices, 1995
Author: Geoffrey Colvin, et al.
Publisher: Brooks/Cole

Applied Behavior Analysis in the Classroom, 1998
Author: Patrick J. Schloss, et al.
Publisher: Allyn & Bacon

Behavior Management: Applications for Teachers and Parents, 1996 (2nd ed.)
Author: Thomas J. Zirpoli, et al.
Publisher: Merrill/Prentice Hall

Creative Strategies for School Problems: Solutions for Psychologists and Teachers, 1995

Author: Michael Durrant
Publisher: W. W. Norton & Co.

Curriculum

Curricular and Instructional Approaches for Persons with Severe Disabilities, 1994
Author: Ennio Cipani, et al.
Publisher: Allyn & Bacon

Curriculum Content for Students with Moderate and Severe Disabilities in Inclusive Settings, 1995
Author: Diane Lea Ryndak, et al.
Publisher: Allyn & Bacon

Deaf

American Sign Language: A Teacher's Resource Text on Curriculum, Methods and Evaluation (American Sign Language Series), 1991
Author: Dennis Cokely, et al.
Publisher: Gallaudet University Press

Encyclopedia of Deafness and Hearing Disorders, 1992
Author: Carol Turkington, et al.
Publisher: Facts on File, Inc.

Issues in Deaf Education
Author: Susan Gregory (Ed.)
Publisher: David Fulton

Emotional Disorders

Characteristics of Emotional and Behavioral Disorders of Children and Youth, 1996 (6th ed.)
Author: James M. Kaufman
Publisher: Prentice Hall

Emotional Problems in Children and Young People (Children, Teachers and Learning), 1996
Author: Linda Winkley
Publisher: Cassell Academics

Unhappy Children: Reasons and Remedies, 1995
Author: Heather Smith
Publisher: New York University Press

General

After Your Child's Diagnosis: A Practical Guide for Families Raising Children with Disabilities, 1997
Author: Cathy Lynn Binstock
Publisher: E M Press

All Kinds of Minds, 1992
Author: Mel Levine
Publisher: Educators Publishing Service

Children with Disabilities, 1997 (4th ed.)
Author: Mark L. Batshaw (Ed.)
Publisher: Paul H. Brookes

Complete Guide To Transition Services, 1997
Author: Roger Pierangelo, Ph.D. & Rochelle Crane, CSW
Publisher: Prentice Hall

The Special Educator's Book of Lists, 1995
Author: Roger Pierangelo, Ph.D.
Publisher: Prentice Hall

Gifted

Gifted Children: Myths and Realities, 1997
Author: Ellen Winner
Publisher: Basic Books

Keys to Parenting the Gifted Child, 1994
Author: Sylvia B. Rimm
Publisher: Barron's Educational Series

Teaching Gifted Kids in the Regular Classroom, 1992
Author: Susan Winebrenner (Ed.), et al.
Publisher: Free Spirit

The Gifted Kids' Survival Guide: A Teen Handbook, 1997
Author: Judy Gallbraith, et al.
Publisher: Free Spirit

The Survival Guide for Parents of Gifted Kids, 1991
Author: Sally Yahnke Walker, et al.
Publisher: Free Spirit

Learning Disabilities

Learning Disabilities and Your Child: A Survival Handbook on Learning Disabilities, 1987

Author: Lawrence J. Greene
Publisher: Fawcett Book Group

The ABCs of Learning Disabilities, 1996
Author: Bernice Y. L. Wong
Publisher: Academic Press

The Misunderstood Child, 1998
Author: Larry B. Silver
Publisher: Random House

Mental Retardation/Developmental Disabilities, 1993

Children with Mental Retardation: A Parent's Guide (The Special Needs Collection)
Author: Romayne Smith (Ed.), et al.
Publisher: Woodbine House

Handbook of Mental Retardation and Development, 1998
Author: Jacob A. Burack (Ed.), et al.
Publisher: Cambridge University Press

I Have a Friend Who Has Mental Retardation (Basic Manual for Families and Friends of the Disabled), 1995
Author: Hannah Carlson, et al.
Publisher: Bick Publishing House

Mental Retardation: Foundations of Educational Programming, 1994
Author: Linda Hickson, et al
Publisher: Allyn & Bacon

Teaching Students with Mental Retardation: A Life Goal Curriculum Planning Approach, 1996
Author: Glen E. Thomas
Publisher: Merrill/Prentice Hall

The Special Child: A Source Book for Parents of Children with Developmental Disabilities, 1995 (2nd ed.)
Author: Siegfried M. Pueschel
Publisher: Paul Brookes

Visual Impairments

Visual Impairment in the Schools, 1984 (2nd ed.)
Author: Randell K. Harley, et al.
Publisher: Charles C Thomas

Index